JOHN STEINBECK

John Steinbeck. (© Hans Namuth Estate. Courtesy of the Center for Creative Photography, University of Arizona.)

JOHN STEINBECK

A Centennial Tribute

Edited by Stephen K. George
Foreword by Terry Gorton

Contributions to the Study of American Literature, No. 15

Westport, Connecticut
London

Library of Congress Cataloging-in-Publication Data

John Steinbeck : a centennial tribute / edited by Stephen K. George ; foreword by Terry Gordon.
    p. cm.—(Contributions to the study of American literature, ISSN 1092–6356 ; no. 15)
    Includes bibliographical references and index.
    ISBN 0–313–32325–9 (alk. paper)
    1. Steinbeck, John, 1902–1968. 2. Novelists, American—20th century—Biogra-
phy. I.
  George, Stephen K., 1965– II. Series.
  PS3537.T3234 Z71547   2002
  813'.52—dc21
  [B]   2002072542

British Library Cataloguing in Publication Data is available.

Library of Congress Catalog Card Number: 2002072542
ISBN: 0–313–32325–9
ISSN: 1092–6356

First published in 2002

Praeger Publishers, 88 Post Road West, Westport, CT 06881
An imprint of Greenwood Publishing Group, Inc.
www.praeger.com

Printed in the United States of America

The paper used in this book complies with the
Permanent Paper Standard issued by the National
Information Standards Organization (Z39.48–1984).

10 9 8 7 6 5 4 3 2 1

Copyright Acknowledgments

Grateful acknowledgment is made to Viking Penguin, a division of Penguin Books USA Inc., for permission to reprint from the following: *America and Americans* by John Steinbeck (copyright 1996 by John Steinbeck); *East of Eden* by John Steinbeck (copyright 1952 by John Steinbeck, renewed 1980 by Elaine Steinbeck, John Steinbeck IV, and Thom Steinbeck); *The Grapes of Wrath* by John Steinbeck (copyright 1939, renewed 1967 by John Steinbeck); *Journal of a Novel* by John Steinbeck (copyright 1969 by the Executors of the Estate of John Steinbeck); *The Log from the Sea of Cortez* by John Steinbeck (copyright 1941 by John Steinbeck and Edward F. Ricketts, renewed 1969 by John Steinbeck and Edward F. Ricketts, Jr.); *Steinbeck: A Life in Letters* by Elaine A. Steinbeck and Robert Wallsten (copyright 1952 by John Steinbeck, 1969 by The Estate of John Steinbeck, and 1975 by Elaine A. Steinbeck and Robert Wallsten).

Grateful acknowledgment is also made to McIntosh & Otis, Inc., and The Estate of John Steinbeck for permission to reprint from *Speech Accepting Nobel Prize for Literature* by John Steinbeck. Copyright © 1962 by John Steinbeck.

For his boys, Thom and Johnny,

For mine, Henry and Charles,

And for Peter and Roy, who gave so much to a beloved author.

In Memory of John Steinbeck

Peter Lisca

Finally, in sleep, his great heart failed him;
but only as hearts fail all good men.

Alive, his flame burned always bright,
whether in wrath at our mutual inhumanity
and wayward understanding of democracy,
or with joy in the people of his valley,
lifting a cup to paisanos, Mac and the boys.
His discontent was never for himself;
he joined battle in the common cause,
too large a man to reign in any private Eden.
Nor did he barter the pearl of his genius
like some commodity for private gain,
but wrote as he himself defined his craft:
to celebrate man's proven capacity
for greatness of heart and spirit,
for gallantry in defeat,
for courage, compassion, and love.

This great man still stirs with these words.
It is we who sleep; he who believed
ourselves true images of His kingdom,
our eyes the nebulae, and universes in our cells,
one with plankton and the spinning planets—
that man cannot die.
He drifts down the dark of some geologic sea
and yet moves with light
across unknown pastures of the Milky Way.

Contents

A photo essay follows page 79.

Acknowledgments

This centennial tribute to John Steinbeck could not have been assembled, edited, and sent off to Greenwood Press in a mere six months without the combined efforts of many people. I particularly wish to thank the Brigham Young University–Idaho English Department and its chair, Kip Hartvigsen, for supporting the idea of this book and for providing funds for correspondence, shipping, photocopying, and telephone calls. I also appreciate the help of the university's interlibrary loan and computer staff, especially Shirley Calder, Alan Young, and David Pfost, and of my colleague Joelle Moen for her facility with Spanish.

The photographs for this volume have been provided by David Laws and Windy Hill Press; Katie Rodger of the Martha Heasley Cox Center for Steinbeck Studies at San Jose State University; Dianne Nilsen of the Center for Creative Photography at the University of Arizona; Jonathon Meredith, surviving son of Burgess Meredith; and Nancy Steinbeck, who also provided the article for John IV and tape transcript from Gwyn Steinbeck. I am also grateful to Peter Namuth, whose enthusiasm paved the way for his father's photograph of John Steinbeck to be used as the cover and the frontispiece of this volume, and to my father-in-law, Dr. Dennis Nelson, who provided financial support along the way.

For various reprints I would especially like to acknowledge Ohio University Press for Elaine Steinbeck's interview; Little, Brown and Company and Kimberly Ingersoll for Burgess Meredith's piece; Dr. Tetsumaro Hayashi and the *Steinbeck Quarterly* for John Ditsky's article; and Dr. Hayashi and Dr. Richard Astro for Webster Street's "Reminiscence." I am also indebted to Peter Jones of Peter Jones Productions, Inc. for acquiring the never-before-published interview of Thom Steinbeck, which was originally conducted for the A&E *Biography* episode "John Steinbeck: An American Writer." And I thank Hendrika Monkhorst for her kind permission to reprint Peter Lisca's poem as an epigraph to the book.

Gail Steinbeck, Thom's wife, has been a constant source of encouragement for this project, as has Joyce Simmonds, who made Roy's delightful "*Of Mice and Men* and (Perhaps) Other Things" available when he was unable to do anything further. Also, friends and fellow critics Michael Meyer and Barbara Heavilin provided me with sound editorial advice at the beginning and end of the process, for which I am indebted.

Finally, when Yevgeny Yevtushenko's usual translator fell ill, my colleague Edwin C. Kumferman capably stepped forward to do the translation. I am also grateful for my editorial board: Professors Luchen Li of Kettering University and Terry Gorton of Brigham Young University–Idaho, who within a month's time (and in the middle of an academic semester) carefully read and critiqued all the selections from Part II and many from Part I, with Terry also graciously agreeing to provide a foreword. This is a better tribute because of them.

Given that this was my first tour of duty as an editor, I had little idea how much time and effort it would take—literally hundreds of letters, e-mails, faxes, and telephone calls; hours upon hours of revising, editing, and proofreading submissions; waking up at 4:00 A.M. with flashes of inspiration and arriving home at 6:00 P.M. completely exhausted. I want to conclude by thanking my children—Louisa, Emma, Margaret, Henry, and Charles—for their patience with the hours dad was away obsessing over Steinbeck. I owe the most, however, to my wife, Rebecca, who believed in the tribute idea from the start, constantly gave me perceptive and honest feedback, and filled in for my many absences at home; she is the unacknowledged third member of the editorial board. To all involved, including the many contributors, my sincere and heartfelt thanks for making this tribute possible.

Foreword

Terry Gorton

Perhaps the most persistent echo among Steinbeck readers is a reminder that life often gets in the way of our schemes and strategies: our best laid plans "gang aft a-gley." Many of the titles—*East of Eden, The Grapes of Wrath, The Winter of Our Discontent, In Dubious Battle*—seem to telegraph this all-too-common irony as a recurring motif. Whether by a casual visit from an itinerant pot mender, a chance encounter with the foreman's wife, or the arrival of the dust storm of the century, Steinbeck shows us how fickle a mistress the future is.

We had a tidy package in mind when we started this collection. But when the various essays, tributes, and reminiscences from family, friends, and scholars arrived, we quickly realized that none of our strategies could encompass the kinds of responses a life like Steinbeck's elicits. We settled on a personal/professional partition for the entire book and (after Susan Shillinglaw's introductory "Why Read John Steinbeck?") arranged the essays in Part II from scholarly to reflective. But as you will see, in Steinbeck's case, friends and scholars, life and art are not so neatly sorted.

So many of those who knew him spoke about his wide-ranging influence. We learn from Yevgeny Yevtushenko, Kiyoshi Nakayama, Donald Coers, and Tetsumaro Hayashi how far from the Salinas Valley and Cannery Row Steinbeck's characters have wandered. "I can't think of another American writer," Arthur Miller writes for this volume, "with the possible exception of Mark Twain, who so deeply penetrated the political life of the country. . . . The

Joads became more vividly alive than one's next-door neighbors, and their sufferings emblematic of an age." Miller's comment suggests Steinbeck's greatest literary triumph: how he manages such an intense focus on particular sufferings, yet still powerfully evokes societal and universal longings. Tom Wolfe, another icon of American letters, agrees: "He conceived of the Joads as types, as specimens, as a cluster of people representing the whole experience of the Okies, and yet Ma Joad and her rebellious son Tom come to life in the pages of *The Grapes of Wrath* as two of the most compelling individuals in American fiction."

Wherever many of the contributors started, they seemed naturally tilted—as trusty cars with their own sense of alignment—to comment on the ethical range and intentions behind Steinbeck's fiction. So, for example, several writers joined John Timmerman ("An Ethics of Fiction") in considering such things as his "outward reach" (Brian Railsback), his Ricketts-inspired "organic" philosophy (Richard Astro), his earthbound spirituality (Barbara Heavilin), his moral conception of the function of fiction (Warren French), and his portrayals of women (Mimi Gladstein). Moreover, a few writers take us on a rather broad, breezy overview of Steinbeck's oeuvre in attempts to suggest his continuing relevance and some of the most important reasons we should read him today (Michael Meyer; John Ditsky). I think Robert DeMott speaks for many readers of Steinbeck when he writes of *East of Eden*: "[It] was the first book that gave me a handle on symbolic experiences, the first to make personal journeys, choices, and continuities seem like palpable endeavors."

Some essays, of course, are not much about Steinbeck the writer at all—they are about John the husband, father, neighbor, friend, paramour, bar buddy, or fellow artist. Here we can learn something about personal passions, insecurities, disappointments, exhilarations, quirks, confessions, dreams. We learn of his wry humor, how he fertilized his garden with a truckload of fish guts, how children adored him because he never "talked down to anyone," of his childlike curiosity, his arm wrestling at bars, the hidden "ocean of sorrow" beneath his eyes.

Finally, one writer expresses an idea that somehow runs through every single selection, an unavoidable way station through which each passes, no matter where else they were headed. "The most gratifying thing he gave me," says one of his sons, John Steinbeck IV, "both before and after he died, was to know that the most refined . . . wisdoms and human knowledge we find in the everyday ordinary world . . . from the guy down the street." It was this guy that Steinbeck wrote about and to. We hope this volume sheds some light on the guy behind the pencil.

Introduction

Stephen K. George

On a cold December afternoon in 1986, with the snow gently falling outside, I began reading a worn copy of *The Grapes of Wrath* on a sofa in my cramped student apartment. I didn't stop until daybreak the next day—it was the most powerful reading experience of my college years. I soon learned, however, from the dearth of any Steinbeck in other classes, that many academics refused to take him seriously; Steinbeck was lightweight, high school material, with little to say in the era of political correctness. This movement to dismiss the author had started in earnest some two decades earlier, most intensely after October 25, 1962. On that day John and his wife Elaine were enjoying a quiet breakfast alone at their Sag Harbor home in Long Island, New York. John, dressed in a robe and pajamas, was concerned about the recent events of the Cuban missile crisis and turned on the television to hear the latest news. According to Jackson Benson, "The first words that came from the set were, 'John Steinbeck has been awarded the Nobel Prize for Literature'" (914).

What occurred next had no precedent in American literary history. Almost in unison the leading critics of the day rose to protest the choice, with the brash *New York Times* running an editorial the very next morning asking why a more significant writer had not been chosen. Particularly shocking was Arthur Mizener's condescending piece on the eve of the Nobel ceremony—"Does a Moral Vision of the Thirties Deserve a Nobel Prize?"—which viciously mocked Steinbeck's many artistic accomplishments while simultaneously trotting out past charges of sentimentality and relevance. Overall, the Eastern establishment's response was both mean spirited and (as Robert Morsberger puts it) unsportsmanlike—a cheap shot on the field of literary criticism when the writer was at his most public and vulnerable. Despite a remarkable reception and ceremony, in which John and Elaine had the distinction of escorting the king and queen of Sweden into dinner, Steinbeck—always a sensitive man—never fully recovered from the critical broadsides of his own countrymen. From that moment until his death in 1968, he never wrote "another word of fiction" (Benson 922).

Yet today, a hundred years after his birth in Salinas, California, on February 27, 1902, John Steinbeck remains one of the most popular authors in all American literature, second only, perhaps, to his favorite, Mark Twain. Of the several dozen works he wrote in his lifetime, there remain a long list of classics, including *Tortilla Flat*, *The Long Valley*, *In Dubious Battle*, *Of Mice and Men*, *The Grapes of Wrath*, *Cannery Row*, *The Pearl*, *East of Eden*, *Travels with Charley*, and *The Winter of Our Discontent*. American Nobel laureates with much less on their literary plate, such as Pearl Buck or Sinclair Lewis, had escaped the Eastern ill will that attended Steinbeck's award. Yet despite the continued critical and academic snubbing, Steinbeck's influence today on readers worldwide remains constant—he is beloved by millions and read in countless classrooms, while adaptations of his novels in film and on stage continue to inspire and challenge into the twenty-first century.

It is this love for Steinbeck and his fiction that sparked the idea for a tribute in May 2001. I found from discussing my idea with several colleagues that in spite of the many anthologies, festivals, and conferences scheduled for the 2002 anniversary, no single volume was planned to celebrate Steinbeck's life and literary accomplishment. My idea has been to edit a unique work—one that would appeal (as Steinbeck did) to the general reader of his books as well as to the scholar and critic. Just as Steinbeck's fiction includes a multitude of voices, from farmers and whores to misfits and minorities, so should *A Centennial Tribute* include as many different perspectives as possible: family members, celebrity friends, esteemed authors, lifelong scholars. More than anything, this tribute seeks to do justice to the complexities of Steinbeck but without pandering or dishonest intellectual praise. I believe there is enough to both the man and his work that contributors need only tell the truth as they see it, flaws and all. Steinbeck, a man so brutally honest as to publicly question his own worthiness for the Nobel, would expect nothing less.

This volume, then, offers a unique portrait of John Steinbeck: his passion for his craft, his struggles as a husband and father, the extraordinary range of ideas and emotion in his fiction, his moral and artistic integrity (George

93). Yet the time in which to put such a tribute together has been unbelievably short given the anniversary deadline. Its publication in a little over a year has been nothing short of a miracle. Some potential contributors regrettably could not participate despite a desire to do so—John Updike declined but shared an anecdote about how he saved his pennies as a boy to buy his mother "the Christmas present she had asked for, a copy of *Cannery Row*." Yet most responded immediately and with a passion for Steinbeck and his work that allowed the many essays, stories, interviews, and photographs to be submitted, edited, and prepared in record time. In particular I am indebted to the contributors in Part II, many of whom have devoted decades of their professional lives to creating societies, organizing conferences, forming journals, writing books and articles, and generally doing all they could to answer those who are too narrow-minded (as Brian Railsback argues) to comprehend Steinbeck's artistic vision. I feel privileged, as editor, to have been able to provide the opportunity for scholarly summations on Steinbeck's spirituality, his ethics and conception of fiction, and his portrayal of women, as well as for the many personal and intimate reflections on the author. One of the contributors, the independent British scholar Roy Simmonds, has offered his last thoughts ever on Steinbeck, having passed away while this book was being assembled; his delightful story about finding a "dream" copy of *Of Mice and Men* is a gem in and of itself. My only regret is that, due to length considerations, more scholars could not participate.

I have also felt privileged to work with the contributors in Part I, particularly Steinbeck's surviving son Thom, his gracious cousin Stanford, the enthusiastic Virginia Scardigli, and the obliging Arthur Miller and Tom Wolfe. It is these entries from those who actually knew the man and loved his books that complete the ruddy hues and shades of the writer's portrait, revealing to us an enormously talented, compassionate, at times tormented man who nonetheless felt compelled to continually refine his art and to speak the truth about the country he so intensely loved. It is by combining the personal with the scholarly perspectives that we may best come to appreciate what Steinbeck has given to the literary world. As Elaine Steinbeck notes, John was a complex person, outwardly simple but not easily understood. This book reveals a further glimpse into the man who wrote so passionately and so well.

Perhaps the best response to Steinbeck's detractors (to return to the Nobel Prize reactions and my own college experience) is merely to note that there is no tribute, no worldwide celebration, no volumes or readings or quiet moments of reflection and appreciation planned for them. Those who dismissed the writer four decades ago are largely silent, while Steinbeck's literary creations—Lennie, Doc, Ma Joad, Cal Trask—live on. A third generation of Steinbeck scholars and readers now carry his torch, finding in the work of this writer a philosophical probing, an artistic craftsmanship, a courage and compassion that make his books come alive despite a twenty-first-century audience's distance from the Great Depression, World War II, and John F. Kennedy's assassination. There is something self-evident about a writer who can touch a lad in London, a Catholic in Chicago, a Japanese reader in Kyoto, and, in my case, a kid from backwoods Kentucky for whom California was another world. John Steinbeck captures the minds and hearts of his readers and continues to inspire today. What more do we require?

PART I
FAMILY, FRIENDS, AND AUTHORS

Wonderfully shy, women adored him, great to travel with, the most entertaining man you want to know. But that's not the man who sat writing the books. And I will never pretend to know that any better than you do.

—Thom Steinbeck

I have to hold a pencil in my fingers. I need to write some pages every day. When you do something for over thirty years, when you hardly think about anything else but how to put your experiences into the right words, you can't just turn it off and go out and play in the garden. I want to write every day, even if—I don't have anything to say.

—John Steinbeck

My Father, John Steinbeck

Thom Steinbeck

Interviewer: Tell me about your father—what kind of man was he?

Thom: Steinbeck's unique. I talk about my father and I talk about Steinbeck, but I don't confuse the two. Because Steinbeck is a very private man that no one really knows. There's no way you can stand in his place or sit at his desk or be in his mind while he's writing. And I never do him the disrespect of calling my father Steinbeck. I call the writer Steinbeck and my father is my father.

Int.: What was he like to be around?

Thom: He's a real funny guy. And he's unbelievably charming and a great raconteur. Wonderfully shy, women adored him, great to travel with, the most entertaining man you want to know. But that's not the man who sat writing the books, and I will never pretend to know that any better than you do.

He loved working with his hands. And he loved his boats, and he loved his solitude a lot. My father thought of himself as a craftsman; he didn't think of himself as an artist. It's a craft. He never got to the point where he believed his voice was the voice of God on any subject whatsoever; he always stayed away from that himself.

Int.: And you saw that your father was more popular abroad than he was in the States?

Thom: Oh, yea, that was scary. I mean arriving at a station and thinking a football team has come in and they're there for Steinbeck. And people picking up your bags and carrying you away. Because my father is the kind of man who owned the same car for ten years, you know. He'd buy a good car but he'd keep it for ten years. He bought his shoes in London and every couple years he sent them back to be rebuilt. He only had three suits. He had them named: Old Blue, Dorian Gray, and something else, and he had them rebuilt every two or three years too. I was stunned to find out that great minds all over the world wanted to meet him, to talk to him. I just never saw him in that context before. I mean you're just a kid, never believing literature to be that powerful.

Int.: Did your father like that kind of attention?

Thom: I think we all like that kind of attention; it's like visiting your own funeral. But he was a very shy man. And he would have hid out during the whole thing. I mean, we used to say, "Mumble a little louder, John" because he'd get a deep voice and grumble and growl a bit, which was just hiding the shyness. It was really very charming—you see this massive bulk, this sea captain, whose handwriting was so small they had to train people to read it. Some of the best literature ever written in America and you can't make heads or tails of it. That's why I think his handwriting was so small, his shyness. He would talk loud if he was around friends and had a couple of drinks, but normally he was a very quiet-spoken man.

He was also so wonderfully boyish. There was a part of him that was the eternal boy, trying to handle attention as politely as possible but basically being very pleased by the whole thing and thinking, "Now can I get a drink and get out of this outfit?" And children adored him. All the neighborhood kids would come over and ask Elaine if he could come out and play. Because he always spoke to them like adults. He never talked down to them. He just walked around and talked to them about the weather and fish and stuff, and they just thought he was the most incredible thing that ever happened. He never talked down to anyone.

Int.: What about Steinbeck as a writer? The scientist in him is what I want to first ask you about.

Thom: Language which is created by a scientist when he's observing a protozoa, it's the way other people describe his technique and style. Actually, it was far more organic than that for him. I don't know any other writer who basically sets out to follow a style and bring you through his story by virtue of a mechanism which he's already pre-determined. He just dove away, very confident in his style, his timing, his language. Very confident in his teachers, by that I mean the people he read and authors he enjoyed, going all the way back to Malory.

Int.: Why would a ten-year-old kid be so attracted to Arthurian legends?

Thom: Possibly because he thought he lived in front of a castle. And if you look at the Gabilan Mountains, the mountains became Camelot and he was ingrained with it from a very early age. Which is why he could take older themes and place them in modern context. That's why *In Dubious Battle* works; it's a very ancient theme just put in modern context. *Grapes of Wrath* is the same thing. Look at his titles—he basically never invented a title in his life. He didn't have to because basically he's talking about the same condition that the other author is talking about.

I discovered this myself when I was in Vietnam. There wasn't a great deal else to do so I went back and found *The Moon Is Down*, a piece which is wonderful. It's about the German invasion and occupation of a Norwegian city, a mining town on the coast. The characters are so well drawn that just for the heck of it I decided to transpose the whole story to South Africa, and it worked—a white dominant military society moving into a black mining community wouldn't have any more success than Germans had in Norway. I didn't have to change the lines, just the characters' names. The people died for the same reasons, the same intimacies took place. And I suddenly realized that Steinbeck was writing in a much cleaner style than I ever imagined. This is all soldiers, all men, all time. I think it's one of the influences Ricketts had on Steinbeck, to see beyond the petri dish. I think Steinbeck was very much micro macro in that sense. What was true on the tiniest scale was true in the largest.

Int.: He has that journalistic eye, that objectivity.

Thom: And simplicity.

Int.: Simplicity in language certainly.

Thom: He doesn't editorialize his model. My father said once, "I don't lie, I just remember big." I know he stole that line but I've always loved it. He had the journalist's eye insofar that he could step back from something. But he had something more—he understood motive and most journalists can't go to motive.

Int.: There's a power to his work that I'd like you to try and explain.

Thom: I've found in many cases when you write something that's terribly moving, it's like a boomerang. It suddenly hits you in the back of the head a half sentence or half paragraph later after he's given you the underpinning for the other side. Steinbeck has such confidence in his readers; I think that's why he has so many fans. Because he lets you bring as much to it as he brings himself. Whereas a lot of writers really close out their readers: this is all mine, that's my pen, that's my paper, and I'm going to tell it like it is. Steinbeck lets you in. I think he's very compassionate about it when a lot of writers are not. He finds the human condition painful; you'll notice a lot of his books are about violent aspects of life. *The Long Valley*, for one, is a marvelous study of violence, both psychological and personal, all the way through the book.

Int.: What were your father's reading and writing habits?

Thom: He adored reading. I don't remember him ever without two or three books at a time, including ending the evening with Malory just to soften the mind before he went to sleep. He was always reading.

Int.: And his writing?

Thom: Dorothy Parker says no one likes writing, everybody likes having written. The point is if you're an artist, everything you do is in progression to a destiny of which you do not know, a place you'd like to be. I think as a writer that commitment was Steinbeck's most of his life. I remember him all my life getting up long before anybody else did, going out and writing, taking a break, maybe go down to get the paper, and then coming back. He would start his day every day with letters to warm up. Get the poetry flowing. And then he'd go to his work and stop around 12:00, maybe 1:00, go fishing or do something. But the rest of the day fishing meant he was finishing that chapter out there. He wasn't going out there to catch any fish. He just put the line in the water with this ugly homemade lure, maybe asked a couple dumb questions of my brother and myself, and sat there and played and wrote in his head.

Int.: What was his attitude about his writing? Completing a book?

Thom: Every time I write something I just think, "Oh, God, this is so far off base." People may say it's fantastic and I still don't know what they mean. Because all I live in, as a writer, is that moment of terror. And I'm sure Steinbeck did too, like, "God, 200,000 words and I don't think I understand a thing in it, you know, and it's not even finished." There's a great line about a Japanese painter who lived for a very long time, who at the age of 89 or 90 said that if the Gods were kind and gave him another dozen years, he might become a real painter. I think that was also Steinbeck's attitude. If he could live long enough, he might become a real writer.

Int.: He had to deal with the problem of people wanting him to write his first successful book over and over again, didn't he? People always held everything up to *The Grapes of Wrath*, but he had no interest in repeating what he had done before.

Thom: No, I don't think anybody really does. I don't think anybody with imagination wants to rebuild the same thing twice. That makes them a factory.

Int.: How would you describe yourself as a reader of Steinbeck?

Thom: I'm one of the biggest Steinbeck fans I know and it has nothing to do with him being my father because, as I said, they're two different people. I love Steinbeck. I sometimes find the style a little difficult because it's the style of another age. But I'll tell you, I cannot finish "Flight" in *The Long Valley* without crying. In *In Dubious Battle* he leads you through the whole story with you thinking that you're talking to the hero and you're not. You're talking to the villains. That's the most marvelous part of that story. He does it in *The Moon Is Down* too, which is one of the greatest war stories ever told. He has a very compassionate view of the German soldiers because they're just soldiers. As he says, the flies have conquered the flypaper. Who's the winner? And that last line in *In Dubious Battle*—"Comrads! He didn't want nothing for himself"—it's like seeing the end of *Hamlet*. It just drains me.

Int.: Why did he so disdain his bourgeois upbringing? He was attracted to Communism.

Thom: Well, I don't think Steinbeck ever flirted with the Communist Party.

Int.: Carol did, I guess.

Thom: Well, in those days you got to remember, it was like *In Dubious Battle*. And when you saw the starvation and the poverty around you and people not getting fed by the fruits of their own labor, you had to ask some questions. My father had more a socialistic point of view, if anything, that people needed the help of government in order to survive. He couldn't understand why they were pouring gallons of milk out in this valley and children were starving in that one, or why they were letting apples rot over here while people were hungry over there. It really was a matter of government balance; it had nothing to do with changing the whole form of government. Steinbeck just couldn't figure out why government didn't function.

Int.: Everybody always said he rebelled against bourgeois respectability.

Thom: I think because respectability is acquired when you have achieved a status which basically immobilizes you. And once a creature or anyone reaches that state it stops growing; it's just going to fill its pot full of roots and die. He thought as long as he remained on the edge, he would never be so comfortable that he wouldn't be driven to change. But I wonder if that really happened in a sense. Because he remained, you know, in Long Island and New York for many years, extremely comfortable. Traveled to Europe a lot. Rarely came back to California. So I wonder if he disdained it, why was he so comfortable in it?

Int.: People have said he spent the first half of his life playing the Black Irish and the second half the Prussian.

Thom: Yeah, I can understand that observation. I certainly know that his trip to Vietnam disheartened me and my brother. Somehow he thought that that was still the Second World War and "Rah, rah, the boys, we're all writing home to our moms in the trenches." And that wasn't how it was. And he suddenly became one of the most unpopular literary figures in America. Not for a very long time, but for a while.

Int.: He became disillusioned with Vietnam, especially after he visited Cambodia.

Thom: Well, I think my brother had more to do with influencing my father than anybody else. He was drafted first. My father went to visit him and my brother started showing him what it was really all about. It wasn't what my father thought it was. He was a total American. There's no question about it; Steinbeck loved America more than anything else. He believed in America and what it did. And he was also close friends with [Lyndon] Johnson. He was writing speeches for Johnson and he'd been advocating the war and writing things for *Newsday*, and suddenly we're all sort of standing back and saying this is not the Second World War, this isn't Korea. This is something else altogether. And Steinbeck's not getting it. And it caused a big division between us for a long while.

Int.: Was there a changing of his mind?

Thom: I think so. I came back before he died, on emergency compassionate leave, and he was in bed with his reading glasses on reading the galley of Johnny's first book, *In Touch*, which is a fabulous book about Vietnam for a 21 year old to write, much better than the first book I ever wrote, my father said. But I think my father might have come to understand that this time he had backed the wrong horse. I think at the very end my father finally got to see a true picture of what was happening.

Int.: Would you tell me about the women in Steinbeck's life. He had been raised by a gaggle of women.

Thom: And very strong and brilliant women, too. But the older sisters were basically out of the house and married by the time he came into a state of rebellion with them. They were gone. And his youngest sister, Mary, of course he was very, very close with. She was Lancelot to his Arthur, Sancho Panza when he was Don Quixote.

Int.: Did you know Carol at all?

Thom: No, I didn't. As a matter of fact, Carol never wanted to have anything to do with me. I think that probably had more to do with the fact that they had lost a child and she probably resented my mother for having my father's children when she didn't. Each of the three wives represents a stage of Steinbeck's development and growth. And Elaine is as different from Carol as night is from day, or from my mother, Gwyn. It's really amazing; it's hard to find the thread of what he was looking for in a woman when you see these three completely different women.

Int.: They're all very strong, smart, and independent.

Thom: Yeah, I would say Carol and my mother more so. I mean because they came from working class backgrounds, my mother singing professionally by the time she was 16 and Carol from a very early age. Elaine came along because my father had no idea who she was. But she had something else too; Elaine had that wonderful Southern quality of great patience with men regardless of how stupid they think they're being. She could just smooth down those hackles and say, "John, you don't want to talk that way, you know," this kind of thing, and suddenly you're blushing. And you just can't help it. And he'd reply, "Okay, I'll get in my suit; we'll go," that kind of thing. Which my mother couldn't have done because she was a heckler and Carol couldn't have done because she gave orders.

I think he was a very lucky man. He got things when he needed them. And each wife had a completely different place in my father's life. Carol certainly from the earliest working days, and my mother as a mother and because she gave up her career for my father. Then there's Elaine, who represents that solid foundation that he really needed in the last third of his life, when "I want a home, I want it to be quiet, I want you to run interference for me, I've got a lot of work to do, etc." And I think Elaine did that brilliantly for him.

Int.: I want to ask you about your mother. John and she were in love but they also butted heads.

Thom: Yeah, they did. They were both, I think, so equally strong and in such dynamic ways. My father was a very emotional man, though he didn't show it on the surface a great deal. And he could be easily hurt. And my mother had a very sharp tongue and she was very smart. She was so brilliant, had a photographic memory, and she loved literature. She would finish a 350-page book in an evening and with total retention. She was a great cook, loved art, and was a great collector of art. Had the best taste in the family. If there was a beautiful tablecloth or beautiful silver, my mother did it.

But my mother wanted recognition in her own right. She felt she'd given up her career long enough. They had a passion for each other, absolutely. But passion can just turn on itself and eat itself up. And I think to a certain degree, as much as I loved my mother, she could be frightening when it came to cutting you off at the knees. And my father was a very sensitive man who wasn't going to take that for very long.

Int.: What about you and your brother? What kind of father was Steinbeck?

Thom: Having children was not one of his favorite things; I mean he just wanted to be a writer. My mother sort of snuck it over on him as women have a way of doing. "John, I'm four months pregnant." "Well, why didn't you tell me sooner?" "Well, I didn't think you'd like the idea." I think for a man who really only wanted to be a writer, he was a tolerably fine father. Because that really was not his prime intention in life. It's like being saddled with something you'd really rather not do and trying to carry it on as gloriously as possible. But I was very proud of him for trying. You know, I think he did his real best.

Int.: He said he wrote *East of Eden* for you and your brother.

Thom: Yeah, Cain and Abel! Typecasting too, it really was. My, I'm sorry you will never get a chance to meet my brother. I think he was one of the most brilliant writers I've read in my life. He had a love/hate relationship with my father that was really amazing. Their humor was so identical, their love of study and scholarship.

I was really stunned when it came to the conflict within our own family, how close Steinbeck came to it in *East of Eden*. My brother's attitude about the family, he was the James Dean of the family if there ever was one.

Int.: How did you find out that you weren't Jewish?

Thom: I thought I was, a name like Steinbeck. I had a circumcision. Who would know I wasn't Jewish? Nobody was paying attention to my religious upbringing whatsoever.

So here I am and I'm Jewish and about 12 and a half years old and my father and Elaine are living on 72nd Street at the Brownstone. And my father would sit down in the downstairs breakfast room, behind the kitchen next to the garden, and read the newspaper. And I came in this one Sunday with this list of things for my Bar Mitzvah, and this list goes on and on. And my father was reading the funny papers; he's totally addicted to Pogo and Dogpatch and Little Abner. My father doesn't say a word, totally indulgent. And I finish this list and notice there's no negative expression on his face. So I figure I'm almost home.

And at that, he flips over the top of the paper. And drops his glasses down on the end of his nose and reaches over and says, "I don't want to break your heart, but you're Episcopalian." And this just devastated me. I mean, I'd been passing for Jewish to all my friends. I didn't know what Episcopalian was. I just thought they were, like, lazy Catholics. But my father's attitude towards this whole thing, rather than being humiliation or outrageous, was just very straightforward. I didn't walk out feeling humiliated by him, but by my own confusion in the matter.

Int.: I was going to ask you about Charley too.

Thom: Oh, Charley was one of the great dogs on the planet, greater than anybody ever knew really, even Steinbeck. Because if you can live with a Steinbeck, get in a truck with him and go around the country, then it's like Job, you can live with anybody. This dog had an incredible sense of patience.

Steinbeck and he were really delightful together. Because he loved to sing to the dog and the dog loved to be sung to. And then, the dog didn't understand a damn thing that wasn't in French. He was so French that if you gave him a command in French and it didn't sound like French, he wouldn't do it. He used to sing, "Oh, Charley dog, they are calling you a frog, such an insult pretty poodle never had. But you sit there in the mud, with your whiskers full of mud, and the polliwogs refer to you as Dad." And this dog would sit there with his eyes open, saying, "Sing it again, sing it again." And this gigantic guy, with the eye up and the monocle and lighter and cigar, singing this stupid song to this poodle, who absolutely adored it. They were a fabulous pair. Why anyone didn't recognize him on the road during *Travels with Charley* I'll never figure out.

Int.: Is there anything else you'd like to say about your father?

Thom: I've known so few people as driven to be a writer as he was. He made a deal once with his dean at Stanford. He said, "I just want to learn how to write." He was going right to the sophomore and senior writing classes. And of course, he went for seven years, which shows a great deal of dedication. He could have graduated if he wanted to. But he only had one course in life, and that was to be a writer.

Int.: He certainly was that.

Thom: Especially abroad. Steinbeck sells five to one in Europe to the United States. As popular as he is here, he's much more popular there. Thousands upon thousands of volumes in 147 languages. He's the only author in America, dead or living, whose every work is published in hardback each year. Not even Hemingway's published in hardback every year.

Int.: Was there a Hemingway thing in the back of his head?

Thom: Could have been. I think there is a little bit of Hemingway in the back of every male's head. But he was always a fan of many writers, including Hemingway, which always stunned me. He always loved Hemingway's work; the first person that turned me on to Hemingway was Steinbeck, before he even turned me on to Steinbeck. And he turned me on to Joseph Heller. You know, he loved other authors too much to take too much credit on his own shoulders for anything.

John Steinbeck Was My Father

John Steinbeck IV

A bulky, bearded man, barefoot, John Steinbeck IV opened the front door, invited us to come in. We wriggled out of our shoes ("You can leave them on if you want," John assured) and followed him across the ivory cotton carpet into a small, white-walled room. Displayed on the south wall was a hanging on which were ranked various avatars in the Tibetan Buddhist pantheon. Rapidly, his voice raspy, John tolled off these avatars' names and histories. On a low table beneath the hanging were bowls that held incense, rice, coins, a pocketknife.

In the house's lower level, along the stairway leading up to bedrooms, books spilled from bookshelves. Had John's father prodded him to read? "Correctly suspecting he had given birth to a petty thief, my father encouraged me to read by locking in a leaded glass-front bookcase books that he thought were essential—the *Iliad*, Lao-Tse's *Tao Te Ching*, Mark Twain, the Bible, *King Arthur and His Knights*, and other tales of chivalry. Then he hid the key where he knew I would find it and threatened me within an inch of my life if he ever caught me in there. Needless to say, I learned to read rapidly."

On the patio, we settled on chairs beneath an umbrella shading a round table. . . . So, what had it been like to be the child of one of the United States' most famous writers? "I didn't know John Steinbeck was my father until the next-door doorman said to me when I was about five, 'Do you know your father is John Steinbeck?' 'Yeah,' I said. But I had no idea what that meant. Steinbeck—" John paused, explained that he spoke of his father alternately as "Steinbeck" and "my father" "—Steinbeck is a beloved writer. People love him. I'm not sure that's all completely deserved, being his son. But people really feel they knew him in a way that's really touching to them."

He'd had, John admitted, "a lot of practice with being John Steinbeck. I've always been very generous with who he is and what that's about. Not my brother. It gets in his way a little more, he's more 'Get out of my face.' " John's brother Thom lives in Los Angeles. He's a screenwriter, "a very good writer, an artist, a painter. He makes things, he has very gifted hands." Are they close? "Our phone bill last month was $750. He's my best friend, the only guy who knows what I know, including Vietnam, growing up with my mother and my father. He's the **only** person who knows what I know. . . ."

About his father, John said, "My brother and I, we talked with him a lot about things, languages and history and cultures and customs. We traveled around the world with him. I had a great education. He had a lot of eclectic interests as I do or my brother does: Why a crossbow arrow will penetrate your breast at a certain number of miles per hour. My love of words and communication I got from him. When I was not doing my homework in boarding school, I was reading encyclopedias. He made me think learning things was not a chore, not a duty, but a really exciting thing to do. Not even that, but excitement itself. . . ."

Was there pressure on John to become a writer? He shook his head, no. "I started writing so close to the time he died that he was surprised by the fact that I was even doing it. The fact that I did it tolerably well was nothing but a source of pleasure to him. He said, 'Oh, the kid can write.' My book was in galleys before he died, and he had the galleys on his bed when he died. Being a writer, I am compared to him sometimes. Fortunately, I write nonfiction."

"I'm sure there are all sorts of deep-seated psychological issues—myself comparing myself to him, being under the shadow of whatever those words are. They aren't crippling at this point, but they're there. I am sure that for children of famous people, there's a certain amount of pathology that goes around. Drugs and alcohol have been fatal to a number of my friends. Artists are by nature not particularly gifted as parents. They can be very self-centered, very abusive often and dysfunctional when it comes to raising children. So the kid kind've [*sic*] has to raise himself. Often it is expecting too much for that muse to operate **and** for the person to be a parent." His father, John allowed, never had to be a parent "except on his time and on his terms, and then he was very good at that, very good. Very Huck Finny.

Had he had to do it day in, day out, he couldn't have made it, no chance that he would've been any good at it."

Oh, yes, John said, his father was a disciplined worker. "He would get up at five in the morning, generally, and fiddle around with breakfast. Then he would sharpen pencils for a long time. He had a box of not such dull pencils here . . ." John reached with his right hand into an imaginary box . . . "and an empty box here." He reached with his left hand into a second, imaginary box. Laughed. "I'm talking about 400 pencils. He had one of the first electric pencil sharpeners every made. He'd take a pencil," John mimed, "put it in the sharpener, and by the time he had them all sharpened, when this box was full, he had gotten over what all writers have: that morning inhibition: 'Am I really going to put my mind on a piece of blank paper?' By the time the 400 pencils were sharpened, he'd negotiated all that. And then he would write, from six or seven in the morning until noon. Then quit and go fishing or whittling or invent. I thought that was really enviable, that he only worked until noon. But he did it with a great deal of discipline. He didn't give himself vacations. He didn't gnash his teeth about stuff. He worked out a lot of his mechanical problems by writing letters to his close friends and editor."

We talked, then, among ourselves, about Steinbeck the writer, how as the '30s passed into the '40s and '50s, he remained popular among general readers, even while, critically, his reputation dwindled. "When my father was a boy," John said, "if you were a farm person, or anybody who didn't live in the city, there were no good reasons to read unless you were reading the Bible or the directions to the combine. If you had time to read, it was because you weren't doing your chores."

"He wrote simply, not in the way that Hemingway is considered to write simply, but he wrote in a way that people who are intimidated by books could actually follow the story. It wasn't playing down to them at all, and his books gave them confidence they could read and understand. It wasn't something that was Greek to them. He kind of made it okay for people to read a book without being ashamed. His place in history is very valuable in that sense."

"He had a very pixie sense, he'd write anything. He liked writing *for* things. So if he saw, say, an outboard motor that he wanted to have but didn't feel he should spend the money on it, he'd call the Evinrude company and say, 'I'd like to borrow one of your motors and use it fishing, and if I like it, I'll say I like it.' And then they'd give him the outboard motor. He thought that was one of the best parts of the job. Of course, he was well into the dollar-a-word category when this worked out for him, but he liked it a lot."

"He liked writing frivolous pieces and he liked writing short stories, the serious, well-crafted ones in the traditional sense. He liked doing send-ups of Poe. He wrote for *Sports Illustrated*—phony sports columns. He wrote a piece for them about what sports meant to him or something like that." In another of his *Sports Illustrated* articles, Steinbeck had discussed racing oak trees. John was visiting him and saw, next to his father's writing desk, a baking dish filled with peat moss and on the peat moss were rows of acorns, turned upside down. "I didn't let him know I'd read the *Sports Illustrated* article," John said, "and I asked him, 'What are you doing here?' and he said, 'I'm racing oak trees.' " John's laughter interrupted his story, then he continued, repeating to us his father's answer, " 'Well, it hasn't caught on yet, but if it does, I have one of the first stables.' It was so strange. He had a very funny private little thing going on. You'd go into the attic where people had mousetraps. *He'd* have a plate of poisoned grain, and he'd have signs all over, 'Mouse Beware. This is Poison. Do not Eat.' He was a funny guy."

John's father was a friend of Lyndon Johnson, and the elder Steinbecks were frequently invited to the White House, as private guests. "There's a picture of us, with me shaking Lyndon's hand. When I was sent off into a very insecure area of Vietnam, I had a copy of this picture and I gave it to my company commander. I had written under the picture, 'Hey Lyndon, why me? Why Vietnam?' "

Steinbeck had supported U.S. involvement in Vietnam. John fought in Vietnam, as did his brother Thom. Their father's support of President Johnson's policies in Southeast Asia infuriated many U.S. leftists. "Steinbeck," John said, "had the reputation of being a conscience for Americans." After John landed in Vietnam, his father asked him if he thought he should visit the country. "I had just arrived. I was quite hawkish at the time, I thought the Communists put bombs in crowded movie theaters and we were doing nothing other than trying to save these people. I didn't realize our bullets didn't always hit just Communists. I was very naïve. And other people, including my father, didn't know much then about the war. So he went over to have a firsthand look. He stayed six weeks and wrote a series of pieces for *Newsday*."

"He was quite pro–U.S. involvement, and he lost a lot of readers. There were more people who were 'Let's get out of here, this is ugly.' I think we both misread the situation. After he left Vietnam, about three months later, and I began learning Vietnamese and actually hanging out with Vietnamese people, I begin to see that this [U.S. involvement in Vietnam] was not cool, and I share that with my father and we had a little parting of the way. But not for long. He came around there." It was a time, John reminded us, when "the so-called generation gap was in full gap."

I asked John about his father's response to the *New York Times'* suggestion, after he had been awarded the Nobel Prize, that the award committee might have found someone better than he to whom to give the literature prize. "I'm sure his feelings were incredibly hurt, that he was incredibly pissed off. I think he had a certain amount of insecurity because he was a Western writer. He lived on the East Coast with the Ivy League literate crowd. But he never pretended to be an intellectual. He was a shy man, and I think it made him insecure and then furious. They were such snobs."

"I do know that one person came up to him in Stockholm, when he went there for the prize, an East Coast kind of lady, and said to him, almost like she was musing over her scones, 'I wonder how long it would take to earn $50,000 tax-free,' and he looked at her and said, 'Forty years, lady. I just did it.' He worked very hard at what he did. He was poor for a long time. His success of any remark was in his late 30s. He worked hard and he worked at a lot of things, did a lot of manual labor, was a night watchman, helped build Madison Square Garden, poured cement for it."

What things remind him of his father? "Some odors—a certain Florida toilet water. I noticed very pleasantly the other day, I walked into my office and it smelled like my father's office. A certain humor—my brother and I share a lot of his humor. My bother is quite like him. Without ever thinking about it, my father, walking down the street, would tip his hat to a dog. My brother does that. It's nice when you know it's spontaneous and genuine, nothing cranked up about it. But when it's most touching is when you see your own hands picking up something in a way that your father did or your mother did. . . ."

Was there a thing you two were working out? "I think everybody has that. I communicated with him a lot better after he was dead then [*sic*] when he was alive. . . ." John gazed past us across the lawn, then returned his glance to our faces. "He's alive when I salute a dog walking down the street."

"After he died, I got some writing lessons from him." In 1970, during a winter and spring offensive in Laos, John was holed up during the monsoon in an old French hotel in Vientiane, and he again read *The Grapes of Wrath*. "That's when I got the most out of the book as a writer. By that time I was writing. So then I actually saw how deft he was. I saw the nuts and bolts of the writing. That was as impressive to me as the historical value of the book at the time it came out and what that did to America in terms of becoming aware of the Dust Bowl and Depression from the farmers' point of view."

"The most gratifying thing he gave me, both before and after he died, was to know that the most refined highest wisdoms and human knowledge we find in the everyday ordinary world, not in a library of Sanskrit, not at Oxford, but from the guy down the street. That guy knows as much. The common wisdom is the most profound. Ordinary mind is enlightened mind. Fortunately, my other training also reinforced that truth."

"John Believed in *Man*": An Interview with Mrs. John Steinbeck

Elaine Steinbeck

Donald Coers: As you know, this interview will be published in a book of essays on Steinbeck's middle and later period—the works written after *The Grapes of Wrath*. You were married to him, of course, during most of that time.

Elaine Steinbeck: Yes, I lived the last twenty years of John's life with him. I met him early in 1949 and he died late in 1968. He was really very famous when I was married to him. I met him in Pacific Grove. People there more or less left him alone, so I don't think I realized how famous John was until I came to New York. And then when we started traveling, the press met every plane that John was on or every train.

DC: That bothered him, didn't it?

ES: He said until the day he died, "The best thing that Elaine ever did for me was not to be shy and to know how to handle this." Anybody who knows me knows that I'm not shy. I would talk to everybody and get everything warmed up. Then I could just disappear, go out and mind my own business, and he could take it up from there, whether we were standing in the open somewhere or in a hotel room. John could handle it here in New York, but when we were traveling, I always did the warm-up. He was very shy at the beginning.

DC: Let me ask you about one of the frequently voiced ideas of critics and scholars about John Steinbeck: that his writing changed fundamentally several years after *The Grapes of Wrath.* Jackson Benson puts that change ten years or so after *The Grapes of Wrath*, about the time Steinbeck met you in California. Benson says the nature of the change, at least in the major works he would write during the remainder of his career, was from a focus on group behavior to a focus on the social and ethical problems of the individual. What are your views on the perceived change? Was the move from California to New York significant? Was he just wanting to get on with something new?

ES: Oh, I have very definite views about that. When I met him in Pacific Grove, John said, "I can't live here. Why in the hell did I think I could come home? You can't go home again. I've lived in New York. I can't live here." And he said to me, "I'm here because I've got a job writing *Viva Zapata!* and I want to write it near the studio so I can help them put it into screen form." But he also said, "One reason I'm here now is that I'm going to write a book. I've been doing research for it a long time. I've been living under such unhappy circumstances in New York that I haven't been able to write." As Jay Parini [author of an upcoming biography on John Steinbeck] said the other day, "He didn't write well with Gwyn because they were so unhappy all the time, because they were fighting all the time."

Anyway, John said, "I still have some research to do out here with the newspaper, in history, about when I was a little boy. I'm going to write a book and put everything in it that I know. I'm going to tell everything I know about my family." Well, I think when he had done that [finished his work on *Zapata!* and the research for his book], even if he hadn't met me . . . I don't think John moved back to New York because of me. I think he may have moved **when** he moved because of me, but he had already said he wasn't going to stay, that he couldn't stay anymore [even though] he was delighted with his house in Pacific Grove on Eleventh Street. Once while he was living there he told me, "I felt so good this morning. That old man next door looked across and saw me in the garden, and he said, 'You Ernst Steinbeck's son?' 'Yes sir, I am.' 'Been away?' " He just loved it. That old man only knew him as Ernst Steinbeck's son. Anyway, I know that he was going to move back here [to New York]. How long can you stay and write about Cannery Row? I don't see why anyone is startled that he moved around. One of the first things I asked John when I first met him was, "When Fitzgerald and Hemingway were abroad, why didn't you go?" And he said, "I'm very glad now that I didn't because I stayed at home and wrote about my own people."

DC: Would you agree with those scholars who say that Steinbeck always insisted on doing what he wanted to do, that he maintained his individualism and didn't look at the critics?

ES: Yes, he did not do what the critics wanted, ever. He never wrote to anybody's formula. Critics faulted him, but he never paid attention to them. He wrote whatever he wanted to write. And I would like to say that I know that's why John did not do more on the Arthurian legend—it's all right to say it now because the people involved are dead. In the first place, John had no idea he was going to die so young. He wouldn't have had a spinal operation the year before if he had known he was going to die. That's one of the hardest things anyone could have gone through, learning to walk again and all that. He had no idea his heart system was going to go out and his heart was going to fail. He certainly meant to finish the Arthurian cycle. His agent, Elizabeth Otis, whom he adored, had never interfered in his writing and neither had his editor, Pascal Covici. The man Elizabeth Otis loved and lived with for many years, Chase Horton, owned the bookstore that supplied John with all of those books, so many books, that he used for Middle English. And suddenly John said to me once when we came back from the year in Somerset, "Elizabeth and Chase have gotten so involved in this. How did I let this happen? I can't work like this. I'm going to stop for a while." I think he stopped and wrote *The Winter of Our Discontent*.

John always meant to go back and finish the Arthurian book. I studied Middle English with him just for fun, and he loved the fact that I did. When we would go to London and visit the British Museum, while he was doing research I'd be reading letters in the display case. And he would pass by me getting a book and he would say, "Having fun?" and I'd say, "I'm reading Queen Elizabeth writing to Queen Mary of Scotland; of course I'm having fun." Anyway, what John had meant to do was this: he had meant to translate the Malory straight as Malory wrote it and then to go back and to fictionalize it, write the Steinbeck version of it. But he simply didn't get around to it. He died; that's the only reason. But he just said, "The people who work with me are getting too involved and they are driving me crazy and I will stop for awhile and write something else and then I'll go back to it quietly and not tell anybody I've gone back to it." That's the truth. These are the things that nobody knows but me, because I lived with him. Then about two years after John died, Elizabeth Otis said, "Let's publish it." She said, "I'd like to publish it and publish his letters to Chase there in the back of the book." I wasn't too with it at the time. I had had a terrible time adjusting to John's death.

DC: So, you're not sure you would make that same decision again?

ES: I'm not sorry; every once in a while somebody loves the book, and it gets better as it goes. Towards the last third of the book John is beginning to have fun and to embroider a little. We had gone down to the coast . . . Southampton . . . no, I can't remember where now, and he begins to write about that because he and I had walked there. And he begins to put his characters into that landscape, and, I think, to have fun. It would have been wonderful.

DC: He certainly has fun with those private jokes he puts in the book—the one, for instance, about Toby Street [Steinbeck's longtime friend], who appears as Sir Tobinus Streat de Montroy.

ES: . . . if John had finished that book, nobody could have said that he had gone downhill. Because that's what he wanted to do and that's what I regret more than anything for his sake—that he never got that done. Remember the story I told you about when he was dying?

DC: About the time you spent in Somerset?

ES: He was in bed and I was sitting beside him. I was reading to him—he had the oxygen tubes in his nostrils—and he suddenly said, "What was the best time we had in our twenty years together?" I started to answer, but then I said, "You tell me first." And he said, "No, I'm dying and you'll agree with me." And I kind of laughed and he laughed. I said, "I'll write it on a piece of paper and put it in your hand." And I did. Then I asked him, "What's the best time we've had?" And he said, "The year we spent in Somerset." And I said, "Open your hand." And I had written "Somerset." It's an incredible story for me to remember during the last hours with John.

I also remember one day when we were alone in the cottage [in Somerset] and he said, "Elaine, can you hear me?" I said, "Yes, I'm on the stairway." He said, "Can you look out the window toward the garden?" And I said, "I'll go quietly and look out." He said, "I'm writing about Morgan le Fey and I want you to see what's in the garden." There was a raven sitting in the garden and he said, "Maybe that raven knows what I'm writing about. That raven is looking for Morgan le Fay." She always rode with a raven on her wrist, you know. The Arthurian legend was all magic to him. . . .

DC: We were talking yesterday about a part of Steinbeck that general readers and even scholars sometimes miss, his humor.

ES: People who knew him knew his humor. And people in California knew his humor and everybody around here knew it. It's just some of the scholars now. They think he's the Great Steinbeck and that everything he wrote has to be taken seriously. I find that a lot of young people or very pompous people or people who are teaching will pick up something that John meant to be ridiculous and think that he was being profound. . . .

DC: Obviously Steinbeck had a common touch for those who knew him personally as well as for his readers. . . .

ES: But you see John was not always able to do that in person. He was only able to do that . . . that's why he liked to write. When we first started seeing each other—I didn't know it at the time but we were falling in love—he took me over to show me his house, and he said, "I started to write in that room." I said, "When was that?" And he said, "I don't remember a time I didn't write." You see, he just did not remember a time that he didn't put words on paper. His common touch came from that. I can't tell you how shy John was. Sumner Locke-Elliott, the Australian writer whom I love, once said to me, "Elaine, I had one opportunity to meet John, and he talked solemnly and I understood about every tenth word. I was too shy to say, 'I can't understand you.' " John *really* mumbled. I would say to him, "Honey, please speak up." And all of his friends would say, "Stop mumbling!" He was *genuinely* shy with new people, but not with his old friends like Otto [Lindhardt]. But his common touch was in his writing. John expressed himself well in words [when he talked]; I'm not saying that he did not. He expressed himself in the most interesting way. He was very witty and very funny. I'm a big crossword puzzler, and I used to ask him for a synonym but I would have to say, "I don't want the history of the word, John; I want the synonym." He loved words and I learned to love words from him.

John was the most fun to travel with of anyone I've ever known. Somebody said to me the other day, "We're going to be in Rome a short time. Should we go out to Hadrian's Villa?" I said, "Oh my God, that is the most important and most interesting—" But then I said, "I don't know whether you should go or not. You won't be with John." When I was there with John we took a bottle of wine and some cheese and some ham and bread and went out and spent the day. The ruins are very sparse and low, and John just filled the whole scene, right in front of my eyes. And we spent the day there, and I was *in* Hadrian's Villa. And although there was just a little of it standing, we would sit and walk in the garden and then sit and drink our wine and have a picnic. Travelling with him was simply wonderful. He always knew what to tell me to read. I always read about what I'm going to see and read about it while I'm there and then read about it more when I leave. He was a marvelous man to travel with. But—and now I'm trying to think of things about him—he was a man who wanted privacy. He didn't want to go out as much as I did. Once when we were getting ready to go abroad for several months and we were living here, he said, "Why are we going out so much?" Then he said, "We're saying good-bye to people I scarcely ever say hello to." He was very funny—and fun to live with—but also very moody. At first when he went through those terrible black moods when he was writing—I found out those were writer's block—I would think, What have I done, what have I done? He was very hard to live with in many ways. But I think most writers probably would be.

DC: You said something yesterday about his being the most complicated person you ever knew.

ES: Oh, his mind went in so many directions. He was very political. He knew world history very well indeed. He was very opinionated, which I liked, and he was very liberal. . . .

DC: You know, those predictions about the collapse of communism [in *Journal of a Novel*]—he was making them at the height of the cold war. And they show the same fundamental faith in democracy and human decency he proclaimed in *The Moon Is Down* during the darkest days of the Second World War.

ES: You see, John believed in *man*. That's what his Nobel Prize speech says. He said, "You believe in the perfectibility of man. Man will never be perfect, but he has to strive for it." That's the whole point. That was his whole point about life. And religion to John was very interesting. He was religious. He didn't believe in any church creeds, but he said to me when he was dying, "Don't you let a bunch of people get together and tell yarns about me. Make sure it's the Episcopal burial service." And I said to him, "Do you believe?" And he said, "I'm like Socrates before he drank the hemlock: I don't know if there are gods or not, but in case there are. . . ."

"The Marriage of His Life": Meeting John Steinbeck

Gwyn Steinbeck

Late in 1939, when I was twenty years old, I worked on staff at CBS studios in Los Angeles and lived with my mother. I mentioned to Max Wagner, a family friend, that I'd read [*The*] *Pastures of Heaven* and since Max knew John Steinbeck, I said I'd like to meet him because the book was a break-through into a kind of literature I had never read and I was very impressed. Max arranged a meeting when John was very ill with back pain. "I told him you were the best cook in the world," Max said. "He's lying in an apartment without any food. Would you make him some chicken soup?" I told him I would, and he took me to the Aloha Arms apartments on Sunset and Highland.

I walked into the room and saw a large man lying on an old Murphy bed. And then it sort of happened—this man fixed his blue eyes on me and before I knew it, I had talked with him the whole night through. What happened between us was pure chemistry. I fed him his soup, I washed him, I bathed him, and I rubbed his back and legs. He had a magnificent physique. John was in great pain and that brought my maternal instincts into play. Whatever I was able to provide was something he needed.

In the evenings I was singing in a nightclub, and John started visiting me at work or during the day at my mother's. We were in the last years of the Depression, and he admired what Mother and I could do with little or no food. Basically, he was a shy man, but he had me hooked. I was smitten; I had never met anyone before like him. One night, he asked me out for dinner. We went to a little place on Sunset Boulevard and he talked to me in very subdued tones.

"What do you want to do? Who are you in love with? What have you read? Where were you raised?" I told him a bit about my background and he said, "You are an Earth Woman."

Our relationship developed spasmodically because he had not gotten a divorce from Carol yet. He sent me his favorite books to remember him by, like *Black Marigolds*, *Green Mansions*, Robinson Jeffers, and all of Robert Louis Stevenson. Then he asked me to come up to Salinas for a weekend. Carol was there at the time, but John and I stayed at a hotel, on the sly. We went on a pub-crawl with Ed Ricketts and when I got tired, Ed paid a little Mexican boy a quarter to borrow his red wagon until midnight. Ed came back and said, "Your taxi is waiting." For the rest of the evening I was pulled around in a little red wagon and John thought it was very funny. We went into another bar, and I sat on the upright piano and sang "Just My Bill" and "Someday I'll Find You." It was a mad, mad weekend.

When I returned to Los Angeles, I suffered with ill health and decided to go live with my father in Florida to recuperate. I wrote to John in care of Ed Ricketts at the laboratory and told him where I was going. It seemed obvious that he had gone back to his wife and I felt there was no room for me at the time. Even though I was very much in love with John, I wasn't going to push things. John was married. I thought it best that somebody drop out of the picture and I seemed to be the logical one. I stayed in Tampa for six months, and then I got a call from CBS asking me to join their staff in San Francisco, where I sang on a coast-to-coast program once a day.

One night, while the show was on, I got a call from John saying he'd heard me sing on the radio. He told me he had to see me. He came up to San Francisco and we went to the Cliff House. He said, "I can't get over you. I am still very much in love with you. Things are not getting any better between Carol and myself. I don't know what to do. Will you wait for me?" I told him I would try.

I went back to Los Angeles to stay with my mother, and soon there was a wire from John. All it said was "Coming." When John arrived, he told me that Carol was going away for a while to work in New York, and he asked me to come to Monterey with him. I went, and John begged me to stay with him; he said that he was very lonesome and upset and that he needed my comfort so he could work. We started to renovate the house. We painted and scrubbed, burned weeds and tore out things. John didn't say anything about what my future was to be with him other than that he was able to work and he seemed to be more at peace, although restlessness did plague him sometimes. In the mornings he worked in the garden and eventually hired a Japanese gardener. He knew I liked roses, so he went down to the fish cannery and ordered a whole truck of fish guts and had it turned into the soil. When he did that, he said we wouldn't have to fertilize for seven years, and he built me a beautiful rose garden.

The guesthouse was directly opposite the living room, and John planned on making that into his nest. He always had to have his nest because he liked to leave the main house to work. He started very early in the morning, usually just a little past daylight. If he had a particularly long piece of work or a passage or chapter or sequence that he wanted to complete, he sometimes got up around 4:00 am. He'd throw on a pair of khakis, leave his pajama top on, and put on some bedroom slippers. He'd make a pot of ranch coffee and drop an egg in to clarify it. It was really a mess to clean up. He'd use canned milk and sugar; if he was really tired he would use a lot of sugar.

Then John would wake me up, and we would sit and talk, not necessarily about his work but about lots of things. If he was working on a particularly tough piece, he would ask me about it, but I don't think he really listened to what I said. I was the sounding board while he thought out loud. Then he'd go hole up in his nest and go to work. Sometimes I went back to bed and slept for another hour and then got up. By then, John would have finished his first pot of coffee, and he'd holler, "Honey, I need more coffee," and the pot would go on again. John never typed his manuscripts. He had written in longhand for so many years that he thought he expressed himself better in longhand. Usually, he would take a break around noon, but he rarely ever ate lunch. If he were going strong, he'd skip the break and call for another pot of coffee. He might stretch and go for a walk in the garden, but he never talked because he was so preoccupied with work. I busied myself all day with house matters or worked outside. John didn't like having anyone around the house making noise. When he worked, he wanted absolute quiet.

John's average word count in those days ranged between twenty-five hundred and five thousand words a day, and when he was finished he would come out of his nest physically exhausted. He would take a long bath and then an hour nap. While I was fixing dinner, he would talk with me or read me what he had written that day. He did not drink while he was working—ever. If what John had written was bad, he knew it before I did. If I said, "I think that part isn't quite right," he would say, "Well, that's the part that's bothering me. I must rewrite it." My opinion was only a confirmation of what John already knew, but sometimes he had to hear the words out loud when he read them to see the problem. I never gave criticism because, in the first place, I was in great awe of his work, and in the second place, I was in love with him.

After dinner we would listen to the news and he would read all the papers. John wasn't very anxious to see people while he was working. Monday through Thursday we never went out. He might have one drink but always at home. During the week John did not want a hangover. His vital time was in the morning. He was like a long distance runner. He was blanched by evening; he was exhausted and had used up all his energy.

John and I would get to bed during the week no later than ten o'clock and usually I read to him. He loved the classics: Tacitus, or Julius Caesar, or something about the Gallic wars, or poetry. John wouldn't read for himself because his eyes were tired from staring at his own writing all day long. Weekends were for friends. On Sunday we usually had an open house and served brunch. John never went to church. He was raised Episcopalian and had both of his sons baptized. But his family was very high church and wouldn't accept divorce, so that made it very difficult for him to walk into church. He was a very spiritual man; his spiritual sense was very deep inside of him. He had a feeling that God was all the forces in nature and that there must always be a balance in nature. People died or were killed, and that was a part of the balance.

In August of 1941, John and I moved to New York. There was never an actual proposal of marriage on John's part to me. He wanted to go back east because Carol was coming back to California from New York. One night, John casually said, in the middle of the conversation, "Well, Carol has finally made up her mind. She's going to get a divorce, so I presume some day we will be married." That's the way he put it. John talked to my mother and told her he wanted to go to New York and make a new life for me there. It was January of 1943 when John's divorce from Carol was finalized. We had already furnished the apartment on 51st Street and we decided we should be married in New Orleans, where we had friends. John and I picked March 29, 1943, as our wedding date. I went on ahead to New Orleans, and John stayed behind to select our wedding rings at Tiffany's. He told me that he wanted an old-fashioned antique gold ring, one of the "got you" sort of rings, because he said that ours was going to be the marriage of his life.

My Cousin, John Steinbeck

Stanford Steinbeck

My name is Stanford E. Steinbeck. My father, Charles Minor Steinbeck, was the oldest of five brothers and John's father, Ernst, was the youngest. I was born on April 15th, 1907, in Templeton, California; that's near Paso Robles. John and I were five years apart in age. When we were youngsters I lived in Hollister and John in Salinas, twenty-four miles away. We saw each other quite a bit during the early days of our lives. I remember one time that made me fully realize that John was a great storyteller. He had fallen in the Salinas River while fishing and had gotten pneumonia. I think I was about fourteen so that would have made him about nineteen. And I went over to Salinas to see him from Hollister and he was just recuperating and still in his bed. And he told me about it in such descriptive terms that I full well realized, at that point, that John was a storyteller—by that I mean a teller of stories. As it turns out, he certainly was.

We also had a period of time in New York. I was living in Washington DC so I saw him quite frequently. Every time I'd go up to New York I would take a pile of his books, eight or ten of them, for autographs. And then I would give them to my friends in Washington. John was, by that time, coming along pretty well and so they were all received with great pleasure. But John, I remember, would get down on the floor and auto-graph these books. I'd ask him to do one for somebody and then he'd do it to "Peter Williams," we'll say, "from John Steinbeck," or he'd just plain autograph them for me. He was very cooperative.

Later I followed him down on a trip to Mexico in 1945 when he went to counsel on a motion picture entitled *The Pearl*. We went down and took over an apartment that John and Gwyn had had in Cuernavaca at a German hotel. At that time Thom, the oldest of the two boys, was maybe a year old. We had such a wonderful time in Mexico together. We used to go into Mexico City with him. Driving with John was an experience—not his driving, but he had comments that were hilarious. Describing some of the people who maneuvered by without much finesse, he had terms that weren't particularly endearing.

The last time I talked to John was in 1968, the year he passed away. My wife and I had driven across the United States from San Diego to Florida. And then we had gone up the coast and planned to go to Canada and then west on Highway 1. I talked to him when we were in New York City and were staying at the Algonquin Hotel; I had read about Ernest Hemingway and many famous authors staying there so we stayed there. We called John and had a hard time getting him because he wasn't in his New York home; he was at his home in Sag Harbor on Long Island. Finally, through his agent's help, I did talk to him, told him about our trip plans, and he said, oh, he'd wanted very much to do that part of western Canada and would we send him a card from there. He was so interested in that country. That was the last time I talked to him. I had realized that he was ill, at that time, but didn't realize he was that ill. This was in June 1968.

I love John's writings. But I can't say I have a favorite book. I thought they were all wonderful. To me, John was a writer, a storyteller. It wasn't a question of pursuing or trying to emphasize any social cause—he was telling a story. John was the friendliest man you could ever know and so worthwhile. He was generous, thoughtful, a friend anyone would be proud to have. I am very proud of him to this day and I think he's worthy of it.

John Steinbeck

Burgess Meredith

John Steinbeck was basically a simple man. He liked good food and he liked pleasant surroundings, but underneath he was a farmer and enjoyed country attitudes. There was a dichotomy in his nature, though. For example, he dined often at the "21" Club and the Colony Club in New York, and yet he never let a meal pass there without making some deprecating remark about New York life. Maybe deep down he felt that he should have never have left California or left his beloved "Pastures of Heaven."

Some critics have said he never wrote well after he came East. John would talk about that problem openly, saying that he often thought of going back, and part of him wanted to, but he could not force himself to do it. Yet he never stopped writing about it, and his books became more and more successful. From memory he could write about Monterey or Cannery Row or Salinas or Soledad with such freshness of mind and sharpness of detail you'd think he'd never left the West Coast—but ended up with homes on Long Island and on the elegant side of Manhattan.

Whether the quality of his writing diminished or was sustained, time will tell. But it's interesting that in the days when Steinbeck was alive and at the top of his career, most critics considered him a lesser talent than Hemingway or Faulkner. As time went on, this estimation began to change. He received the Nobel Prize. And today, bookstores sell more Steinbeck novels than those of Faulkner and Hemingway. Even some of his shorter works like [*The*] *Pastures of Heaven* and *Cannery Row* and *Tortilla Flat* are more highly regarded now than they were when they arrived on the scene. Steinbeck was always famous—he was always a star and always a best-seller—but high acclaim and deep respect come to him more and more as time rolls on. American authors do not ripen as well as the English and Irish authors, but time seems to favor John Steinbeck.

Odds and ends of memories of Steinbeck float into view: I recall his childlike pleasure with tricks and gadgets. Once he conceived the notion of bringing helium tanks into his house, not for therapeutic purposes, but for the purpose of changing the quality of people's voices. If you inhale helium and try to talk, something fantastic happens to your voice. It becomes eerie and strangled, an octave above its natural range. The first time Steinbeck tried it on himself, he took a gulp of helium, and spoke the words, "It is a far, far better thing that I do than I have ever done." He sounded like a suffocating cat or a querulous corncrake. It was one of his favorite amusements, and often in those carefree days when we went to Steinbeck's house all of us would amuse ourselves by inhaling the stuff and saying foolish things in an altered voice.

This so intrigued me that years later, when I was directing a play called *The Frogs of Spring* (a play by Nathaniel Benchley, about Steinbeck, by the way), I had one of the characters come on stage with a lungful of helium and say something or other in the hopes that it would brighten the act. The audience laughed at the gimmick but the critics were not amused. They said we were trying to cover up a bad plot with secondary tricks—but right or wrong, we had fun doing it.

The other thing I recall about John was his early fascination with his sons. He had wanted very much to have children—he said he felt incomplete without them. He wrote a play about it, *Burning Bright*. It had to do with a circus performer discovering he could not have children. Then one day his wife became pregnant by someone else. At first the performer was murderous and vengeful, but in the end he was persuaded that all men are related and all children everyone's sons and daughters. That was the plot . . . but John personally would never have been guided by such a gentle philosophy. His own children meant a lot to him.

I made up a poem about John's son Tom [*sic*], when the lad was five or six years old. It went: "Tom, Tom, the writer's son, stole a plot and away he run." For the life of me I don't know why this struck John so funny, but it did, and I can only guess we were easily amused in those carefree times.

John was a seeker after women and he enjoyed them. I had the sneaking feeling that John liked to appear more unbridled than he really was. This, of course, is a tendency of many artists and, I guess, nonartists. But artists particularly, because they are in the public eye and often feel they should hide their sensitivity and their shyness. John's defense was to thrust out his chin very hard after he had a few drinks—I think he believed his chin receded a little. It looked to me like a perfectly good chin, but he wanted it to be more than that. Finally, in the last fifteen or twenty years of his life, he grew a full, thick beard. After that he apparently didn't feel the need to act pugnacious.

John was usually a humorous man. He gazed on most events with an antic eye. He wrote seriously when he wanted to, and his serious writings are probably his best—but in his life, John had a humorous slant on people and events. He enjoyed most of the things that happened to him and many of the people he knew. It comes back to me strongly, that enjoyment. When he laughed, his face got red, like Santa Claus's. It did not get rosy, it got painted red! There is a portrait of him that Lewis Milestone owned which caught John's high coloring exactly.

There was another, darker side, that sometimes showed through; underneath, there seemed to be an ocean of sorrow. Yet I never saw John out-of-hand while drinking. I did not ever see him totter or stumble or show hostility, as they tell me Faulkner and Fitzgerald sometimes did. I never witnessed him disagreeable or dangerous. He was a large man, over six feet, and well built, but he never took exercise. I don't recall him running or playing outdoor games. Yet I feel he often fancied himself a rugged individual resembling many of the characters he wrote about. One time in a pub, I saw him arm-wrestle quite a few people and get beaten regularly, which seemed to surprise him. A lot of us act that way. We think we are in better shape than we are. And, of course, until late in life John's eating habits didn't always encourage good health.

On the other hand, his writing habits were disciplined and very scheduled. In the years I knew him he wrote early in the morning—from five to noon. Originally, he wrote in a wonderful longhand on legal paper with fine blue lines—his earlier manuscripts are handsome as a monk's scroll. His handwriting was small and tight, and he seldom had to rewrite. It is interesting to note that Maxwell Anderson's handwriting and John's writing were somewhat similar. They both wrote in small careful script and they both used a finely lined legal paper; a coincidence that interested me, because otherwise they were totally unlike.

Years after John and Gwyn separated and she was living in Palm Springs, she showed me the original manuscript of the novel *Of Mice and Men*. It was faultless, with few corrections, and handwritten. Gwyn was about to sell the manuscript to a college or a university or to a collector for $50,000. She was, she told me, broke. Her health was bad and despite suffering from emphysema; she smoked constantly.

John wrote passionately and with absolute concentration. He seemed to be totally involved in the process of creation and in the formation of words. In the 1950s, when John moved to New York, he confessed to me that he was starting to use a dictating machine. He said it felt pretty good. He told me that *Travels with Charley* was partly dictated. His manuscripts are now extremely valuable—particularly his early ones that had to do with California and were written in his clear, precise hand. I have a half a hundred unpublished letters from him written in that very fashion.

East of Eden was finished about 1951 in New York at the Bedford Hotel of all places, but I don't recall if it was written in longhand. He told Nathaniel Benchley and myself he wanted to write it for his children, to make them aware of their heritage. He struggled to make it instructional and simple. In the end, with his editor's urging, Steinbeck the novelist took over. *Eden* was his last long look back at California. He wrote it while his powers were still mighty and while his feelings about the West Coast were vivid.

Three fine motion pictures were made of the works of John Steinbeck: *The Grapes of Wrath, Of Mice and Men*, and *East of Eden*. I was with Elia Kazan and John at the Bedford Hotel, when they phoned Darryl Zanuck and made the deal for *Eden*. I felt left out of the proceedings, a poor cousin.

After the death of Doc Ricketts, John took over the laboratory and assumed the financial obligations of Doc, who had not been a great hand at making or saving money. I remember John phoning me about Ricketts's death. He spelled out the details of the tragedy with great exactness: how a train from Monterey had run into Doc's car and killed him instantly. Knowing Doc as I did, and knowing how close he was to John, it was moving to hear John tell it so slowly and so clearly. I wish the exact words he used were in my memory; in times of tragedy, the mind can't always hold the full picture.

The two of them collaborated on *Sea of Cortez*. The original book was an expensive edition with many color pictures taken by Doc of the sea creatures they collected on the famous voyage to the Sea of Cortez. A beautiful book it was. I still have a copy of it and I look at it often. John's words are the fourth dimension.

One day I was sitting in the "21" Club with Harold Ross, editor of *The New Yorker* magazine. *Sea of Cortez* had just come out. I talked about it with some enthusiasm to Ross. He said to me, in his shoulder-raising, head-scratching manner: "That book is nonsense. It was just an excuse for Steinbeck to get away from his wife with some jackass friends of his. You can't expect much of a book under those circumstances." This is not a precise quote, but it is the exact gist. It was not an accurate observation, since Carol, Steinbeck's wife, was the cook on the trip. I was taken aback, because I respected Ross's opinions, but recently I reread *Sea of Cortez* and to me it is one of John's most enduring works.

Steinbeck, whatever his reasons for writing the book, had enjoyed the trip. Later, he told me—and this was after Ricketts died—that Ricketts had not written any of the diary, and so John felt justified in reissuing it without Ricketts's pictures and scientific data. In the original edition, there are many technical descriptions given in the enormous index at the end of the book. Apparently that index, plus the pictures, of course, were the extent of Doc's contribution. John also told me that his publisher begged him not to use Ricketts's name as co-author, but that John had insisted that his friend be so designated. John immortalized that trip; he was the one who made it work. He did it for Ed Ricketts's sake, and all of us have benefited.

One time I was sitting up in Doc's laboratory with John and Doc. We were drinking California wine. Martin Ray, a winemaker and a colorful character, had just made some Chardonnay and we were tasting it. John was in a wistful mood and started to talk about the golden past of California. He regretted that much of the beauty had disappeared. He said that the Spaniards came here to find the fountain of youth and they found gold in the ground and they found gold in fields and golden weather as well. The California hills were gold and the earth was gold, and so California attracted adventurers from everywhere—she seduced them with golden promises.

But then, in less than a century, the scene changed. The mines were closed, the gold rush was over, and the hills and the valleys were overlaid with cement and asphalt; the golden groves of oranges were covered with housing developments and factories; the Pastures of Heaven were subdivided . . . and so California, the seductress, took away the platinum weather and bright sun and covered the gold coast with a veil of smog. The shiny beaches and the adjacent palisades looked gray and foggy . . . California wasn't the same golden gal she once had been.

I said to John maybe California was not as pristine, not as virginal as before, but didn't he think there were other seductions still around . . . like the golden movies, the golden aura of Hollywood? John said he didn't think movie studios were seductive to begin with, but whatever they were before, now they were dismal and commercial.

"But there is one bright promise," John said. "There are the vineyards . . . the gold and rose and red grapes of California. Vineyards are good." He looked at the goblet of Chardonnay he was holding in his hand and said, "I like vineyards very much . . . and they will stay here for a long, long time." He proved to be right. Vineyards are beautiful to look at and, for the moment, they are holding off the ruthless cementers.

A last thought about Steinbeck. He had been "schooled," but his was not a professionally trained, intellectual mind, like Huxley's or Anderson's or Shaw's. Sometimes John would surprise you with his knowledge about books or facts, but his talent was raw and native. He said he had not been a steady reader when he was young, but later he read everything he could.

So far in this century, Steinbeck's writings hold up with the best of American authors, which should make him happy—particularly if it includes Mark Twain, his favorite.

John Steinbeck: A Reminiscence

Webster Street

In addressing people, I usually assume that they don't know the facts, but when the verdict comes in I often find that they know them better than I do. Well, anyway, these facts I am going to go over rather briefly concern my association with John Steinbeck from the year 1923 until the time of his death. And at the same time, since it sort of overlaps, I shall discuss my acquaintance with Ed Ricketts.

I first met John at Stanford in the spring quarter of 1923, and at that time he was living in a woodshed on San Mateo Creek. The next time I saw him was at Stanford where he was staying for a full quarter. He went to class, but I am pretty sure he did not register. The reason that he kept coming back to Stanford even though he did not have the funds to register in regular fashion was because he had so many friends on the faculty of the English department who had great hopes for him. . . .

We first became good friends at the English Club meetings on the Stanford campus, presided over quite often by Dr. Margery Bailey who was an authority on eighteenth-century literature, but whose love for the century was sort of telescoped from the sixteenth century. She never gave a lecture without going back to the germ of the Elizabethan spirit, and of course John was very enamored with that period of literature, although one would not know it to read his books.

I lived in Palo Alto from 1922 until 1935, and I often went down to see John and Carol where they lived in a tiny house on Eleventh Street in Pacific

Grove that belonged to John's family. John's father was Treasurer of Monterey County, and since the job didn't pay a big salary and because he had three daughters as well, he could never afford to send John to college. When I got married in 1925, John was my best man. I have never seen any record in any biography of Steinbeck where it even mentions the fact that he was on the west coast during 1925; he seems to have been someplace else, but the truth is that he was there. Then, after that, we worked together during various summers at Fallen Leaf Lodge, a resort near Lake Tahoe and now the Stanford Alumni Summer Camp.

He and I also met quite often at what we called "the Lab." Now I think that it would be a good idea simply to describe this "Lab" because it was a general meeting place; for us it took the place of the eighteenth-century coffeehouse. Moreover, we didn't have to pay anything, so it was a real Mecca. It was a very small room and it was occupied almost entirely by a large bed which served as a place for people to sit. In addition, there was a shelf for Ed Ricketts' books and a very tiny kitchen behind that. Ed had formed Pacific Biological Laboratories in 1924. He and a group of young scientists had gotten together and shared it. And since I'm on that subject, I might say that in 1939 John bought quite a large block of stock in that corporation and also loaned it a substantial sum of money which it needed very badly.

Ed Ricketts was a very good businessman, although we called him the mandarin because he would sit and listen to what we were saying and would nod his head and close his eyes—he seemed to agree with everything anybody said. He was a good businessman, but not in the general sense of achieving monetary success; rather he was meticulous and very precise in everything. He had a profound influence on John, but I don't know if it had too much relation to the tide pools. What they discussed was Nietzsche, Schopenhauer, and Kantian philosophy, what's right and what's wrong, and all the other kinds of things people talk about when they're young. Ed's views on these things were largely based, I think, on Marcel Proust, at least that was the way it seemed to me at the time, and John listened very attentively because he admired Ed a great deal and had a very strong inclination toward Ed's form of scientific investigation. They would get into some kind of discussion and would go to the shelf and pick out a book, and Ed would say, "No, that's a sea rabbit," and so would pull the discussion together. We also discussed, and this was one of Ed's fetishes, I suppose, the idea that the moon had a very vital effect on what man did, not because of any mystic quality, but because it had a real gravital effect on man's bloodstream and his body. John would listen to this, and I don't know whether he agreed or not, but those were the kinds of subjects they talked about. In fact, in all the time that I listened to John and Ed discuss things, I never heard them mention political views.

We had, as a matter of fact, what might be called a nonliterary association. We went to bars together—he would introduce me as Toby, "my learned friend at the bar when it's open." He would not discuss at all one of his books with me once it was written. On several occasions, he did write to me while a book was in progress, and I remember particularly his talking about *East of Eden*, which he thought was the best thing he had ever done.

Actually, he was a very bad critic, and I imagine that was why he did not want to speak about his own works. He also wrote to me when he was writing *Cup of Gold*, but he didn't discuss the book very much except to say that it was sort of based on the Arthurian legend which he and another mutual friend of ours, A. Grove Day, later an English professor at the University of Hawaii, were very hep on at the time.

Before I get to something else here, I want to point out that in writing *Tortilla Flat*, John firmly believed he was writing folklore, but the truth is that his characters were real people, and proof of this can be found in the police records of Monterey. These men that he was discussing were before the police courts about once a week, particularly on Monday mornings after spending their weekends in the tank. John was careful about these characters. He knew them and saw them on the streets in various positions, usually lying down with a jug beside them, and so he checked with the man who was then Chief of Police, Monty Hellam. I think Monty filled him in on the actual activities of these people. Another man who helped John in this regard was Steve Field, a descendant of the first Chief Justice of the Supreme Court of California, and who, because his father was English and his mother was Spanish, was a real *paisano*. He told John all kinds of stories—if I had the time I could tell a lot of stories that John never wrote, but Field did give him a great deal of background

Another person who gave him a lot of information (particularly with respect to the writing of *The Pastures of Heaven*) was Sue Gregory, a schoolteacher who had taught in a good many places in the school systems of Monterey County. She discussed things with him; paisano stories about the little kids in school—all their troubles and problems. The frog story in *Cannery Row* is also based on fact. Ed Ricketts had to have specimens; he had to have cats and dogs and frogs because that was his business. He would prepare these animals for histology classes and for dissection, and often these vagabonds came to his laboratory with bags full of things, most dead animals of one kind or another. John and I met them there a lot of times; besides, many of them lived across the street in the pipes. That was Cannery Row, and when a boiler would burn out (they are quite large and quite high) the cannery would just lay the pipes in rows right across the street from Ed's laboratory and these people would just crawl in and establish their homes.

On the academic or cultural side, I think John's short story teacher at Stanford, Edith Mirrielees, had a great deal of influence on his early writing in that she taught him to be simple and direct. Basically, she had three criteria by which a writer could evaluate his own work. First, the writer must determine whether or not he accomplished what he set out to do. Secondly, he must write a short story and not a novelette (she insisted a short story ought to be short). And finally, she believed that the story's conclusion had to be true as well as convincing.

In this regard, there is a curious thing that has always seemed to run through John's writing. This is his fondness for the spontaneous human expression, as, for instance, when somebody gets in a jam and says something and you think, "Well, that's a hell of a thing to say." In many cases, say at the end of *The Red Pony* and thoughout *In Dubious Battle*, John relies on the truth of the spontaneous human reaction in speech. Critics might contend that he made up these passages, but a good many times I think he took them right from what people told him, because when you talked to John, you were conscious that he knew you a great deal better than you would ever know him.

There are a few other things I was fortunate enough to witness. Anyone who knows Steinbeck's work is, of course, familiar with the story of "The Snake." I was there when that episode took place, and I mention it to show how John had the ability to relate an incident from real life to something he created. That snake thing took place in Ed's laboratory. He had two big rattlesnakes in a cage in the lab, and he had a bunch of white rats running around. He went in and got a white rat and put it in the cage. A girl who was one of the dancers from a local vaudeville team that was passing through Monterey was there. She was just fascinated by the whole thing, but she didn't say a word. The little rat went in there, and the snake waited and pierced the rat behind the ear. The snake pulled back and the fang caught and pulled him over to one side. The rat ran around for a little while, unconscious of the fact that he was mortally wounded, and he finally died and the snake took him. That girl never said a word, and when it was over, she just got up and left and we never saw her again. Now John, I am sure, made that episode into the story of the snake and gave it sexual implications which you could not help doing if you had seen that girl.

One day we were coming back from Palo Alto on the way to Salinas and we stopped for a beer at a bar just outside Castroville. We were sitting there talking, and suddenly we heard the bartender speaking to somebody wearing bib overalls. We listened for a while. The bartender said, "And then what did you do?" and the guy went through all sorts of motions. He didn't talk with his fingers as in sign language, rather he illustrated what he did. He was mute; he could hear but could not speak. I'm certain that John based the story of "Johny Bear" on that episode. As a matter of fact, on the way back he said, "Did you pay attention to that fella, the guy in the overalls? You know he could do a lot of harm, that guy!"

In connection with *To a God Unknown*, I had been staying in Mendocino county for two vacations from college (1923–1924). I was enamored with the country because it was so green and wonderful, and I tried to persuade John to write a story about it. But he wouldn't take my word for it. I said it was like the country down by the Big Sur, but he wouldn't believe me, so we had to go and see it together. We got to Laytonville where they were having a big party and the orchestra consisted of just a piano player and a drummer who had lost his drumsticks. So John said, "That's nothing," and he went though the kitchen and took a chair (John was awfully strong) and took the rungs out and brought them back to the drummer, and the drummer went ahead with it. Then John wrote his novel.

We had all sorts of these kinds of things happen to us. The sad part of the whole business, though, is that he quit writing. I wasn't convinced of that until June of 1968 when I went back to see him at Sag Harbor. His wife Elaine, who was very protective, heard me scolding him in the garden one day. I had said, "John, with all the places you have been and all of the things you know, why have you quit writing?" Elaine lit into me and gave me "what for" for trying to get John back in the harness. She knew he was ill and I didn't.

While I was there, the editor of *Life* magazine called up. John was in the garden in one of his tool sheds, and when Elaine told him about the call, John asked, "What does he want?" "He wants you to go to Brussels with him," Elaine said. "When?" "Tomorrow!" John said, "Nuts, what does he want me to do?" "He wants you to write something for him." John said, "Tell him when he gets back to tell me what happened and I'll give him a hundred lines free."

I don't really know anything about literary criticism; but I have a lot of ideas about it, and if I had the time I would probably put them in print. But coming back to this question of the soil, I was convinced that while John was writing about the people and places he knew, he was writing well; but when he left California and started to make it up, as in *Burning Bright*, he fell apart. I talked to him once when he was out here on the coast and told him, "John, you've never answered my letter about coming back here; I've got a letter of yours that asks me to try and find you about five or six acres where you can build a house—you wanted it near the sea, not too close to any town—what happened to all that?" John said, "I feel about Monterey like Amy Lowell thought about Oakland." He went on, "In the first place, the Monterey I knew isn't there anymore, the people aren't there anymore; they are all different." And if you want to know what Amy Lowell said about Oakland, she said, "There's no *there* there."

"I Think I Just Saw God": Thoughts on John Steinbeck

Virginia Scardigli

John and I shared so many things. We had a similar background in that we both went to an Episcopal Sunday school but didn't swallow things just because they were told to us in a church setting. John busted up a church business there in Salinas once because he felt the minister was a hypocrite and told him so. We also had the same sense of humor. When John and Carol built their first house up in Los Gatos, they had a separate building that was the guest room. When Remo (my husband) and Carol would get together, John would say to me, "Come on, I got something to show you." The entire wall going up to the second floor of the guest room was lined with old comic strips, and it took us an hour and a half to walk upstairs because we had to discuss them first.

John was a big, rough-looking guy with a very gravelly voice. He did a film introduction to "The Chrysanthemums" and a few other things and spoke way down there. We had many crazy times together. He and Carol once had a Rosewood piano that they took an ax to and hacked up. Also, he and Ed Ricketts were up on the porch at the Los Gatos place once and were looking across to Mount Hamilton. They had this stunt of sneaking up there when the astronomers were gone and hiding something that they would see when they went up the stairs to look through the lens. But it would be such a strange thing that they'd show up with that one by one they would make all the astronomers absolutely crazy.

I first met John in Ed Ricketts's lab. I was trying to figure out how to support myself after losing a job. I had done a lot of posing for artists; once I was in three different art galleries at one time. One night, at an art class in Monterey, a guy who was the assistant postmaster of Carmel came up and said to my husband, "You know, I think you'd like to meet my brother-in-law, and I'll give you a ride home if you will come over with me." So we thought, "Good, that means we don't have to walk the six miles back." So we get there and it was the lab, and his brother-in-law was Ed Ricketts.

It was love at first sight with Ed because here was a working lab, which always interested me, and lots of good music. By the time John and Carol got back from celebrating the success of *Tortilla Flat* in Mexico, we were part of the lab crowd. I would see John there, but the center was always Ed, not John. It was his place, he had the records, he was very outgoing—Ed was an amazing kind of person. Also on the row was Flora Woods, who was almost directly across from the lab. And down further toward Monterey was a two-story building with a long balcony on top that was Rose and Grace's. John never wrote about Rose and Grace; he wrote about Flora Woods and Lee Chong and the gal at the far end. We thought her place was just a beer joint, but it turned out to be a whorehouse.

When John was around the lab, he loved (as I did) the live creatures, and part of the fascination of Ed was that he was always working with live creatures. We would go down there and Ed would have a job for me to pick up so many different kinds of animals (he always said my eyes were better than his) for him to work on. John and I were just fascinated with the life in those animals. One time when we were sitting in the lab sharing a stool, Ed brought out this ghost shrimp, which is a transparent little animal. John looked at this thing, turned to me, and said, "I think I just saw God."

I had a friend who was acting in a play in Carmel, and I brought her over to the lab to see Ed, and John was there. John could be cool at times, so he said to her, "Are you an actress?" And Ann said, "Well, I'm working on it." And he said, "Well, read this to me." And he gave her the book he pulled some verses from to close *Cannery Row*, verses from *Black Marigolds*. He just threw her the book. And by gum, she got through it, the whole darn thing. And John's response, instead of saying, "Oh, that was very good," was, "Thank you very much." He didn't say another word.

Despite what some people have said, John could cook. I picked up this one dish John used to make and it was marvelous. It was coarse-ground potatoes and onions with some salt and pepper in a cast-iron skillet. And you turned the thing on very low and it cooked and never burned, so your conversation could go on forever; it got better and better.

We didn't have enough dishes to have lots of people up at the house on Fourth Street, but Remo made fantastic spaghetti sauce. We never bought anything terribly expensive, it being the Depression, but John, having a good nose for sniffing, adored that sauce. We'd say, "Everyone, we're having spaghetti tonight," and I would make up a dishpan full of lettuce, get some French bread, and then the spaghetti. John just fell like a ton of bricks for it! He would turn up at our door the next morning and say, "Come on, I know you still got some. It's better cold than hot!" And we'd still be in bed.

He was always turning up at the house with fascinating people. He and Louis Paul, a wonderful writer he met in New York, arrived at my doorstep there in Pacific Grove saying, "Well of course Louis worked for a pickle factory." And I said, "John, will you give me a reason why he worked for a pickle factory?" So he said, "Well, we were walking along the East Side of New York and Louis would lift up the wooden cover and take a sniff and then put it back and go on until finally he would lift up one and say, 'Ah, these are the pickles!' " So I said, "Well, that's a good reason. But why did he leave New York?" And John was ready to kick me down the hillside for having stopped his great story, which was going to last him for days!

John wrote his stories, his books, in his head. Remo and I were there once when he did this. We didn't call on any of the artists or people until after 5:00 P.M.; that was supposed to be the legitimate time to quit whatever work you were doing. We had just come down to John and Carol's place on Eleventh Street, knocked on the door, and John's old gravelly voice spoke up and said, "Who's there?" And I said, "It's Remo and Ginia." And he said, "Well, come in." So we came in and John was sitting stretched out on this brown leather chair. Carol was up in the window seat drawing some of her fantastic nudes. There was this horrible feeling in the room. In the corner there was a black-and-white pup named Toby (after the nickname of John's lawyer friend, Webster Street). And Toby was there with his paws over his nose. Well, I knew that John would never hurt a dog, so I said, "What happened?" John just pointed at Toby and said, "He ate the book." He was talking about *Of Mice and Men*.

Later that night John came up for spaghetti and he said, "Can I borrow a book?" And I said, "Sure, it's just my college books and a few of my books from childhood." So he finally got up to the front door where I was saying good night to people and he said, "This is the only book worth reading in your whole damn library." And I looked down and it was *Raggedy Ann*. He read it for a purpose—to not read a book that would make his mind start thinking about what that author was talking about. He wanted to keep focused on what he was writing in his head.

That was the only time I ever talked to him about a book because that was part of my unspoken vow—I recognized that he didn't like talking about what he was doing. But this time I said, "John, how long is it going to take you to rewrite it?" And he said, "Oh, I'll be about three months." He wrote for three months, and then *Of Mice and Men* comes out, and there were three words different from the version Toby ate. I know this because Carol told me and she did all his typing. That's why there isn't one wasted word in *Of Mice and Men*—that book, to me, is the pearl of his writings.

John also used to come over to the house because my husband was a wood-carver, and he had a big six-foot table where he taught John how to chip carve. To chip carve you cut at an angle and then you lift out the piece that you have cut from both sides. When they had the celebration for John's stamp, I went up to his son and said, "It's been a long time since I've seen you." And he looked at me with a blank stare. I said, "My gosh, you wouldn't remember, you were just a baby. But my husband was the one who taught your father how to chip carve." "Oh, he did that until the day he died," he said.

I envied John's ability to go out and work for hours on his writing, to stick with it; I can't pretend to do it. But he could—he wanted to write. I ran into a woman one day who lived two or three doors down from their house in Salinas, and she said that John's father took some copy off of John's desk down to her father's and said, "Will you read this and tell me whether it's any good or not?" John's father didn't trust himself to know whether he had a writer–son or somebody who was just being a kid. In the lab we were all concerned with accuracy, and John wanted the same thing to happen with words, which I think is why he enjoyed writing in his head. What he was doing was searching for the right word that would communicate *exactly* what he wanted to say. In the lab we would do this, for example, in discussing the exact meanings of the words "good," "right," and "proper."

The last time I saw John was at Ed's funeral. John and I were the only ones dressed for a funeral. There was the gal that Ed married at the very end; her name was Alice. There were Ritch and Tal Lovejoy and a few others. We were drinking coffee before the funeral, and John and I talked a little about the snowstorm that he'd run into, which was why he was late getting there, and what the weather was like in the East. And then we finally said, "Well, it's time to go." And that was when John or I said (I don't remember which), "Ed wouldn't have gone," meaning to the funeral. So we walked from Ritch and Tal's house over to the little chapel, which is on top of a rise there in Pacific Grove. We walked over to the door of the chapel, and there we saw this gray coffin with shiny black leaves, and John and I just stopped cold at the doorway. We turned around and walked down to the coast and each of us got ourselves a rock and had our own meditation service. This was the last time I saw John.

I think that anyone who teaches Steinbeck, if they have enough sense to hand the book to their students, should realize that even if it seems so easy, it isn't. John's work is full of deep thought. People complain that there are no realistic women characters. But when I pick up "Flight," I see one of the beautiful women characters in literature. My favorite book to teach was *The Pastures of Heaven*. In the high school where I taught in Palo Alto, the kids preferred Steinbeck. This was at a time when at the college level they were all talking about Hemingway. But there is a hopefulness in Steinbeck that isn't in Hemingway, though Steinbeck doesn't run away from painful things.

I loved John Steinbeck. It was one of those relationships in which you saw each other and hugged, but you didn't necessarily say anything. You just communicated volumes.

John Steinbeck:
Footnote for a Memoir
John Kenneth Galbraith

I did not meet John Steinbeck until just after Christmas in 1953–1954. With my wife I had been in Puerto Rico at the university, and we went on to St. John in the Virgin Islands for a holiday. My wife returned from her regulation dawn patrol to report that there was only one other couple in the hotel and adjacent cottages. Their name was Steinbeck. You don't suppose. . . ?

It was, and the beginning of a friendship. I can add little on Steinbeck as a writer, for he did not like talking about his work, at least to me. But I can tell quite a bit more about a shrewd and perceptive man, much interested in politics and contemporary anthropology and not only droll but very, very funny. He was a large man, still clean-shaven, exceedingly homely, and in 1954 looked older than I had imagined or he was. He spoke in a carefully subdued mumble. Elaine, his wife, was intelligent, tolerant, devoted, and lovely.

At Caneel Bay the Steinbecks too were on holiday, and John regularly took a mask and snorkel, and looking from shore like some terrible accident of marine miscegenation, went out along the reef to explore the underwater life. It was an interest which had developed many years before on the California coast near Monterey and is reflected in many of his stories. One day, however, my wife and I set out to tour the island on foot, and John abandoned the sea to accompany us in a Jeep that he had requisitioned for the purpose, along with the owner. (The latter was an acquaintance who had secluded himself on the island to write a novel. In face of the failure rate, it is astonishing how many people can be persuaded that solitude is a substitute for art. This was possibly an instance, but John deferred to the unhappy man as to Proust.) We explored the ruins of the old sugar plantations and heard of the great revolt of 1733 when the slaves seized the island and penned their erstwhile masters up in a small enclave around Caneel Bay. Eventually, a commando of soldiers righteously representing the several civilized powers with interests in the area was sent in to restore order. It was a fine example of international cooperation. The slaves, however, had the last word. They went to a high promontory at one end of the island and dashed on like lemmings into the sea. The island went back to wilderness. John thought, on any rational calculation of their personal future, that their decision was sound. He predicted that, within a measurable time, a similar calculation would be made by the inhabitants of Manhattan, and certainly of Miami Beach, with similar results.

We also talked a good deal about politics. John liked [Adlai] Stevenson and believed Joe McCarthy, then in peak form, strictly a flash in the pan. To exercise power through fear, he thought, required commanding intelligence and great diligence. Joe had neither. I seem also to recall that even at this stage Steinbeck thought he [McCarthy] would prove a bit vulnerable to the bottle.

Then, as later, John developed a favorite theme, which is that the world owes more than it realizes to shared greed. Since there is an infinity of visions of the future, and also of how any one vision can be made real, ideology divides men. But they are brought together again by pursuit of their common interest in income, power, position, or the prospect of an invitation to eat at the White House. It is a shrewd point. New York and California liberals quarrel hideously because, being happy where they are and not wanting to go to Washington, they are influenced more or less exclusively by ideas. Elsewhere shared greed makes men more tractable.

In the ensuing years we saw the Steinbecks at intervals, and I heard from him often—as there must be many who will testify, he was (in small but legible script) one of the last good letter writers. We were brought together at John F. Kennedy's inauguration, because someone had the idea of beating out a covey of artists, writers, and certified intellectuals to attend the rites, a project with a heavy portent of disaster for President Lyndon Johnson and Professor Eric Goldman. The Steinbecks were in the flock and joined us for the day.

We were also joined by a television crew whose principals had the idea of covering the event by immortalizing the responses of a highly unrepresentative set of spectators—as I recall, besides the Galbraiths, Scottie Lanahan, Janet Leigh, and Senator and Mrs. Hubert Humphrey. Having Steinbeck show up was, from the point of view of the producer, roughly equivalent to discovering [Arnold] Toynbee in the studio audience at the Johnny Carson show.

To have a television camera on you all that day (and in the front seat of the car as we were stalled in the traffic jams) was an unbelievable mark of political status. We attracted attention second only to President and Mrs. Kennedy and well ahead of Douglas Dillon, Dean Rusk, or the Secretary of Commerce. We both made the most of it, but John more than I. He told one or two people who got up the courage to ask why the attention that he had just been named chairman of the Joint Chiefs of Staff and had not yet got his uniform fitted. To others, he said he was the new Secretary of Public Morals and Consumer Education. (I think that was it.)

When asked by the television men for his reaction to the Inaugural Address, he said, "Syntax, my lad. It has been restored to the highest places in the republic." Inspired by the prayers of Cardinal Cushing and other prelates, he also offered an allegory on that evening's situation meeting in heaven. The briefing angel would say, "Well, it was a pretty quiet day down there until noon, my Lord. Then we got one hell of a blast!" I was sad that John did not live to reflect on the way the doors and windows of heaven were shaken by the Reverend Billy Graham on January 20, 1969.

A few weeks later as I was about to leave for India, I received a letter from John—which alas, I seem no longer to have—which impressed me as much as any communication I ever received. It said that no writer, teacher, or man of required independence of mind had any business becoming an ambassador, and that definitely included me. It wasn't necessarily that I would louse up the job or dislike it. Rather, I would like it too much. The bonds and constraints of bureaucracy would become too comfortable. Presently one would relax in them and cherish them. Thus, the end.

Meanwhile I began to get letters forgiving me for my decision and offering me advice. An undated one from Babylon sur Rhone, which evidently was Avignon, must have coincided with the shelter-building flap of 1961–1962. He began with a reference to this. I have Elaine Steinbeck's permission to quote him. On the shelters he said: "I have my own shelter worked out in New York. At the first suggestion of a bomb, I'll pry open a manhole cover and there are a thousand miles of shelter. And the rats there aren't likely to draw a gun on me. . . . Furthermore, after a couple of days, the sewers are going to smell sweeter than the upper air."

Later, proposing that all writers unite to modernize the clichés about peace—he urged that henceforth we beat swords into portable typewriters and ballpoint pens—he asked me to arrange him a diplomatic appointment. He had decided that he wanted to be ambassador to OZ.

Now OZ has another secret weapon we could well use on all levels of government and diplomacy. The Wizard of OZ is a fraud who admits he is a fraud. Can you think what this would do if it got into chancelleries and general staffs. There would be a major break-through. I can think of a dozen other advantages and rewards of my Embassy to OZ but I think these two would justify it. The simple expedient of dying different countries different colors so we would know whether we were for or against them would be worth any outlay by our government. It is even possible that a discreet traffic in emeralds could make my Embassy self-supporting if not profitable.

Then came what, with some effort, I considered a compliment: "I trust you, Ken, to handle this matter for me with your usual discretion and subtlety."

In the next letter, not having been notified by President Kennedy of his appointment, he thought probably Senator Dirksen had got it. "Maybe he can do the job better than I can. . . . It's just one more small heartbreak."

A year or two later he reported on his triumphant journey to the Soviet Union and returned to a favorite theme.

We got home from our culture-mongering completely exhausted and with a very vague idea of what had happened. . . . I developed the only diplomacy that has ever worked outside of total conquest—that of finding areas of mutual greed. I found I enjoyed the Soviet hustlers pretty much. There was a kind of youthful honesty about their illicit intention that was not without charm. And their lives are difficult under their four party system. It takes a fairly deft or very lucky man to make his way upward in the worker's paradise.

In the last year or two his letters were shorter. The X rays which led to spinal surgery in the autumn of 1967 he reported as looking "like a snake fence after a tornado." With some misgivings I sent him a pamphlet I had written on *How to Get Out of Vietnam.* To my delight he approved, on the whole, although he thought my solution—basically that we recognize error, pull back, and negotiate our withdrawal, assuring ourselves only of the safety of those remaining behind—a bit reminiscent of a recommendation that came out of a big meeting in Washington in World War II. It was to consider what could be done to arrest the rapid increase in venereal diseases. Everybody was stumped. Then Gene Tunney came up with an idea that "was a beauty and would work." He proposed continence.

My last letter was in the spring of 1968. The political prospect was for

Mr. Johnson against Mr. Nixon. He [John] was reminded of a little Indian girl in Salinas watching a wrestling match. In great excitement she said, "Jeses Chris' they're both jus' as good." Then, though recognizing that the need had long since passed, he got back to advising me on diplomacy. He had just heard about the perfect diplomat. Two men were discussing Green Bay, Wisconsin:

First man: It's a real nice place.

Second man: What's nice about it? Only things ever come out of Green Bay is the Packers and ugly whores.

First man: Now, wait just one minute, you son of a bitch. My wife is from Green Bay.

Second man: She is? What position does she play?

Steinbeck

Arthur Miller

I thought of him as a friend but our lives ran parallel and never really crossed. I had read him in college; he was legendary by the time we met, sometime in the early fifties, a world celebrity whose life was filled with famous friends and the powers that come with fame. But close-up it was his uncertainty I found surprising and his shyness and sensitivity, especially when he was so physically large and so deliberative in his views. We lived in a time distorted by obligatory and defensive patriotism, an atmosphere unimaginable anymore, the contest with the Russians being at its height. John, after all, had begun as a radical writer, and the guilts inherent in that kind of alienation were compounded by the strident demands of convention in our time. It was perhaps inevitable, given the near-hysterical state worship of the hour, that he should have come to feel alien to both past and present ideologies; filled with feeling, he tended to seek out goodness in the world and to some extent to sentimentalize the underdog rather than drawing attention to the threat always inherent in him. Steinbeck, utterly American, had a suffering conscience: his moral life was always vital to his work and his daily existence. So at times he would feign a toleration, if not acceptance, of any and every kind of behavior; the alternative was an isolation only an ideologue would cherish.

As a native New Yorker, I couldn't help seeing in John a grown-up country boy. He had read philosophy and much classical literature and enjoyed talking about arcane matters, but he liked to sit carving wood, and it was when he was talking about farm or small-town life that a certain genuine warmth poured out of him, a kind of easy familiarity and joy. I could be mistaken in this, but I often wondered if he wouldn't have been better served as a writer and happier as a person had he stayed home, as Faulkner and Welty tried and often enough managed to do. To be honest about it, I often felt Steinbeck, in the last part of his life, was feeling much of the time like a displaced person rather than a cosmopolitan at home anywhere. But it is a very rare thing for an American writer to stay home. We tend to use up the energies of a particular place, then to leave home in the attempt to capture a wider America for our work. But in the end, America is perhaps only a lot of little places, the undistinguished streets and neighborhoods and countrysides of native ground.

I can't think of another American writer, with the possible exception of Mark Twain, who so deeply penetrated the political life of the country. *The Grapes of Wrath*, as I recall, stopped a deaf Congress from babbling on about very little and turned its attention to the masses of people being forced off their native lands by the Depression, then to be turned into desperately ill-paid itinerant farm labor, attacked and murdered by thugs employed by harvest contractors intent on squelching protest of any kind. The Joads became more vividly alive than one's next-door neighbors, and their sufferings emblematic of an age. Steinbeck's picture of America's humiliation of the poor was his high achievement, which for a time challenged the iron American denial of reality.

As I say, we were not privy to one another's private life, but our paths on a few occasions did cross in an illuminating way. I had broken my relationship with Elia Kazan after his cooperating testimony before the House Committee on UnAmerican Activities. Some weeks or months later (I can't recall how long exactly), John, who was a friend and sometime collaborator and intimate of Kazan's, wrote declaring that I ought to resume a friendship that had been so deep and a working relationship as productive as ours had been in the theatre. He saw, correctly, that we were both wounded by what had come between us and hoped to do what he could to heal the breach. For myself, in the struggle of that time, I could see no way to go back over that broken bridge, and I have never known what Kazan's reaction was to Steinbeck's attempt. But within a week or two, a second letter from Steinbeck arrived. This apologized for his having suggested what, on thinking about it, he realized was and had to be impossible. Taken together, both letters reflect the two sides of Steinbeck, perhaps the two eras of his development: the struggle within him between an overflowing sympathy for suffering, a veritable embrace of those in pain, and a hardheaded grasp of moral dilemmas from which, with all the good will in the world, there is no escape.

But I think Steinbeck's whole life was a hard struggle, first to achieve recognition and then to dig in against easy and shallow popularity and the wiles of show-business values that in so many ways have triumphed in our culture. Even when mistaken—as in my view he was when declaring support for Lyndon Johnson's doomed Vietnam policies—the way he chose was far from easy. In a word, he was not outside the battle, safe in his fame, but in it to the end.

Full-Body Wine from the "Grapes of Wrath"

Yevgeny Yevtushenko (Translated by Edwin C. Kumferman)

The year 1937 was a tragic one for both America and Russia. In Oklahoma there was the terror of drought and dust storms, which drove so many disparaging farmers to the California valleys where it was possible to cough the dirt from their lungs and begin a new life under a new roof, which—God willing—would turn out more hopeful than the previous one. This is what John Steinbeck wrote about in his saga of the Joad family, *The Grapes of Wrath*. For Russia, 1937 was also a terrible year because another, more merciless, terror—Joseph Stalin—sent one and one-half million people who had not confessed anything, who were called "enemies of the people" without any evidence, to be either executed or sent behind the barbed wire of labor camps. Their wives (if they themselves weren't arrested), their children (if they weren't sent to special "homes" for children of the enemies of the people) were thrown out of their apartments, their belongings completely confiscated, and were deported to distant regions where they, like the Joads, also had to start all over again.

Exposing the egotism of the capitalists, who destroyed vegetables and fruit and even pigs so that they wouldn't fall in price during the Great Depression, Steinbeck wrote:

The people come with nets to fish for potatoes in the river, and the guards hold them back; they come in rattling cars to get the dumped oranges, but the kerosene is sprayed. And they stand still and watch the potatoes float by, listen to the screaming

pigs being killed in a ditch and covered with quicklime, watch the mountains of
oranges slop down to a putrefying ooze; and in the eyes of the people there is failure;
and in the eyes of the hungry there is a growing wrath. In the souls of the people
the grapes of wrath are filling and growing heavy, growing heavy for the vintage.
(449)

The Russian translation of *The Grapes of Wrath* was published in soft cover
on newspaper-like pages with a circulation of millions by the state-run publisher Novel-Newspaper. In the opinion of ideologists of that time, this
novel exposed the inhumanity of capitalism and therefore objectively worked
as Communist propaganda. Following precisely such logic, Stalin personally
recommended the films of Charlie Chaplin for multiple distribution as a
symbol of the solitude and helplessness of the little person in the face of the
capitalistic machine, which pulls him into itself, threatening to grind him
into powder with its gears, like in the film *Modern Times.*

Yet despite his inquisitorial, Machiavellian mind, Stalin erred. He forgot
that true art possesses a force of magnetic self-identification of readers or
viewers, that most people in the world don't think of Hamlet as Danish,
Don Quixote as Spanish, or Anna Karenina as Russian, but relate to Hamlet,
Don Quixote, or Anna Karenina independent of their nationality. The Soviet
people (to whom Stalin gave a highly dubious compliment, calling them
"cogs of socialism") saw on the screen not Chaplin but themselves squeezed
between gears, not of an American but a Stalinist machine. Indeed, in this
was the secret of success of Theodore Dreiser's *An American Tragedy.* Its
hero, Clyde, believing that the girl in love with him was hindering his career,
pushes her off a boat into a lake. Clyde was a type for those who, during
the Stalinist purges, for the sake of their careers, renounced their relatives
and loved ones, pushing them into nonexistence.

The secret of the grandiose success of *The Grapes of Wrath* in the USSR
is concealed in this unpredictable, subconscious identification by Stalinist
ideologists. When I was about fifteen, my father stunned me by telling me,
"We don't have any kind of Socialism. This is state Capitalism." I looked
around and, despite my age, realized he was right. Our government was
swelling with capitalists–monopolists, manufacturing everything from shoe-
laces to the atom bomb. All people became private property of the capitalist
government, and it did with them what it wanted. The government decided
whom to glorify and whom to kill off. If Steinbeck saw with his own eyes
how they slaughtered pigs in California and discarded them in ditches, then
in the forests and cemeteries of Russia the executed, having had no trial,
were also discarded into pits to be covered with quicklime. Having miraculously survived a similar execution, Soviet intellectuals, whose numbers

were quickly thinning out, read *The Grapes of Wrath* in particular—not only sharing the pain of the Joads but seeing in them (as with themselves) unnecessary elements that their own government wanted to get rid of. But if Steinbeck was successful in 1939 in publishing the history of 1937 America, the first anthology of Stalinist crimes, Aleksandr Solzhenitsyn's *The Gulag Archipelago*, would have to wait until 1987 to be published in the Soviet Union—a half century later. Our "grapes of wrath" became overripe and turned out to be tinged with rottenness. Hence, today's "wine" that we in Russia call democracy is still very far from the full-body wine that is worthy of grapes of wrath.

But let us return to the past when Steinbeck, who had already become a Nobel laureate, came to Moscow. I believe it was in 1965. At that time the whole intelligentsia of Russia had not long before become engrossed in reading Steinbeck's translated novel *The Winter of Our Discontent*, which was printed in sections in the journal *Foreign Literature*, which had 300,000 to 400,000 subscribers. *Travels with Charley in Search of America* and the early works *Tortilla Flat* and *Of Mice and Men* had also appeared in Russian. When Steinbeck arrived in Moscow, he was surrounded by American correspondents and representatives of the embassy as well as, naturally, our KGB, yet at the same time he experienced a reverential worship from his Russian readers that, by his own admission, he didn't find in America. Nevertheless, the Cold War was in full swing and Steinbeck felt some uneasiness over the enthusiastic display—he suspected a certain "organization of enthusiasm." Beginning a meeting with some young writers at the editorial office of *Yunost*, he suddenly said, with the sly cannibalistic smile of an old pirate before a willing dinner of cute pink children, "Well, guys, I know of course that you love Russia. I also love America. But let's not talk today about what we like in our countries, but about what we don't like."

It was amusing to see how the faces of the representative of the American embassy, who resembled a Doberman pinscher, and of the chief editor of *Yunost*, who looked like a relatively liberal Muscovite watchdog when compared with literary sheepdogs, fell anxiously and with rare synchronization for the Cold War. For three-quarters of an hour Steinbeck criticized severely ("neck and crop," as they say) his own government, American society, and the press, and then finally stopped, took a breath, wiped his perspiring brow with a handkerchief, and encouragingly winked to us: "Well, I have revealed to you what I don't like in my country. Now it is your turn—what don't you like in yours? Well, wolf cubs, show your teeth!"

However, we "wolf cubs" exchanged embarrassed glances with each other, blushed, panted, smiled absurdly, but didn't show any teeth, as if, having lost our baby incisors, others had not grown in. The representative of the American embassy immediately cheered up and, with victorious condescension, looked at us as those who clearly had not grown into the openness of Western civilization. Trying to smooth out the situation, the editor of *Yunost* spread his hands, saying, "They are bashful over here, Mr. Steinbeck." Steinbeck understood perfectly all the advantages of his position in comparison with us wolf cubs, with whose political upbringing a whole army of wolfhounds had kept up. Osip Mandelstam, having been tormented in a labor camp, wrote about this, foreseeing beforehand his end: "The century of the wolf hound has been thrown upon my shoulders." And Vladimir Vysotsky sang out a hoarse requiem to a whole generation surrounded with the red stains of hunters' flags.

Nevertheless, Steinbeck continued to provoke us with the cunning of an incorrigible tramp from his own pages: "Well anyway, guys, do you absolutely like everything in your country? Even unhappy situations? Even sicknesses? Even droughts or floods?" The wolf cubs held their tongues. The situation was becoming simply stupid. Then Steinbeck caught sight of a girl slanting her eyes, who on that day had found herself not in the mood. She was smoking long thin cigarettes one after another, breathing out smoke from her lips, which were closed angrily, perhaps reminding Steinbeck of the ladies hanging out in the bars of *Tortilla Flat*. The ashtray in front of her was a breeding ground of cigarette butts with scarlet borders from her lipstick.

"What's with you, dear child?" Steinbeck said as he turned his attention to her. "Why are you so sad if you like everything in your most wonderful, most irreproachable, most unique country without even the least fascinating imperfection?" The girl, whose name was Bella Akhmadulina, didn't lose her head: "My rights have been taken away Mr. Steinbeck, therefore I am so sad." The translator, panicking from the responsible work entrusted to her at this historic meeting, translated the word "rights" literally as "driver's license." However, here, finally, a chance was presented to the American embassy representative to show that the special federation grant awarded to him to study Russian at the military college of Monterey was not money thrown to the wind. With lightning speed he bent over to Steinbeck's ear, lowered his voice, and in an official way articulately explained about the thin double meaning of the Russian expression "my rights have been taken away" that may mean not only to take away a "driver's license" but also to take away "human rights." Steinbeck burst out laughing and teased us no more with indelicate tests of civic bravery. He understood everything perfectly.

In the evening he was with his wife visiting at my place. He drank a lot and even then continued to laugh, remembering that day's meeting at the editorial office. We rose up and suddenly the doorbell rang out and a completely unforeseen guest sprang in—my uncle Andrei, a truck driver from the Winter station, who carried a veneer suitcase tied up crosswise with a rope. As it turned out, he had received a travel voucher to the Black Sea resort as a type of prize and decided to peek in on his nephew on the way. I adore my uncle. He possessed several patents for different inventions and was one of those who during the war directed the transfer from trucks with gasoline fuel to a steam system in which thinly chopped firewood blocks were used in the capacity of fuel. The boys were the stokers. The front part of the basket was filled with blocks. Two iron trash tanks were welded to the back part of the basket. We placed the blocks into these tanks and the trucks, shrouded in white clouds of smoke, moved along majestically like steamships.

Uncle Andrei was the main driver of all Siberia and didn't lose his head a bit when I introduced the great writer to him. Steinbeck, upon seeing such a rare extraction for an American Cold War author as a real Siberian proletarian, immediately lost interest in me and seized my uncle in his greedy hands, using me only as a translator. I translated my uncle's words from Russian to Spanish, and I translated Steinbeck's from half English–half Spanish to Russian. I also tried not to drink, but in the company of Uncle Andrei plus John Steinbeck this was impossible.

Steinbeck asked my uncle whether he had read any of his books. He asked nonchalantly, as if by chance. To my surprise, my uncle answered that before the war he had read *The Grapes of Wrath*, but if his memory had not changed, in the photograph in the book Steinbeck had only a mustache and didn't yet have a beard. "Right!" exclaimed Steinbeck. "I didn't have this gray broom then! In that photograph I looked like Clark Gable!"

But then anxious sparks appeared in his eyes. As I subsequently realized, Steinbeck was trustful as a child but also suspicious as a child. Couldn't this appearance of my proletarian uncle turn out to be skillfully staged Soviet propaganda? Steinbeck began a meticulous interrogation of my uncle about the contents of *The Grapes of Wrath*. Uncle Andrei, to my even bigger surprise, completely passed the examination. The suspiciousness in Steinbeck's eyes gave way to tears. He was touched, as well as marginally drunk, and his wife, Elaine, apparently used to his emotional splashes, whispered something delicately into his ear. But he was already unrestrained, like a big ship during a major excursion. "You made my day, Andrew!" he exclaimed to my uncle. "Would I have ever thought that even drivers of Siberian trucks would read me!"

Then Steinbeck asked my uncle who his favorite writer in the world was, perhaps with a secret hope that it would be him. My uncle completely took me aback, naming as his favorite writer Miguel de Unamuno, a philosopher–

idealist from Basque who died in 1936. Then Steinbeck pressed my uncle to his heart and shed more tears—for, it turned out, he had once met Unamuno in Spain and also adored him—and said that absolutely the greatest people in his life were Don Miguel and Uncle Andrei, and for this reason it was necessary to drink again. Then he asked my uncle for whom he would have taken Steinbeck if he had not known his profession. "For one of our Siberian foresters," uncle answered, causing Steinbeck to be in an even bigger euphoria. "And who would you have taken me for?" asked Mrs. Steinbeck, with a coquettish curiosity. "For one of our milkmaids," my uncle answered unequivocally and proposed a toast to her, ruthlessly having filled my drinking glass with vodka too, which was never my favorite beverage. But in the company of a great Siberian driver and a great American writer there was no place for champagne.

"And is there a problem with freedom of speech among the working class of Siberia?" asked Steinbeck, returning to his "civic mission" and again beginning his "testing," which was now familiar to me.

"Look here, Mr. Steinbeck," answered my uncle, eyes gleaming. "We Russians are like children—after every other word mama is mentioned. At our auto base there is such freedom of speech that one could cut it with a knife."

"And how does the working class conceive Communism?" Steinbeck drilled him.

"Is it really possible to conceive it? One has to experience it first of all. And how can one experience it if it doesn't exist? It's like paradise, but so far no one has returned from paradise and no one has reported what is there exactly," my uncle said, shrugging his shoulders.

"Well, and what do the Siberian drivers think; will there be a war between America and Russia or not?" Steinbeck asked intently.

"There is enough of the world both for us and for you. We Russians have nothing to share with you Americans except stupidity," smiled uncle, knocking back yet another shot of vodka with Steinbeck.

"Why is it necessary to share stupidity?" Steinbeck asked, as all the wrinkles on his forehead gathered.

"Simply because only the one of us who has more stupidity will begin the war. Therefore, it is necessary that our stupidity is equal; then there won't be any war. Well, let's start!" and like magic two shots filled to the brim appeared in my uncle's hands. "For me and for my American mate."

"You Russians have a national love of slogans. Why not hang out a slogan of your uncle's, 'stupidity is equal,' " Steinbeck burst out laughing. "To the working class of Siberia!" he said. "And look at you not drinking—you are a bad nephew. Let me pour you a shot." Everything was swimming before my eyes.

Meanwhile, it was approaching morning and Steinbeck, having been energized by the rays of daybreak, announced that he had heard about one interesting Russian drinking custom, "*pollitra na troikh*" (a bottle of vodka for three), when three people not acquainted with each other go in on one bottle of vodka at the door of a store and drink it in turn from the bottle. Taking opportunity of the fact that his wife had curled up comfortably on the sofa, Steinbeck demanded that I take him, together with his "mate" Andrei (Steinbeck had already learned that Siberianism), to the opening of the closest store in order to put this unique Russian custom of morning trio solidarity into practice. I presented myself in the capacity of the third member, but Steinbeck announced that *pollitra na troikh* was a tradition of the proletariat, and they needed "only the working class man."

I remember vaguely what happened later. It seems that I left Steinbeck and my uncle at the "Young Communists" store for about an hour. I don't know what language they conversed in with each other, but when I returned, having worried about them quite a bit, I saw an idyllic group like a sculpture seated on a garden bench. In the middle of the bench, with the already destroyed bottle of vodka gleaming shyly underneath, sat the singer of *The Grapes of Wrath* in a deep sleep, and on his fatherly knees two heads were resting peacefully—one of my uncle, already growing bald but with still some submissive remnants of his former forelocks, the other completely unknown to me, with hair the color of burning kerosene, belonging to an average-size person in rubber boots who even in his sleep wouldn't drop the fishing pole from his hands. I understood the historical confluence of the singer of the American proletariat with the Russian proletariat that had just taken place. I can't say for sure if it was really so or if it was simply a dream or hallucination, but a few of my neighbors who were walking to the "Young Communists" store at such an early hour for such a delicate reason claimed that they saw right there on that bench a person who very strongly resembled John Steinbeck.

In 1966 the newspaper *Newsday* published an article about Steinbeck's later trip to Vietnam under the headline "A Letter to Alice." I knew that Steinbeck flew to Vietnam in order to see his wounded son, and I could imagine how the blood and wounds of the young Americans in that hospital stunned him. He could have seen such blood and wounds at the other side of the front also—in North Vietnamese hospitals. But Steinbeck's fatherly emotions took precedence over reason, and when soldiers invited him to take part in a helicopter ride over the territory controlled by the Vietcong, he didn't refuse. Having read his article, I was startled most of all that Steinbeck, finding himself in an American helicopter that had bombarded Vietnamese villages, compared the fingers of the machine gunner with those of the great musician Pablo Casals, whose fingers flew on strings. This was a sharp dissonance in the background of the gigantic demonstration in the United States for peace in Vietnam in which Benjamin Spock, Martin Luther King Jr., Arthur Miller, Joan Baez, Bob Dylan, and Allen Ginsberg took part. In July 1966 *Litgazeta* published my poem, "A Letter to John Steinbeck," in which I recalled his entreaty to the young Russian writers, "Well, wolf cubs, show your teeth," and called on him to come forward for peace in Vietnam: "So show your teeth, John's teeth!" The poem, which was written in a bitter but also friendly tone, was published in the United States in *Harper's*. Unfortunately, many American leftists, who hadn't done a tenth of what Steinbeck did for his own people, began to cruelly insult Steinbeck for this perhaps only moral mistake in his life. The liberal terror at that time was little better than the medieval Inquisition.

In the fall of 1966 I managed to visit America through the rusted but still existing Iron Curtain. The organizer of my poetic performances in twenty-eight American universities, Albert Todd, told me that John Steinbeck had called and very much wanted to come with his wife to the first performance at Queens College in New York but was afraid that his attendance would cause me some political troubles. I understood how persecuted he felt because I had been insulted more than once both from the right and from the left so that sometimes I was even sick. I immediately called Steinbeck and said that I would be happy to see him during my first evening. There was only one thing that worried me—that Steinbeck was offended by my poem.

"No," he answered, "it hurt me, but it didn't offend me. You know, in my opinion we are both wrong in this story—both you and I. And do you know how? In such situations one shouldn't take either side because both sides are guilty of something. It's a pity that I have understood this too late. You will also understand this sometime."

When I was shown the auditorium, I looked around for Steinbeck, and before I began reading any poems, I jumped off the stage, embraced him, and kissed the hand of his wife. The next day one of the New York papers, it seems to me that it was that same *Newsday*, published a photograph of my embracing Steinbeck with roughly this caption: "Yevtushenko asks Steinbeck for forgiveness for his poem." All of this was presented as if I had renounced my antiwar position and took the point of view expressed in "A Letter to Alice."

"I will have to answer," I said somberly. "I don't want to, but I have to—only so as not to injure the old man. After all, he is not guilty of this."

"Yes, you will have to answer," Todd agreed, and we took to composing the letter, but the words were resisting and wouldn't come together.

"It would be ideal if Steinbeck himself wrote them an answer," Todd said.

"But I can't request that of him," I said. "It is already hard for him without this."

And suddenly right at that moment the telephone rang and I heard that so familiar, somewhat hoarse voice of the American "mate" of my uncle Andrei.

"*Eugenio, que cabrones ellos son*" (Eugenio, what bastards they are), he forced through in Spanish. "They would like us all to argue to the death, because they only know how to envy those who love each other. Don't pay any attention to this provocation. I wrote an answer to them myself. You will read it tomorrow. And I have your autobiography here. I noticed that it was written in a hurry, having only half its ass on the chair. But there is one chapter—about Stalin's funeral—I immediately saw all of it as if I were there myself. Who knows, maybe in twenty-first-century encyclopedias it will be written about you: 'Famous Russian prose writer, who began as a poet.' Also, your poem about three old men, "In 100 Versts," is really and truly a strong short story. Maybe I will retranslate it. *Pero recuerda, Eugenio— quando escribes prosa, hay que usar sobre la silla el culo completo . . . claro, que juntos con el corazon.* (But remember, Eugenio—when you write prose, you must plant your ass firmly in the chair. Of course the heart has to be with it too.) My wife and I will expect you on Thursday—your free day. I want to show you my old film *Viva Zapata!* Maybe Marlon Brando will be there if I can find him. Don't forget the call from *The Jungle Book*: 'We are of one blood—you and I.' "

I haven't forgotten that call, John.

John Steinbeck and the American Novel

Tom Wolfe

The crowning triumph of Steinbeck's career was *The Grapes of Wrath*, his novel of the Great Depression of the 1930s, published in 1939. He had already written a best-seller, *Tortilla Flat* (1935), and sold it to the movies, plus the highly praised and reasonably well-selling *In Dubious Battle* (1936), and was completing *Of Mice and Men*, which became an even bigger best-seller in 1937 and subsequently a play and a hit movie, when he accepted an assignment from the *San Francisco News* to write a series of newspaper articles on the Okies, who were pouring into California from the drought-stricken Southwest, seeking work on California's sprawling agribusiness farms. Steinbeck was not interested in the money or the journalism but in amassing material for what he envisioned as a "big book," a novel on a grander scale than the comparatively spare books he had written so far. He bought an old pie truck, as he called it, stocked it with food and blankets, and prepared to do his fieldwork among the Okies, who were living in squatters' camps and working for wages as low as twelve and a half cents a day. At the time, the existence of the camps was not public knowledge, much less the appalling conditions in which the Okies lived.

Steinbeck was fascinated by the "organismal" theory of a biologist friend, William Emerson Ritter, who believed that the individual human inevitably lived, without knowing it, as part of a larger social organism, after the manner of the multiunit "superorganisms" known to marine biology, and that the whole was inevitably greater than the sum of its parts. For the same reason, no single organism could be understood without observing and comprehending the entire colony. (Which is to say, Ritter was a half century ahead in what is currently one of the hottest fields in science, "sociobiology.")

So Steinbeck headed out into the farm country in his pie truck and toured the camps day after day, documenting the entire "organismal" complex and looking for the individual "organisms" who would bring the whole alive in story form. It was at a squatters' camp in the San Joaquin Valley that he came across a man, his wife, and their three children living in a lean-to made of willow reeds and flattened tin cans and sleeping under a piece of carpet. The wife had just given birth to a dead child, her second stillbirth in a year. Their degradation gave him the idea for the tragedy of the Joad family. He conceived of the Joads as types, as specimens, as a cluster of people representing the whole experience of the Okies, and yet Ma Joad and her rebellious son Tom come to life in the pages of *The Grapes of Wrath* as two of the most compelling individuals in American fiction. Without departing from the Zolaesque naturalism of his approach, Steinbeck manages, by book's end, to make Tom the embodiment of the Okies' will not only to live but to fight back. Ma Joad and Tom became the soul, in Ritter's terminology, of the whole that is greater than the sum of its parts. *The Grapes of Wrath* is a textbook American demonstration of [Émile] Zola's method of writing the novel: leaving the study, going out into the world, documenting society, linking individual psychology to its social context, giving yourself fuel enough for the maximum exercise of your power as a writer— thereby absorbing the reader totally.

The Grapes of Wrath proved to be the end point of a forty-year period in which the American novel rose to an eminence it would never enjoy again. The era began with Theodore Dreiser's *Sister Carrie* in 1900 and would see the flowering of John Dos Passos, Edith Wharton, Sinclair Lewis, Ellen Glasgow, Sherwood Anderson, Willa Cather, Ernest Hemingway, Scott Fitzgerald, Zora Neale Hurston, Thomas Wolfe, James T. Farrell, Richard Wright, James M. Cain, John O'Hara, and William Faulkner. It was the period in which American fiction not only began to be taken seriously in Europe for the first time but also began to influence European writers. Sartre was so impressed by Dos Passos that he wrote his World War II trilogy— *The Age of Reason*, *The Reprieve*, and *Iron in the Soul*—in unabashed emulation of Dos Passos's great trilogy, *U.S.A.*

What is the vein that runs from Dreiser to Steinbeck? It was Alfred Kazin, writing in 1942 in his critical literary history of the period, *On Native Grounds*, who first isolated "the greatest single fact about our modern American literature—our writers' absorption in every last detail of their American world together with their deep and subtle alienation from it" (ix).

Their "absorption in every last detail of their American world" never varied, no matter what their mood. Steinbeck may have felt angry when he wrote *The Grapes of Wrath*, Dreiser may have felt disillusioned when he wrote *Sister Carrie*, Sinclair Lewis seemed to have a Menckenesque sense of the absurdity of the spectacle all around him when he wrote *Main Street*, *Babbit*, *Elmer Gantry*, and *Arrowsmith*, for which he became the first American to win the Nobel Prize in Literature. But all immersed themselves wholeheartedly in that spectacle, relished "every last detail" of it, and recognized the importance of going beyond the confines of their own personal experience to get novelistic material. As Kazin put it, "They were participants in a common experience" who "gave the American novel over to the widest possible democracy of subject and theme" and had a "compelling interest in people, Americans, of all varieties" (207–8).

That the most influential American novelists of the second half of the twentieth century would turn their backs on this triumph in favor of that tabescent failure, the "literary" novel, is the great paradox of American literary history. When Steinbeck won the Nobel Prize in 1962, fashionable literary figures of the day were openly scornful. By now they regarded Steinbeck's realism as vulgar. Already the American novel was withering away into the "isms": absurdism, fabulism, minimalism, magic realism. Steinbeck's "vulgarity" consisted precisely of his "compelling interest in people, Americans, of all varieties" and his stance as a participant "in a common experience." By 1962 fashionable novelists were using "literary" fiction as a means of elevating themselves above the mob, which was now known, of course, as the middle class. Steinbeck's gaffe had been to thrust his hands too deeply into the earthiness of American life.

John Steinbeck: "A Lion in Winter"

Budd Schulberg

A single best seller can ruin a writer forever.
>—John Steinbeck's reaction to the 150,000 hardcover
>sale of *Of Mice and Men*

There's no luxury quite like having something to say.
>—John Steinbeck

No overnight volcanic upthrust but a long ranging mountain was John Steinbeck. When I came to New York fifteen years ago, I picked up a newspaper and saw that my old friend John was in trouble.

Strike One—He was on his back in a hospital bed on the eve of an operation that sounded as if he was bucking the "Big C."

Strike Two—One of his sons had been arrested for possession of drugs. Actually it was marijuana, but from the size of the headlines one would have thought the lad had been caught with a million bucks of the heavy stuff: FAMOUS AUTHOR'S SON NABBED ON DOPE CHARGE!

Strike Three—? Well, Steinbeck was a big man, built for power and, despite years of literary fame and city living, still a raw-boned country boy from the ranch lands of Salinas, California. He was a ruddy outdoorsman, good at growing things, fixing engines, handling boats. He looked like a cleanup batter, a grizzled, bearded, sixty-year-old Duke Snider. Life had pitched him some pretty good curves, even his share of spitters, had tried to throw fastballs past him like a celestial Bob Gibson, and hadn't been able to strike him out yet.

I called his wife, Elaine, who confirmed what kind of day he had had. Reporters hounding him for statements on his son's public embarrassment. John fuming and setting his bulldog jaw, harassed by searing pains of the body and of the spirit. The doctors had already begun to drug him against the crucial morning probe. She didn't know whether or not he would want me to see him in that condition. He was a physical man, furious at having to be in bed. He didn't mind if people saw him gloriously drunk once in a while, but he was as prideful about his physical well-being as he was about his loving care for language. Still, she thought he might like to hear from me and gave me the room number.

A gruff, impatient voice on the other end of the phone said, "Yes? What do you want?" In the tone was a baseball bat waiting to swing at persistent reporters who would invade a man's most private moments to get their story.

I identified myself, said I had just come to town and—though it is always an empty question to ask a strong man who is made to lie down—wondered how he was feeling. "Rotten," Steinbeck said. "It's been one hell of a day. Where are you?"

I said I was about ten blocks away and didn't want to disturb him if—

"Hell, come on over."

Twenty minutes later I was walking into one of those depressingly antiseptic single rooms in an enormous, impersonal hospital on Manhattan's East River. There on his back lay the only living male Nobel Prize winner for literature. With his craggy mountain of a face, his powerful chest, his sturdy body, he looked too big for that hospital bed.

I said I had always enjoyed our talks. We had exchanged ideas, travel bits, book notes, gossip over friendly booze at Elia Kazan's parties, in the kitchen of his town house on 72nd Street, and other places over a bunch of years.

He grunted, closed his eyes in pain, cussed a little bit and snapped open and shut the blade of a large pocketknife.

"Don't know how much sense I'll make. The medics shoved a lot of pills into me. They're rolling me into surgery first thing in the morning."

He pointed a gnarled finger toward a white metal medicine cabinet. "You'll find some vodka in there. Make yourself a drink."

Glass in hand, I went back to the bedside. "I've brought you the book from the Watts Writers Workshop, John, *From the Ashes*. At the last class James Thomas Jackson and the other writers wanted to autograph it for you."

He picked it up and ran his hand over it. "A book. That's great. I want to read it. When you see 'em thank 'em for me."

The book was no token gift to the most distinguished author in America. Steinbeck had been in direct contact with our Watts Workshop. When he saw *The Angry Voices of Watts* on national television he had taken time to send me a note:

I was astonished at the quality of the material. Some of it was superb. . . . I am so tired of one-note writing, sad homosexuality is not enough as a working tool for a writer. Your writers have learned early that one [cannot] . . . scream with pain [without having] glimpses of ecstasy.

Our workshop in Watts—called "Douglass House" in honor of the ex-slave Frederick Douglass, who became a powerful writer and orator in the abolitionist cause—originally had been supported by contributions from fellow writers, Harry Golden, James Baldwin, Irving Stone, and Paddy Chayevsky. Steinbeck's check arrived with a practical suggestion. Instead of my taking so much time writing to hundreds of individuals, apply to the National Foundation for the Arts. He was a member of its council and would put in a recommendation for us at the next meeting. It had been John Steinbeck's characteristic combination of enthusiasm and practicality that had helped to make Douglass House more than just another fly-by-night creative venture in the ghettos. Now, with pain and a dread of the unknown he faced in the morning interlacing his comments—at times punctuating them with disconcerting clicks of the knife he clenched in his hand—he spoke about the Watts phenomenon and black writing in general.

"I tell you something, I know they're angry and feel on the bottom that they've got nothing because we took it all—but I envy those young writers." To my surprise he reeled off the names of three or four from our Watts anthology. His memory, like his colleague John O'Hara's, always had been prodigious. "They don't have to search for material. They're living it every day. The subject matter is built-in dynamite. There's no luxury quite like having something to say."

He took a deep breath that expanded his chest against the straining sheet.

That's my trouble. I don't think I have anything to say anymore. And yet, I'm like an old tailor. Put a needle and thread in my hand and a piece of cloth and I begin to sew. My hands have to keep busy. I have to hold a pencil in my fingers. I need to write some pages every day. When you do something for over thirty years, when you hardly think about anything else but how to put your experiences into the right words, you can't just turn it off and go out and play in the garden. I want to write every day—even if I don't have anything to say.

Watching John Steinbeck lashing at himself in that frustrating hospital bed, I was reminded of the stag at bay, wounded possibly unto the death, but still flailing out with his antlers and refusing to go down.

"John, that's ridiculous. I don't see you often, but every time I do we talk for hours. I don't believe this crap about 'nothing to say.'"

"Go fix yourself another drink," he said. "You've got to drink for both of us. These damn pills." As I made my way to the makeshift bar, he asked, "How do you teach that class? I'd like to see it. I'd like to drop in. But I don't think I'll ever get to California again. Salinas is getting too big. Monterey—I hardly recognize it. I wonder if you feel that way about going back to Hollywood. Thomas Wolfe said it for all of us. 'You can't go home again.' I felt pretty low when I tried." He flipped the knife savagely. He always had been a strange amalgam of gentle and violent man.

"Damn it, got myself off the track. I was talking about your class. How do you teach 'em? What can you tell 'em about writing except putting things down honestly, precisely? 'I looked at the dog. The dog looked at me.' You can try fifty different ways, but you'll never be able to say it any better than that."

We talked about writing and what writers we admired and what writers we could live without. John was impatient with the Mandarin writing that is coming back into style, and with homosexual writing, impatient with excessive flourishes and deviation. In the thirties, with *In Dubious Battle* and the epic *The Grapes of Wrath*, he had been a darling of the Communists and the social avant-garde. Now he had become a curmudgeon to the "Now Generation," who called him a warmonger for his stand on Vietnam and an old fogey for his attitude toward marijuana, acid, and speed. We disagreed about the war, but he was articulate on South Vietnam's side of it. He was hoping for peace, always had believed in peace, but there were times when man had to fight—as the Norwegians stood up to the Nazis in *The Moon Is Down*. I don't think the two wars were analogous. I didn't say it, but I thought in this area John was living in the past.

We half-disagreed about the hippies. He was troubled by their indolence, their self-indulgence, their tendency to do more talking about art than actually to produce any. "This generation that thinks it's so hip could be the real 'Lost Generation,'" he said. "The proof will be in what they produce—and what kind of next generation they produce. We thought we had it bad in the thirties. But I've never seen a time when the country was so confused as to where it's headed. The trouble with the young people seems to be, they're trying to swing the wheel around and take off in some opposite direction. But no one was ever able to do that successfully without maps, without charting a course, taking readings, and knowing the next anchorage."

John Steinbeck was a good sailor, a good map reader, a dreamer with practical hands who knew how to moor his boat at Sag Harbor against the impending storm when neighbors were letting theirs swing and crash into each other. A mapless revolution, a chartless voyage offended the Yankee man of action in whom still beat the heart of a poet.

Tacking a little, while urging me to help myself at his white enameled bar, he compared the wandering hippies to the knights of the Middle Ages. John had made a lifelong study of [Sir Thomas] Malory's *Le Morte d'Arthur*. With his usual thoroughness he had studied fifteenth-century English so he could read the Arthurian tales in their earliest translation. Fascinated by the material, he had planned a major work on the days of chivalry. And as always he had something of his own, uniquely original, to bring to what might have been either a romantic or an academic subject.

You know in a lot of ways, Budd, those days are not so different from our own. An old order was on the way out. Something new was in the air, but no one knew exactly what lay ahead. The concept of chivalry was essentially a humanistic idea— going forth to do good deeds. Not just saving damsels in distress, but protecting the poor. It's no accident that Kennedy's court was also called Camelot. But aside from the courtiers there were these individual knights roaming the land and searching for their own individual values. And there were the bad knights who only pretended to fight for the chivalric myth but were actually using the thing for their own selfish purposes. Maybe on the street corners today are our own Galahads and Mordreds. But it needed an Arthur, a Round Table, to hold them together and—

"Hell, John, that could be a fascinating novel. In a strange way, a kind of *Grapes of Wrath* of the Middle Ages. I never thought of the period that way before!"

John worked his teeth together and stuck out his jaw defiantly. The pills were taking effect, and he was fighting them too. "I don't know . . . nothing to say. . . . Did you see what the *Times* wrote about me?" On the medicine table near his bed was an editorial from the gray eminent *New York Times* wondering in print whether John Steinbeck deserved the Nobel Prize.

I tossed it back impatiently. "Who the hell are *they* to judge *you*? Could the pipsqueak who wrote that stupid paragraph ever write *Pastures of Heaven* or *Tortilla Flat, The Red Pony, The Long Valley, Cannery Row, East of Eden,* and now *Travels with Charley?*"

"Charley [his black poodle] helped me a lot on that one," Steinbeck grinned, and then grimaced. "And here's one from the *Post*."

Another editorial, from the *New York Post*, was putting the great writer down for forsaking his old liberalism on Vietnam. The tone was snappish and unforgiving, as only a religiously liberal journal can lecture a prodigal son.

"John, if I were you I'd throw those lousy clippings away. It's like you're running your own anti-clipping service. Only saving the put downs. But they can't take the Pulitzer Prize away from you. Or the Nobel. Or *Grapes of Wrath*. Or two dozen books that make a monument. You'll be remembered in the twenty-first century, when nobody knows the name of the current put-down artist for the *Village Voice*."

John Steinbeck made a kind of growling sound in his throat and flipped open his blade and made a gesture with it toward his belly. "I don't want to come out of this thing in the morning a goddamn invalid. When I'm not working on a book I've got to be outdoors, working on my boat, growing something, *making* something."

I looked at this big man imprisoned in this small, depressing room oppressed by nagging headlines and notices. It was no accident that his last novel had been entitled *The Winter of Our Discontent* and that the aging protagonist, significantly descended from sea captains but now subserviently tending a small grocery store, thinks to himself, "Men don't get knocked out, or I mean they can fight against big things. What kills them is erosion. They get nudged into failure" (14). It seemed incongruous for me to be searching for words to try to nudge a great man, and incidentally a marvelously warm human being, into a sense of his own glorious success.

A young black nurse appeared to administer some medicines. "You know it's after midnight," she said. "I wasn't supposed to let you stay so long, but you two were so busy talking together, and Mr. Steinbeck seemed to be enjoying himself—"

Maybe the *New York Times* no longer appreciated John Steinbeck, but clearly this young nurse dug him, not for who he was but what he was.

After midnight! I had been there five-and-a-half hours. And the man who had "nothing to say" had done most of the talking, on a score of provocative subjects. I only wish in this electronic age we both feared that I had been able to tape it for our literary history.

When I got to the main floor all the hospital doors were locked. I phoned my wife from the main reception desk to tell her I seemed to be locked in for the night. Finally, a watchman let me out through a basement emergency door.

A few months later I was on my way back to New York again. I told a mutual friend I would call Steinbeck as soon as I arrived. I had heard he was back in that hospital. While I was packing I turned on the TV news and learned that I was never going to see him again.

We arrived in New York the morning of the funeral. It was in a small Episcopalian church in midtown Manhattan. The ceremony took about twenty minutes. Henry Fonda, once the youthful star of the film version of *The Grapes of Wrath*, read a few favorite poems of John's and a relevant passage from *East of Eden*. The small church was half filled. There were [*sic*] a smattering of celebrities, John O'Hara, Frank Loesser, and Richard Rodgers. Paddy Chayevsky said to me afterward, "I never knew him but I thought as a writer I should stop work for an hour and pay him homage."

But he seemed the only one. One might have thought every writer in New York would have turned out, and others from across the country. Of the out-of-towners, I recognized only Joe Bryan III, a gentleman writer from Virginia who is not ashamed of old-fashioned sentiment, not to mention old-fashioned virtues—like loyalty.

In the family room, Elaine Steinbeck embraced the score of friends who had shown up on this bleak Monday afternoon and said, "All I ask is, remember him. Remember him!"

"Remember him!" a European friend of mine said as we joined unconcerned passersby on Madison Avenue outside the church. "Maybe I should not say this as I am a guest in your country, but if John Steinbeck had been one of ours there would have been a great procession down the Champs-Élysées, all the members of the academy would have marched, yes, and the young artists, too. Like when [Albert] Camus died. The whole country went into mourning."

"Well, in our country we seem to reserve that kind of funeral for generals and motion-picture producers, and Cosa Nostra executives," I said. A few days earlier the Walter Wanger funeral had been SRO [standing room only]. But, of course, he had been married to Joan Bennett, had lived in a world of movie stars, had taken a potshot at his wife's lover, and had produced *Cleopatra*.

I had made my peace with Walter Wanger. And surely I would not begrudge him his funeral due. But it does seem incongruous that his passing should be marked with more pageantry and attendance than was granted to Steinbeck. But whether our farewell involved thousands of admirers, or merely the few hundred who were there, John Steinbeck was truly a "lion in winter." Grizzled, wounded, but unbowed, he stormed forward even to what he feared was a losing battle in the final winter of his discontent.

The Steinbeck family home, 132 Central, Salinas. John was born in the home in 1902 and lived there until he left for Stanford University in 1919. (Photograph by David A. Laws. Courtesy of Windy Hill Press, publisher of *Steinbeck Country: Exploring the Settings Behind the Stories.*)

Stanford and John Steinbeck with an anxious Thom in between. (Courtesy of the Center for Steinbeck Studies, San Jose State University.)

San Juan Grade and the foothills of the Gabilan Range at the north end of the Salinas Valley. A young Steinbeck loved exploring these slopes. (Photograph by David A. Laws. Courtesy of Windy Hill Press.)

The Salinas River, setting of the opening and closing scenes of *Of Mice and Men*. (Photograph by David A. Laws. Courtesy of Windy Hill Press.)

Burgess Meredith and Olivia DeHavilland at the Motion Picture Academy Awards Dinner in Hollywood, February 26, 1942, the night before Meredith was inducted into the army. (AP/Wide World Photos)

The Steinbeck home in Sag Harbor, Long Island, with the pool John had built for Elaine at the bottom right. The inscription on the pool's stepping stone reads, "Ladye, I take reccorde of God, in thee I have myn erthly joye." (Courtesy of the editor.)

Steinbeck's writing desk in Joyous Garde, the writing haven he built at his Sag Harbor home. Notice his reading glasses, files, and still sharpened pencils. Here he wrote his last novel, *The Winter of Our Discontent*. (Courtesy of the editor.)

Steinbeck receiving the Nobel Prize. (AP/Wide World Photos)

John and Elaine, October 25, 1962, thrilled by the news that John has been awarded the Nobel Prize for Literature. (AP/Wide World Photos)

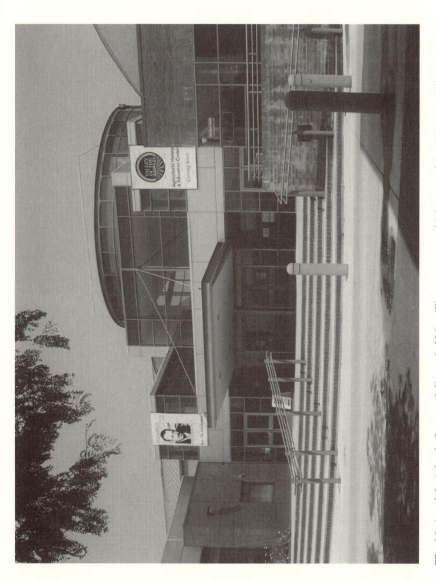

The National Steinbeck Center, Salinas. A $12 million museum which opened in 1998, it celebrates Steinbeck's life and art and stands just a short distance from where the town's citizens once burned his books. (Photograph by David A. Laws. Courtesy of Windy Hill Press.)

John with his poodle Charley. (© 1991 Hans Namuth Estate. Courtesy of the Center for Creative Photography, University of Arizona.)

PART II
CRITICS, SCHOLARS, AND BIBLIOGRAPHERS

Hemingway influenced the way people wrote more than John Steinbeck did, but what people write about, I think John was a much greater influence—the humanity and the caring about the underdog. [However,] for my generation he was certainly not the critic's darling. I went to Columbia where you were forbidden to utter the words "John Steinbeck." American literature stopped with William Faulkner.

—Terrence McNally

It's enough for me if a writer is honest, enormously talented, tells the truth, and has some stuff to say that if people would pay attention to it, could affect their society for the better. John was one of these; what more do you need?

—Edward Albee

Why Read John Steinbeck?

Susan Shillinglaw

John Steinbeck "brings together the human heart and the land."
—Barry Lopez

That phrase, written by environmentalist and writer Barry Lopez, has resonance for today's readers of John Steinbeck. Lopez urges us to consider two primal landscapes: external landscapes—our relations to the land, to oaks, to the whir of night frogs—and interior landscapes—often shaped by the places where we reside. John Steinbeck's work brings together both of these in extraordinary ways, ways that may deeply affect those of us living at the cusp of a new century.

Steinbeck loved the burnished Salinas hills and the churning Pacific. Like some of America's greatest writers—Henry David Thoreau, William Faulkner, Willa Cather—Steinbeck made his childhood haunts vividly real. In book after book, he charted his course in the letters or journals he wrote as "warmups" to the day's writing. Steinbeck wanted his prose to recapture a child's vision of "where a toad may live and what time the birds awaken in the summer—and what trees and seasons smelled like" (*East of Eden* 3). He asks that readers pay respectful attention to an external landscape. He invites us to look: "Orange and speckled and fluted nudibranchs slide gracefully over the rocks, their skirts waving like the dresses of Spanish dancers" (*Can-*

nery Row 31). Passages of stark beauty are found in every Steinbeck novel, sentences that record the rapt attention he paid to the natural world.

And then he asks that we shift perspective. American literature is full of conquest narratives—John Smith as Virginia cavalier, Natty Bumppo as pathfinder, Ernest Hemingway as marksman. But for John Steinbeck, nature is not a commodity, animals not for slaughter. For his is not a man-centered but a holistic universe, with humans seen as simply another species bound intimately to the places where they live, breed, drink, love, suffer, and catch frogs. In Steinbeck's California novels, characters inhabit communities and are connected with one another: Sam Hamilton with Adam Trask, "Doc" Ricketts with Mac and the boys, the Joads with all immigrants. And all of these characters are shaped by the places they live—Soledad, Tortilla Flat, a bone-dry King City Ranch—or to the roads they travel—Route 66, Highway 1 to the Carmel Valley. Steinbeck's is a vision of ecological cooperation, of human's interdependence with nature and one another.

As important to Steinbeck is the internal landscape, often one shaped by isolation, loneliness, failure. I always ask my students to look carefully at the first paragraphs of Steinbeck's novels, where the external and characters' internal landscapes coalesce: *Of Mice and Men* in particular. The "strong and rocky" Gabilan Mountains are in the distance. George and Lennie take shelter in a glade that has nurtured tramps, boys, and deer. That scene evokes their lowly status—throughout the book these lonely men seek shelter from the "strong" in the bunkhouse or the barn. Steinbeck understood such desolate interiors. But his is never the language of despair but of empathy. George and Lennie are great friends—of each other, of each reader. Steinbeck reaches out a fictional hand. Emotional bonds are forged between book and audience. Pauline Pearson, who spent countless hours interviewing Steinbeck's Salinas associates for the Steinbeck Library's oral history project, told me once: "John Steinbeck saved me. I was suffering, and in his work I found solace." Solace and laughter and commitment are what many readers discover in Steinbeck's work. "In every bit of honest writing in the world," he wrote in the late 1930s, "there is a base theme. Try to understand men."

So why do these Steinbeck landscapes, external and internal, matter to us in a new century? We live in an imperiled world. Many New York and California chefs have agreed to take the endangered swordfish off menus. Mining rugged interiors poses a new threat to the environment. Steinbeck's voice, curiously contemporary thirty and fifty and sixty years later, urges us to take heed, to appreciate that external world and our bonds to it. And Steinbeck's ghostly voice of understanding and solace endures, inspires. In his album *The Ghost of Tom Joad*, Bruce Springsteen pays tribute to the power of those interior landscapes—characters whose lives are often desolate, besieged, unacknowledged. "I'll be ever'where," promises Tom Joad, "I'll be in the way guys yell when they're mad."

Other reasons, equally compelling, ensure that John Steinbeck's voice will not diminish. A distinguished scholar of American literature, John Seelye, repeatedly intones: "Steinbeck is a great read." Stories are readily understood. Characters engage, inspire, enrage. Of all Steinbeck's novels, my students love *East of Eden* best: "It's like a soap opera," one said this spring. "Cathy's a kick." Good and evil face off in this book and others. They live. Recently, a class spent fifty minutes discussing whether George needed Lennie as much as Lennie needed George. Readers return to books that are, like close friends, reliable, accessible, entertaining, and—let Steinbeck never again be pilloried by the old complaint that he's a writer only for adolescent readers—challenging and perplexing.

The Japanese have a vigorous Steinbeck Society, over 150 strong. Why are his books so popular there? For many international readers, Steinbeck's work captures the elusive American psyche: bonds to land, the need for a place. Many of Steinbeck's stories are archetypal—restless migrants moving west to begin anew. Some characters, such as [F. Scott] Fitzgerald's Gatsby, are unflinching American visionaries—Jim Casy, Joseph Wayne, Adam Trask. Others are ordinary people, workers, migrants, a few homeless—the Americans celebrated in Walt Whitman's "Song of Myself." At the Fourth International Steinbeck Congress held in San Jose and Monterey in 1997, Asian and other participants read papers that noted Steinbeck's affinity for Buddhist or Taoist ideals—acceptance of what is, not grappling for solutions. Indeed, few twentieth-century American writers seem as relevant, as representative.

Finally, reading Steinbeck may provoke essential dialogue about ethnicity. Early on he wrestled with the issue of California's diversity. At Stanford University in 1924, he published his first story, "Fingers of Cloud," about the marriage of a white girl and a Filipino worker, Pedro. It is an emblematic tale, for much of his work is about cultural tensions. He ended his career with *America and Americans*, writing about America's racial crisis. Over one-third of his work is set in Mexico or about Mexicans. He loved Mexico: "There's an illogic there I need," he wrote at a low point in the 1940s.

Some of my students have trouble reading *Tortilla Flat*, that knotty book that both engages and, for some, repels because it's about drunken, lazy *paisanos*. Stereotypes, they complain. But in class we discuss those problems head on: Is Pirate sterotypical? Does Steinbeck mean these *paisanos* to represent all Mexicans? Are Danny and Pilon demeaned by drink or is that jug the catalyst for something far more significant, some bond linking these *paisanos*—a bond that, for Steinbeck, eludes more socially prominent individuals? Steinbeck wrote, "they want the thing wine does. They are not drunkards at all. They like the love and fights that come with wine, rather than the wine itself." They love life.

Steinbeck endures because he does not permit readers to dig in complacently, like the hermit crab. He embraces the fullness of life. With compassion, tolerance, and humility, he surveys landscapes—of place, of spirit, of a nation.

Sharing the Immeasurable View with John Steinbeck

Brian Railsback

Life sets us up to admire and read certain authors, if we bother to read at all. Grow up in Oxford, Mississippi, and William Faulkner will find you; in Asheville, North Carolina, Thomas Wolfe is inescapable; Robert Frost is there in the trees about Franconia, New Hampshire; try to dodge Leslie Marmon Silko if you grow up in Laguna, New Mexico. When I was a teenager, my family spent Thanksgivings in Monterey, California, and summer vacations on the northern end of the Sea of Cortez. In the souvenir shops on Cannery Row, paperback books by John Steinbeck waited on spinning kiosks. How could I not pick up a copy of *Cannery Row* on that very street, where the last tattered remnants of the canneries leaned over the sea and a faint whiff of dead fish hovered in the air? After two weeks at Bahia San Luis Gonzaga, I had to go to the library and find a copy of *The Log from the Sea of Cortez*. John Steinbeck had my attention.

It is one thing for an author to command us in our youth, as we try to retrace fictitious steps in the parallel nonfiction world around us. The key question comes later: Is something there to sustain us over the long haul, when "home" is a few jobs, a couple of decades, and several hundred miles away? Or can the author even reach those who have never been to the home ground, who have only the words to stand on? After avidly reading several of Steinbeck's books in high school, he lost me with *In Dubious Battle*—I did not understand it and I stopped reading halfway through. As an undergraduate, taking several English classes, I only encountered him once, when we halfheartedly contemplated "Flight" during a fifty-minute discussion. By their selections on the syllabi, my college professors demonstrated again and again that Steinbeck was no match for Edith Wharton, T. S. Eliot, William Faulkner, Ernest Hemingway—the "serious" writers.

As a doctoral student at Ohio University, two serendipitous things happened: Professor Lester Marks had us read *In Dubious Battle* for his seminar on American literature of the 1930s and Robert DeMott, an internationally recognized Steinbeck scholar, worked just down the hall from my office. Soon my creative dissertation (aborted novel) evolved into a project on John Steinbeck, directed by DeMott, despite the fact that the author was a "DWM" ("Dead White Male") and I had been convinced that following Steinbeck for a career in academe was a long walk into the sea. Nearly finished with graduate work, I attended my first professional conference: a 1989 celebration of the fiftieth anniversary of *The Grapes of Wrath*, held at San Jose State University (right there in "Steinbeck Country"). The keynote speaker was Leslie Fiedler, and he spent his hour observing that Steinbeck was a middlebrow writer for middlebrow critics. Several people walked out. I stayed, listening with fascination, reminded of the old Firesign Theatre album, *Everything You Know Is Wrong*. I owe the late Fiedler a career; his speech propelled me forward to find out what, if anything, was right with the works of John Steinbeck.

I have been far from alone in this reaction to the novelist's numerous detractors. Steinbeck's greatest critics and defenders, among them Richard Astro, Jackson J. Benson, DeMott, and Peter Lisca, all took on the question of why Steinbeck has received the Pulitzer and the Nobel Prize, why he has continued to be a best-seller, why many of his works have been made into movies and plays, and yet he is treated with disdain by the literary establishment. I began my own book, *Parallel Expeditions: Charles Darwin and the Art of John Steinbeck*, asking the same question (what critic Donald Noble finally called *The Steinbeck Question* in a 1993 book he edited). In 1995, I encouraged a young MA student at Western Carolina University, Jenny Baumgartner, to do a thesis on the negative critical reaction to Steinbeck. A hardworking, meticulous woman, Baumgartner plunged into a gigantic assignment, but four years later she finished her work, discussing critical confusion over Steinbeck's use of science, his non-teleological philosophy, his pseudo Marxism, hawkish conservatism, his use of allegory, use of language, his hard realism, his soft sentimentalism—altogether the man who produced *The Grapes of Wrath* as Fiedler describes it: "problematical, middlebrow" (64).

Though Steinbeck at times angrily lashed back at his critics, he rather quietly provided the best answer to the widespread confusion over his books.

"A good writer always works at the impossible," he noted in his *Journal of a Novel.* "There is another kind who pulls in his horizons, drops his mind as one lowers rifle sights," he continues, "Whether fortunate or unfortunate, this has not happened to me" (4). Working at the impossible implies the strain to grasp at huge things too large to hold, and it implies occasional failure. To add to Steinbeck's trouble with the critical establishment, he lacked the ego to promote his successes; what other writer of his age would have stood at a press conference after winning the Nobel Prize and responded to the insulting question posed to him, whether he deserved the prize, by answering, "Frankly, no" (Benson 915). Yet for a writer going after an ever-expanding artistic horizon, his answer makes perfect sense.

John Steinbeck grew up looking out over great vistas, whether out of Salinas to vast flat farms up to the rolling hills or out from Cannery Row to the wide sweep of Monterey Bay and the Pacific beyond. He began his life with these long views and he ended it on a couch high in a tower on East Seventy-second Street in New York City, just a few steps away from breathtaking panoramas of east and south Manhattan. When I think of Steinbeck in this way, I am drawn back to Ralph Waldo Emerson's *Nature* and the assertion that "[t]here is a property in the horizon which no man has but he whose eye can integrate all the parts, that is, the poet" (815). The Steinbeck problem is not what the critics have said about him but more one he was well aware of: his attempt to pull in the entire horizon, all the parts. To do this, in good Emersonian fashion, one must be rid of "all mean egotism" to become that "transparent eyeball" that is nothing but sees all (815). To truly understand Steinbeck, one must consider him as an artist always straining toward the horizon, looking as far out of himself as possible. In a humanist era when the artist was applauded for looking inward—Robert Frost's examination of our internal "desert places" or Faulkner's fascination with the human heart at war with itself—Steinbeck peered outward, to a fictional landscape where the first-person point of view almost never appears. Unlike Thomas Wolfe, Steinbeck has no Asheville to yearn for; unlike F. Scott Fitzgerald, no personal past or faded romance to lament; unlike Hemingway, no comfortable stylistic smoking room to inhabit again and again. John Steinbeck's life, art, and philosophy expands ever outward and to follow him requires taking in a vast, often bewildering view.

In my opinion, the greatest book written about John Steinbeck is the biography by Jackson J. Benson; beyond its weight as a fabulous resource for anyone wanting to study the author's life, *The True Adventures of John Steinbeck, Writer* exists as an artifact of a serious critic's desire to track down John Steinbeck. Benson labored for thirteen years to research and write the book and it came in at over one thousand pages. The biographer tried (and

I think succeeded) to contain the life of an artist within an ever-expanding horizon. In terms of geography, discipline, and artistic form Steinbeck spread out from an early age. As a child, Salinas was a home point between Pacific Grove on the shore and his uncle Tom Hamilton's inland ranch. For the rest of his life, home becomes a series of points, from places in California throughout the 30s and into the 40s to Mexico, Europe, Russia, and Asia. "I have homes everywhere and many I have not seen yet," he wrote in 1949. "This is perhaps why I am restless. I haven't seen all of my homes" (Steinbeck and Wallsten 382). Toward the end of his life, when he was ill and slowed down by serious heart trouble, remarkably he was still on the move, traveling in 1966 with soldiers on the ground for six weeks in Vietnam. Even in his last year, 1968, he traveled to Grenada and according to his wife, Elaine, was still pining for a trip to the Great Barrier Reef (personal interview). In his 1949 letter to Elaine, he summed himself up neatly: "I am not patient. So much to do and so little time" (Steinbeck and Wallsten 382). He wanted to see it all and, like the transformed Tom Joad at the end of *The Grapes of Wrath*, he wanted to be everywhere.

He also wished to write in many genres—to even create a new one (the play–novelette)—and to write across the disciplines. In 1939, after the publication of *Grapes* and at the top of his game as a novelist, Steinbeck declared in a letter (to friend Carlton "Dook" Sheffield) his artistic independence from all form. In this oft-quoted pronouncement, I find the quality of creativity and *courage* that I most admire about John Steinbeck:

I have to go back to school in a way. I'm completely without mathematics and I have to learn something about abstract mathematics. I have some biology but must have much more and the twins bio-physics and bio-chemistry are closed to me. So I have to go back and start over. . . . I'm going on about myself but in a sense it's more than me—it's you and everyone else. The world is sick now. There are things in the tide pools easier to understand than Stalinist, Hitlerite, Democrat, capitalist confusion, and voodoo. So I'm going to those things which are relatively more lasting to find a new basic picture. (Steinbeck and Wallsten 193–94)

In this same letter, he declares that he has worked the novel as much as he can and will search out "the form of the new" (194). Great but lesser writers typically stick with what is working well; Steinbeck, to his credit but no doubt to the detriment of his assessment by critics, looked at *The Grapes of Wrath* and turned to something completely different. Like his travels across the globe, Steinbeck journeyed across the disciplines and artistic forms. He broke through the boundaries of the newspaper article, the short story, the essay, the novel, and extended into film, plays, musicals, and photo books. He worked with scientists, strike organizers, actors, directors, producers, and photographers. He enjoyed gardening, gadgets, and new technologies; had he lived long enough, I believe he would have beaten Stephen King as the first major novelist to sell a book independently online. In his last book published in his lifetime, *America and Americans*, Steinbeck wrote a long sermon to his fellow citizens, urging them to stir from self-complacent lethargy and do what they do best: push forward. "We have never sat still for long," he writes, "we have never been content with a place, a building—or with ourselves" (143). This statement, written at the end of his career, is at once an exhortation to his people and a declaration about himself.

Steinbeck's best illustration of his own thinking—his lifetime goal of widening his perspective to arrive at greater and greater truths—occurs in *The Log from the Sea of Cortez* after he has observed a Japanese dredge boat operation during his and Ed Ricketts's 1940 collecting expedition in the gulf. As the nets pull in countless dead marine animals that are not part of the catch, Tiny, a fisherman aboard the *Western Flyer* (the boat Steinbeck and Ricketts chartered) decries the waste. "We discussed the widening and narrowing picture," Steinbeck writes (*The Log* 217). From Tiny's perspective, there is waste, but as the view widens what appears to be waste goes into the sea and feeds a variety of species from bacteria to sea birds: "in the macrocosm nothing is wasted" (217).

This impulse to step outside oneself, even one's own species, to enter into the whole is the great achievement and philosophical infrastructure of Steinbeck's work. "It is advisable to look from the tide pool to the stars and then back to the tide pool again" (179), Steinbeck writes near the conclusion of *The Log from the Sea of Cortez*. Throughout much of his work, from *The Pastures of Heaven* to *America and Americans*, he considers the individual view against the larger, universal one. In *The Grapes of Wrath*, for example, he shows us the realities of a great migration and of Depression-era despair from the narrow view of the Joad family and the omniscient, wider vista of the intercalary chapters. To attain this view himself, Steinbeck was a collector of experiences, stories, and ideas. His trip to the Sea of Cortez was literally an expedition of scientific collection of marine animals; his road trip across the country in 1960 leading to *Travels with Charley in Search of America* was a collection of observations and stories; and his library—as DeMott's *Steinbeck's Reading: A Catalogue of Books Owned and Borrowed* demonstrates—contained books spreading across the disciplines, including anthropology, biology, Eastern mysticism, history, philosophy, physics, and sociology. "The process of gathering knowledge does not lead to knowing," Steinbeck writes in *The Log from the Sea of Cortez*, "A child's world spreads only a little beyond his understanding while that of a great scientist thrusts outward immeasurably" (137). From childhood on, Steinbeck traveled outward immeasurably and he knew that the more he learned the bigger the questions would be. Each book he wrote would only suggest another book, another answer, another form.

In true Whitmanesque fashion, Steinbeck writes as much about himself as he does everyone when he makes this observation in *The Grapes of Wrath*:

For man, unlike any other thing organic or inorganic in the universe, grows beyond his work, walks up the stairs of his concepts, emerges ahead of his accomplishments. This you may say of man—when theories change and crash, when schools, philosophies, when narrow dark alleys of thought, national, religious, economic, grow and disintegrate, man reaches, stumbles forward, painfully, mistakenly sometimes. Having stepped forward, he may slip back, but only half a step, never the full step back. (192–93)

In books such as *Cannery Row* or *East of Eden*, Steinbeck stepped forward; and indeed, he slipped back a half step with *The Short Reign of Pippin IV* or his version of the Arthurian legends. Yet in the current of an Emerson, Melville, Whitman, or Silko, Steinbeck pursued the largest picture and used whatever form he needed to present what he found. I take John Steinbeck to heart, and I have come to believe what he believed. When I hear a critic try to pigeonhole the novelist or make light of him, I suspect I'm hearing from a mind not large enough to handle Steinbeck. And when I find myself hesitating, afraid to step forward, scared of my own idea, I like to look out the picture windows of my house on Savannah Ridge in North Carolina—looking miles across the valley to the Blue Ridge Parkway—and I think what John Steinbeck made of the vistas before him, and what his work asks us to make of our own vistas.

Steinbeck's Spirituality: A Sense of the Ending

Barbara Heavilin

I believe that there is only one story in the world, and only one. . . . Humans are caught . . . in a net of good and evil. . . . There is no other story. A man, after he has brushed off the dust and chips of his life, will have left only the hard, clean questions: Was it good or was it evil? Have I done well—or ill?

—John Steinbeck, *East of Eden*

The writer is delegated to declare and to celebrate man's proven capacity for greatness of heart and spirit—for gallantry in defeat, for courage, for compassion, and love. In the endless war against weakness and despair, these are the bright rally-flags of hope and emulation. I hold that a writer who does not passionately believe in the perfectibility of man has not dedication nor any membership in literature.

—John Steinbeck, *Speech Accepting the Nobel Prize for Literature*

Spirituality is a popular topic nowadays, bandied about by everyone from personal mystics whose 900 numbers are available in television advertisements to ecumenical gatherings of theologians of all denominations and faiths—with few definitions of what the word means. Often it seems to have as much to do with personal dynamics and charisma as it does with things of the spirit. For purposes of this discussion of Steinbeck's spirituality and his sense of the ending, I am going to define the word "spiritual" as an awareness of God—someone higher than humankind—who requires something of us and to whom we are finally accountable. Although I am not sure that Steinbeck himself would define spirituality in just this manner or that he would be altogether comfortable with the personal application, this concept is the center around which many of his writings revolve. With the voice and authority of a poetic bard and prophet, he did not often invoke the name of God, but he did draw living portraits of God by other names. Like the seventeenth-century mystic poet George Herbert, he drew images that show God in action through His creatures and His creation, and he called Him other names, not capitalized, of course: Love, Joy, Truth, Goodness, Light, Beauty. For Steinbeck, where God dwells is "the other side of home where the lights are given" (*Winter* 275).

With a certain, clear sense of what human beings ought to be, Steinbeck draws God's love in action as Ma Joad shares her family's meager supper with a group of hungry children at the Hooverville Camp. And when he shows Ma's passing on a pair of treasured earrings to her daughter, Rose of Sharon, piercing her ears and assuring her that this rite indeed has great meaning, he pictures a ceremonial and holy joy. Abandoned by her husband and fearful for her unborn child, Rose of Sharon receives with gratitude not only the earrings but her mother's comfort and joy as well. When Steinbeck delivers the famous jeremiad in *Grapes*—warning of the consequences of looking the other way when people are starving in a land of plenty—and when he assures readers in *Eden* that there is no story other than one of good and evil, he speaks with the authority of one who has received truth that he must tell.

In *The Winter of Our Discontent*, when he portrays Ethan's grieving over his family's loss of virtue and praying to go "to the other side of home where the lights are given" (275), he provides a testament of the reality of goodness and light. In the preface to E. W. Tedlock's 1969 edition of *Steinbeck and His Critics: A Record of Twenty-Five Years*, Tedlock muses on the mixed critical reception of Steinbeck's works, asserts that there is "a special love and tolerance" which art requires, and provides an "insight" on the experience of reading Steinbeck: "There is at times in Steinbeck an experience that I think of as purely existential and native or basic to him, beyond cavil. It can be seen in a note of his on an early morning encounter with some farm laborers camped by the road. The note is of great objective purity, and is also most humanly attractive." Feeling this "atmosphere," he maintains, is a "marvelously fresh, non-conceptual awareness . . . so beautifully natural and yet so vulnerable" (5). Tedlock thus testifies to a captivating beauty that the reader discovers on occasion in Steinbeck's writing.

Love, Joy, Truth, Goodness, Light, and Beauty are among God's other names. And Steinbeck defines these names for us in unforgettable cinematic scenes that have a haunting power to draw readers in as participants in what he has called "the actuality." For Steinbeck this actuality often involves a mystical "breaking through," seeing the tide pool and the stars, and on occasion may result in transcendence or rising above the circumstances of here and now. Unlike the exhausted stoicism of Ernest Hemingway, who continually returns to disillusionment and the loss of faith and hope, Steinbeck writes of human beings who at times demonstrate the attributes of God Himself.

Steinbeck's spirituality, then, is sharply focused on the present and on this world. Particularly, he wrote with a passionate love for and belief in his country and his fellow Americans, whom he saw as engaged in a continuing psychic battle between good and evil, most specifically between greed and magnanimity, self-absorption and compassion. And he persistently, passionately believed in their "perfectibility," their ability to transcend and rise above their failures. His vision of this battle and passionate belief in his nation's perfectibility most clearly occurs in the endings of three novels that together may be considered an American epic—a trilogy beginning in medias res with *The Grapes of Wrath* and the Oklahoma Dust Bowl, continuing with the nation's beginnings in *East of Eden*, and concluding with the nation's contemporary struggles with immorality in *The Winter of Our Discontent*. Each novel occurs against a somber biblical backdrop: *Grapes* against the backdrop of the Children of Israel's escape from Egypt and journey through the wilderness; *Eden* against the story of the Fall in Genesis; and *Winter* against the New Testament story of Holy Week and the sufferings, crucifixion, and resurrection of Christ. In each of these novels clearcut battles between good and evil lead to an ending in which human beings either transcend their circumstances or in which the possibility of their transcendence is strongly implied. In *Grapes* the battle revolves around the struggles of the dispossessed in a nation of plenty; in *Eden*, around the freedom to choose between good and evil; and in *Winter*, around one man's struggle between darkness and light.

The critical debate over the ending of *Grapes* in which Rose of Sharon, breasts swollen with milk for her stillborn child, nurses a starving stranger in a deserted barn began with the editor's protest before the novel was published and continues today. Some critics have found this ending uncomfortably "sentimental." Nevertheless, the final sentence in this scene takes the novel into the realm of a nation's mythic history: "She looked up and across the barn, and her lips came together and smiled mysteriously" (581). In 1989 the title of Studs Terkel's introduction for the Viking Deluxe Edition of *Grapes* proclaims, "We Still See Their Faces" (v). We still see, too, the steadfast gaze of this exhausted, feverish, sick young woman as she takes on her mother's mantel as a "citadel," a source of refuge and strength not only for her family but for anyone in need. As Ma, Pa, Winfield, and the stranger's son wait outside in the tool shed, the reader waits also. Warren French has called the Joads' experience an "education of the heart," and so it is. Now acutely aware of the needs of others and of the human/humane responsibility to respond to those needs, the Joads have transcended their present circumstance, but in this final cinematic scene their story is frozen in time, unended. As Joseph Fontenrose deftly pointed out in 1963, "Perhaps the story has not ended yet" (83). Further responsibility, this ending implies, lies with the novel's reader, listener, and participant.

Although the ending of *East of Eden* is a deathbed scene, it, too, is a time of transcendence when Adam sets his son, Cal, free of his fear that he is like his mother, a prostitute who seems darkly predisposed to evil throughout the novel. Finally freed from her wickedness, as though "she had never been" (705), Adam and Cal exult in their freedom from her as Adam whispers his parting word, "*Timshel*," a word symbolizing the human ability to choose one's way, the power to triumph over evil. There is another cinematic freezing here (as in *Grapes*) as Lee, Cal, and Abra surround the dying Adam—all representative of Steinbeck's optimistic belief in the power of transcendence. As paralyzed Adam summons the strength and courage to speak a final word of encouragement to his son, the shared love in this group takes the sting from death. Like Viktor Frankl's vision of communing with his dead wife during his experience in the Nazi death camps of World War II, Steinbeck's ending suggests that "love is as strong as death." Certainly there is in this final scene a transcendence over death and evil and an assurance of Samuel and Adam's continuing legacy of goodness.

In the ending of *The Winter of Our Discontent*, his own plan to rob the town bank thwarted, Ethan Allen Hawley has learned that his son has plagiarized an award-winning essay in the national "I Love America" contest, and he fears that the light of his family's moral legacy is going out. In a reversal of Othello's "Put out the light" speech before he kills Desdemona, Ethan moves from the temptation to commit suicide and extinguish his own light to the realization that he is himself a "light-bearer" for his family, that it is up to him to pass on a moral heritage of uprightness. What follows is a paean to light and light bearers: to Marullo, his Italian boss; to "old Cap'n," his grandfather; and to Aunt Deborah, whose lights all burn brightly. But Ethan's own moral light is now "out . . . blacker than a wick" (275). In a wish that is at once a prayer and a suicidal desire, he first wants "to go home" and then "to the other side of home where the lights are given" (275). Reaching into his pocket for the razor he has brought along to slash his wrists, he finds that his daughter, Ellen, another light bearer, has placed in his pocket a luminous and translucent stone, his family talisman, and that it now gathers "every bit of light" in the rapidly flooding cave where he has come to commit suicide. Experiencing an epiphany of light, he struggles against the tide, fighting his way out of the cave to pass on to Ellen, its new owner, the talisman that symbolizes the light of the Hawley family heritage. Although he is in the midst of the escape from the rapidly rising tidewaters as the novel ends, it follows by implication that both he and Ellen are now light bearers.

There is a simplicity and straightforwardness in these endings that stands in stark contrast to the cynicism and disillusionment in many of the writings of Steinbeck's peers. And they certainly have nothing in common with T. S. Eliot's "Hollow Men," in which the world ends "not with a bang but with a whimper" (2630). Considered sentimental, the concept of transcendence was certainly not the hallmark of his times, and Steinbeck well knew that he was taking a less traveled road, listening to a different drummer. In *Journal of a Novel: The East of Eden Letters*, he wrote before *Eden* was published that it would "be considered old fashioned and old hat." Further, he had not intended to keep pace with his peers, maintaining that "in pace it [*Eden*] is more like Fielding than like Hemingway. I don't think the lovers of Hemingway will love this book" (29). The comparison to Fielding is applicable to more than the "pace" in *Eden* and to more than just this one novel. Like the eighteenth-century novelists, in *Grapes*, *Eden*, and *Winter* Steinbeck holds the mirror so that people can see themselves as they are, with the hope for reform. Such a role is definitely an "old fashioned and old hat" position in the eyes of those critics who have labeled him "sentimental," but it is also the stance of one who speaks simple truth in an age when Pontius Pilate's cynical question "What is truth?" is the more popular view.

Steinback's harshest critics would label as "sentimental," too, his passionate belief in the perfectibility of man as shown in the characters in these novels who transcend their circumstances and failings in the end. But times are different now. As Roger Rosenblatt wrote in the September 24, 2001, issue of *Time* magazine, the age of irony—the time when "nothing was to be believed in or taken seriously"—has come to an end, and we have been confronted with the actuality of "kindness," "honor," and "fair play" as an aftermath of great terror, suffering, and evil (79). After the fall of the Twin Towers in New York, the assault on the Pentagon, and the fallen plane in Pennsylvania on September 11, 2001, an ironic stance does not work quite so well anymore. Perhaps the facile dismissal of Steinbeck's portrayal of these virtues as sentimental does not work either. In the endings of *Grapes*, *Eden*, and *Winter*, Steinbeck has shown the triumph of good over evil. In them he has shown us God by His names of Love, Joy, Truth, Goodness, Light, and Beauty. By these names the "Every Americans" in these novels have risen above their faults, have behaved heroically in the face of opposition, and have shown the possibility of emerging out of darkness into light—an aspiration that is both a hope as well as a prayer. Similarly, in the midst of the horror of that sunny September day in 2001, hundreds of thousands of Americans lived up to Steinbeck's highest aspirations, hopes, and prayers for them. There were heroes and saints and martyrs—doing their jobs, acting out of love, behaving sacrificially. They are the actuality of what Steinbeck so passionately believed, and their stories, like his, have no end.

John Steinbeck: An Ethics of Fiction

John Timmerman

Ethics, morals, codes of conduct, are the stern rules which in the past
we needed to survive.
—John Steinbeck, *America and Americans*

That John Steinbeck was, throughout his career, an ethical writer—concerned with right and wrong choices and the consequences of those
choices—is a common assumption. Yet relatively little has been done with
the assumption in understanding the aesthetic nature of ethics in his work.
When ethical contexts do occur, they often come obliquely: the role of
conflict and paradox, the relevance of biblical/religious allusions, individual
freedom and cultural oppression, and the like. To a large degree, the diver-
gence of such issues into simple "topics" in Steinbeck studies is due to an
inadequate language and consequent framework, philosophically and liter-
arily, for understanding Steinbeck as an ethical writer. My aim in these few
pages is to suggest that elementary, ethical lexicon and to provide a framework of ethics and art that might lead to some future directions of study.

In a special issue of *PMLA* (January 1999) devoted to the topic "Ethics
and Literary Study," general coordinator Lawrence Buell observed in his
introduction that "Ethics has gained new resonance in literary studies during
the past half dozen years, even if it has not—at least yet—become the
paradigm-defining concept that textuality was for the 1970s and historicism
was for the 1980s" (7). Consequently, Buell points out that "[a]s with any

groundswell, particularly when the central term of reference already belongs to common usage, the challenge of pinning down what counts as ethics intensifies as more people lay claim to it" (7). If, as Buell notes, the study of ethics and literature is impeded by the lack of a common set of terms, the particular instance of our concern with Steinbeck is further complicated by those later works in which he postulates his own ethical claims.

The last decade of Steinbeck's life is often referred to as his "moral phase," marked by his infatuation with the chivalric code of *Le Morte d'Arthur*, his sudden and intense writing of *The Winter of Our Discontent* from March to July 1960, and his reflections in *America and Americans*, a prose retelling of *Winter* in which he overtly addresses the moral contortions he perceives in America. Throughout such works he espouses a sort of "moral manhood." The glory of Camelot as a shimmering beacon of moral rectitude in a world blasted and darkened by moral perfidy grew in his mind as an analogy to America. Reflecting on the disparity between the Arthurian age and his own, Steinbeck wrote to Elia Kazan in 1959: "The values have got crossed up. Courtesy is confused with weakness and emotion with sentimentality" (Steinbeck and Wallsten 631). Obviously the statement begs the question, What, exactly, "crossed up" our values? *Winter* and *America and Americans* provide an answer, but that answer may be conveniently summarized in Steinbeck's letter to Adlai Stevenson of November 5, 1959, in which he excoriated American greed: "Having too many THINGS they spend their hours and money on the couch searching for a soul" (Steinbeck and Wallsten 652). In *America and Americans*, Steinbeck voiced it: "We are poisoned with things" (172).

Whatever the degree of truth in Steinbeck's moral speculations and outrage, and of course it also appears in such antecedent works as *Cannery Row*, they are in themselves of little help in constructing an ethics of literature. In fact, I include them here precisely because moral statement is often confused with ethics. A pronouncement of what is morally right or wrong in an author's perception may be important to understanding an author's beliefs and may bear relevance to the thematic structure of a work, but it fails to encompass the literary nature of the work itself. Let me be more specific here on certain traits commonly misunderstood as qualities of ethical literature and Steinbeck's specific responses or alternatives to them.

To bring shape to Steinbeck's ethics of fiction, it is helpful to separate our approach into two parts. The first of these I will call "intrinsic ethics," that is, what qualities inhere in the work itself to guide our understanding of the ethical positioning of the work. Such elements, for example, might include the motivations of a character to action, the action taken, and the consequences of that action. The second approach we may call "extrinsic ethics," that is, how the author presents the work to the reader. Here a host of authorial choices enter: How much of the story to give over to metaphor, or even ambiguity, for the reader to resolve? What degree of intimacy is delivered by the narrative point of view? In this case, then, the work itself functions as metaphor, involving the reader in solutions and conclusions to which the author points rather than directs.

It should be obvious, furthermore, that we are in error if we construe Steinbeck's fiction as allegory. Even in those works packed most densely with symbolism (for example, *The Pearl*, *East of Eden*), Steinbeck never confines the reader to the strict parameters of allegory where every symbol on narrative level A, for example, has to point to or fit into a meaning on level B. Symbolism, in Steinbeck's literary artistry, is mythic, identified with human experience, tradition, aspirations, and significance. Thereby, Elisa Allen's "planter's hands" represent not only her gift of gardening but also her creative artistry. Furthermore, her gardening gloves represent not only protection of those gifted hands but also the repression of her femininity and creativity by culturally expected roles of the female. Steinbeck structures symbolism as signs stirring the reader's imagination and conclusions. Consequently, the very richness of his fiction lies in the multivariant, and sometimes opposing, interpretations that readers construct.

INTRINSIC ETHICS

A number of twentieth-century ethical systems might be entertained here, each with some degree of relevance to Steinbeck's fiction. Although Rationalist ethics, which posited that the human mind itself was the guide to right and reasonable actions, had been fairly well shredded by early twentieth-century modernism, remnants certainly remained. As such they were subject to Steinbeck's unremitting scorn and attack as "the system," or as *Cannery Row* has it, "civilization." Contrary to rationalism, then, an existential ethics might seem fitting, particularly when one considers the carefree Mack and the boys. But in their case, the ethical properties are actually self-interested rather than pursuing "authenticity" as Martin Heidegger and Jean-Paul Sartre had it, or "good faith" as Simone de Beauvoir put it. Their rejection of and escape from civilization grants a degree of individual freedom but fails to measure the consequences or engage society with any redemptive value.

Apart from *The Grapes of Wrath*, few examples of disinterested ethics occur in Steinbeck's fiction. One could make a good case for Steinbeck holding to a social ethics, particularly as it has been redefined by recent philosophy as how one "holds" or brings a right attitude to others in a

social context. Many of Steinbeck's novels are clearly driven by a social conscience. However, for the sake of narrowing the argument here, consider a
distinction between theological and deontological ethics, since they most
frequently come to bear on symbolic readings.

Perhaps the foremost, and most easily dismissed, of the misunderstandings
regarding Steinbeck's ethics arises from the rippling current of biblical/re-
ligious allusions that flows through his novels. In *To a God Unknown*, they
occur in such turgid and convoluted succession as to render the novel merely
opaque. In such works as *The Grapes of Wrath* and *East of Eden*, they form
deliberate substructures (by Steinbeck's own admission) that guide our understanding of the whole. Yet, as I have argued elsewhere, such allusions
are artistic tools for Steinbeck and not at all evidence of personal belief.[1]
Rather, we must disavow a theological ethics in Steinbeck's work. Theological ethics takes its name from the perspective of religion, which offers an
interpretation of the nature of God and such God–human–nature relationships as sin, evil, goodness, and salvation. The defining nature of such relationships focuses on some transcendent but always immanent source. This
ethics begins with a faith act: that there is a divine being who has encoded
standards of right and wrong behavior, who has revealed them to humanity,
and who expects humanity to walk in those standards for relational ends
between divinity and humanity.

While no sense of a theological ethics is manifested in Steinbeck's work,
an acute sense of right and wrong behavior does appear. That is to say, Tom
Joad picks up Jim Casy's fallen banner because he believes he "ought to."
Instead of a theological ethics, Steinbeck most frequently positions us at a
deontological ethics.[2] Instead of asking the familiar ethical question of what
is the right or wrong choice, deontological ethics asks where one obtains a
sense of rightness or wrongness itself. Is it simply a utilitarian pattern (what
would bring about the most good for the most people) or a cultural norm?
If one feels that certain acts are right (compassion for the needy) and certain
others are wrong (genocide of a needy people), how do we know we ought
to do one and not the other? To extend the issue, why do we see the
genocidal tyrant as an aberration of some moral quality, not just doing
wrong but being evil? Deontological ethics begins with an investigation of
where the "oughtness" behind right and wrong human actions originates.

The modern shaping of deontological ethics occurred in Immanuel Kant's
The Critique of Practical Reason, a response to his own *Pure Reason* that
shaped his epistemology by marrying reason and experience but left no room
for shaping ethical values. In *Critique*, Kant argued that every human has a
sense of oughtness, or what he calls the "Categorical Imperative," the "thou
ought." Humanity needs this to make sense and order out of life, to validate

an ethical existence. Therefore, Kant postulates these universals derived from his Categorical Imperative: that everyone has freedom to seek the universal; that everyone has a soul that is free and that seeks; and that this soul has an underlying cause that is God. The cause of human knowledge in ethical choices, unlike Pure Reason, lies outside of the natural world.

For the deontologist, ethical values are not merely good suggestions; they are obligations morally required of us. The right act, then, is to say this ought to be done. But how do we know that? One option derives from H. A. Pritchard's 1909 essay "Does Moral Philosophy Rest on a Mistake?" in which he argues that we apprehend what we ought to do intuitionally. We can see immediately or intuitively that certain actions are right without having to examine these acts as utilitarian. The source of oughtness, then, is intuition, an innate quality of human nature itself. One can see the correspondence between Pritchard's and Kant's views but also sense that each leaves a problem. If this sense of oughtness originates in human nature, then the "right thing" is not always clear, which is where we find the majority of Steinbeck's characters ethically positioned. In response to Kant and Pritchard, however, others attempt to correct the intrinsic ambiguity by the standard of "disinterestedness." We are to be interested in the consequences of our actions upon others; we are disinterested in that we refuse to allow personal interests to outweigh the good of others.

It should be manifestly clear, albeit not directly articulated by Steinbeck, that his is a deontological ethics. In fact, his sense of intuited oughtness strikes a chord already in the *Sea of Cortez*, his otherwise futile attempt to adapt marine biology as a matrix for human action. Nonetheless, he writes there, "For the ocean, deep and black in the depths, is like the low dark levels of our minds in which the dream symbols incubate and sometimes rise up to sight like Old Man of the Sea" (31). The "dream symbols" here are precisely those myths or stories by which we hold fellow humanity. Or again, "There is tied up to the most primitive and powerful racial or collective instinct a rhythm sense or 'memory' which affects everything" (34). But this voice—preconscious or whatever—is also, in the fiction, a markedly disinterested voice. The clearest expression of this, beyond question, is through Ma Joad and her belief in the "family of man." Self-interest, the quality of the landowners, Ma offsets and rejects by sacrificial living. No special rules govern Ma's behavior. She does it, even to directing Rose of Sharon to the starving man, because it ought to be done.

We discover first, then, that instead of taking biblical/religious allusions as the measure of Steinbeck's moral beliefs we see them functioning metaphorically and anagogically in the work. Furthermore, instead of a theological ethics expressed by a divine being to humanity, we find a deontological ethics of humanity responding to a sense of intuited oughtness. Beyond question, Steinbeck explored the nooks and crevices of human nature, bringing the hidden to light, exposing lies and fabrications, and exploring the costs of pursuing dreams. Such qualities in and of themselves might warrant the appellation of a "moral writer." But it was not Steinbeck's aim to reduce these investigations to a set of axiomatic truths or didactic principles.

EXTRINSIC ETHICS

If the first area of investigation treated the ethical means by which characters discern good and evil in the novels, the second area, extrinsic ethics, treats the way the stories of these characters are offered to the audience. Steinbeck testified often, and throughout his career, that his primary aim as a writer was to tell a story. The stories varied as he felt compelled to tell them. He was unpopular with critics because he was unpredictable. When *In Dubious Battle* was perceived as a Marxist screed, he surprised everyone by writing the quiet little tragedy *Of Mice and Men*. He wrote the bright and rollicking *Tortilla Flat* during a brief interlude while composing the shadowed landscape of *The Long Valley*. Yet in ethical as well as in critical appraisal we are left with the question, To what ends are the stories told? If we have rejected an allegorical reading of Steinbeck's fiction, neither do we expect an Aristotelian argument of truthful ends and right actions. Nonetheless, story as such requires a teleology; the very nature of story narrative initiates a progression toward certain ends.

In a particularly helpful study of the ends and purposes of story, "The End of Literature: Reflections on Literature and Ethics," Clarence Walhout works out a careful synthesis between teleology and ethics in literature. Walhout defines "teleology" in terms altogether applicable to Steinbeck: "Teleology does not require an Aristotelian conception of an ideal or universal *telos* or end or goal. It does not even require that the *telos* be a certain or determinate good. It does imply, however, that living in time entails some sense of purposeful movement toward desired goals" (459).[3] Such a view circumvents the common understanding of teleology as a fixed or transcendent goal, and thereby outside of human endeavor.[4]

Assuming then that teleology is the pursuit of ends or goals enacted in one's life—and consequently also in one's art—how does this belief affect what we make of ethics in literature? Again, Walhout expands his view in a way that also might apply directly to Steinbeck:

Though universal truths and values may be important for the study of literature, the primary purpose of literature is not to convey or represent such truths or values but to explore the possibilities and consequences of specific human actions and thoughts in a narrative situation. Whatever we may mean by universal truths and values in literature, they are qualities that serve the end of literature and are not themselves the end. The end is the narration of actions that have ethical significance. . . . Actions that are narrated in literature are often taken as illustrations of universal truths and values rather than as what they are—the uncertain and often stumbling efforts of characters to find a way to act in a confusing world. (461)

Thereby, as Walhout points out, literature dramatizes for the reader the conflicts and choices universal to the human condition. Literature may be described as a searching out, rather than a positing, of universal truths or values.[5]

If such may be judged to hold for Steinbeck, it bears certain implications for his extrinsic ethics. A sense of teleology that is ongoing draws a reader into possibilities the author holds forth. Into a narrative the author provides conflicts and choices that the reader works through, thereby placing his or her own personhood into the possible resolutions or effects of those conflicts and choices. The reader participates in the story. While symbolism may guide possible choices, it is not structured in an exclusively determinative way to admit one choice only; for example, consider the conflicting meanings and choices provided by the symbolic gem in *The Pearl*. In arriving at an ethical position, then, both artist and reader necessarily work through the ambiguity that grants freedom of choice. To be sure, often the work ends in a tension of unresolved options. This is precisely the point to which Steinbeck often leads the reader (again, consider Pepé in "Flight"). Nonetheless, that very act of pondering conflicting values, of weighing alternatives, and of abandoning untenable responses constitutes an ethical act.

We see, then, that in terms of the intrinsic qualities of the narrative, Steinbeck's artistry is suggestive rather than declarative. Through the use of such constructs as metaphor, symbolism, and character action, he poses conflicts for the reader. Moreover, in terms of extrinsic qualities, he leaves many such conflicts and ambiguities for the reader to resolve. The author tells the story; the reader determines to what teleological ends the story is told. Steinbeck's call to the reader, fundamentally, is to come with me and follow this narrative road on a process of self-discovery. On that road the reader confronts a host of metaphorical and symbolic qualities, many of which emanate from biblical/religious sources. But here too, rather than determinative as a theological ethics, such sources are a call to a reflective plane of deontological ethics, requiring the reader's determination of what ought to be done. For John Steinbeck the reader is an essential participant in both the narrative as well as the ethical understanding of the work.

NOTES

1. See "John Steinbeck's Use of the Bible: A Descriptive Bibliography of the Critical Tradition," *Steinbeck Quarterly* 21 (Winter/Spring 1988): 24–39.

2. My summary of deontological ethics here is necessarily brief. Several of the best introductions to the philosophy include Nancy Davis's "Contemporary Deontology," Charles Fried's *Right and Wrong* (Cambridge: Harvard UP, 1978), and John Rawls's *A Theory of Justice* (Cambridge: Belknap P of Harvard UP, 1999).

3. See also Jeffrey Stout, who in *Ethics after Babel: The Languages of Morals and Their Discontents*, similarly argues that the *telos* need not be "a fixed conception of the good, derived once and for all from a philosophical view of the human essence" (237). For Stout, the *telos* is only worthwhile if it is in fact attainable in human affairs.

4. As I have pointed out elsewhere, Steinbeck's convoluted theory of "non-teleological thinking," as espoused in *The Log from the Sea of Cortez* and several letters, is in fact philosophically teleological thinking (see *John Steinbeck's Fiction* 16–23, 158–59). Steinbeck's fear was of ironclad moral systems that denied individual freedom. His non-teleological thinking comports nearly perfectly with Walhout's analysis.

5. In *The Company We Keep: An Ethics of Fiction*, Wayne C. Booth contends that "[e]very appraisal of narrative is implicitly a comparison between the always complex experience we have had in its presence and what we have known before" (71).

Steinbeck and the Woman Question: A Never-Ending Puzzle

Mimi Gladstein

It is some thirty years since the problem of John Steinbeck's depiction of women in his fiction first crossed my critical radar screen. It has remained a provocative puzzle, one that provides rich resources for continuing analysis and exploration. In those days, before we had the benefit of Jackson Benson's massive biography, there was a tendency to decode the life by reading the fiction. There were few women in the fiction, a fact that had been noted by early readers such as Claude Edmonde Magny, who pointed out that as male couples played such a predominant role in Steinbeck's fiction, it acted to create a sense of the exclusion of women from the human community. Or there was Peter Lisca's observation about the prevalence of male relationships, with the added caveat that Steinbeck relegated such women as did appear in his fiction to the limited roles of either housewife or prostitute. A 1974 dissertation by Angela Patterson analyzed Steinbeck's depictions of and attitudes toward women. Finding few women of worth in their own right, she concluded that Steinbeck was reflecting his own life and times. My own dissertation of the previous year (1973) acknowledged the dearth of women but argued the consequent significance of the few who were accorded some narrative stature. Patterson's unsubstantiated position that Steinbeck was portraying reality as he knew it was replicated as late as 1988 by Beth Everest and Judy Wedeles, who excused Steinbeck for his limited portrayal of women by asserting that the historical realities of his life and of the times he is writing about limited "the roles he could assign them" (23).

Once Jackson Benson had published his massive and painstakingly re-searched biography in 1984, it became difficult to sustain the exculpatory explanations for the short supply of women in Steinbeck's fiction. Benson provided such an abundance of information about the many women in Steinbeck's life that I was moved to question the strange disconnect between the life and the fiction in a presentation at the 1989 conference "The Stein-beck Question." This initial exploration presented some possible reasons for the inexplicable disparity between the many women who played key roles in Steinbeck's life and the paucity and limited possibilities of those in his fiction.[1] The subject was so intriguing that I began to study the historical context for two of his key novels: *In Dubious Battle* and *The Grapes of Wrath*.

The facts of Steinbeck's life easily refute the idea that he was simply re-flecting his personal reality and the social and political situation of his time when he presented no evidence of women professionals, activists, or public figures in his narratives. Women were key players in the drama of his life and in the resources for his fiction. Most recently, at the 2001 Steinbeck Festival that kicked off the celebrations and conferences of the centennial year, I presented information about the women instructors, not the least of whom was his schoolteacher mother, who were instrumental in the forma-tion of the man and the writer. These include Edith Brunoni, his piano teacher who nurtured in the budding writer a strong appreciation for music, and Ora M. Cupp, who did likewise for his writing talent. But no greater tribute can be paid to a teacher's influence than Steinbeck's own acknow-ledgment of Emma Hawkins: "I suppose that to a large extent I am the unsigned manuscript of that high school teacher" (". . . . like" 7). Teachers such as this do not appear in the fiction. I've always wondered why.

Another factor that has complicated the issue of Steinbeck's depiction of women is the contradictory nature of that depiction. There are many ap-parently misogynistic characterizations; indeed, I credit him with the most vicious female villain in American fiction—the amoral Kate Trask of *East of Eden*. Yet at the same time Steinbeck is the creator of some of the most positive female characters who ever graced the pages of twentieth-century literature. Certainly Ma Joad has few equals in terms of a characterization of woman. The portrait the narrator draws of her is a paean to woman as mother, a source of strength and love for her family—assertive, steadfast, and compassionate. Steinbeck's narrator portrays her as goddess, judge, and citadel; one could not ask for a more durable role model of endurance and indestructibility.

Also weighing in on the side of Steinbeck's positive depiction of women is the resolute and enduring Juana of *The Pearl*. Juana is made all the more significant in that fable because she is purely a manifestation of Steinbeck's creative resources. The parable of the Indian boy who found the pearl of great worth that serves as the inspiration for the novelette is recounted first in *Sea of Cortez*. That version does not include a wife and a child. In it, after the boy experiences the greed and violence incited by the pearl, he curses it and throws it back into the water. A freer and wiser man, "he laughed a great deal about it." In Steinbeck's retelling of the tale, he adds a wife whom he invests with the wisdom of the boy in the original parable.

Add to Ma Joad, Juana Abra from *East of Eden*, a character Steinbeck constructs because he needs a "strong female principle of good." Abra has few, if any, analogs in Steinbeck's fiction. She is a young woman characterized as "a fighter and an effective human being" (*Journal* 195). Her function in the novel is as a force for good, an incarnation of Steinbeck's *timshel* principle. Whereas Adam cannot find an appropriate Eve for his dream of a garden, Abra represents the new Eve who, together with Cal, will be the mother for new generations.

There are other inspirational female characters—ones who approach the status of heroines. Certainly Suzy, the spunky whore who wins Doc's heart in *Sweet Thursday*, is a character drawn with compassion and caring. Steinbeck uses her to show how resilient not just women but all humans can be, speaking through Doc: "My God, what a brave thing is the human!" (248). There are more women who seem to transcend the ordinary rules of morality with their creator's approval, such as Mordeen in *Burning Bright* and Rama in *To a God Unknown*.

But just as one gets ready to categorize Steinbeck's women as positively depicted, their appearance is equaled or outweighed by a cacophony of sometimes monstrous, sometimes vapid women. For example, what are readers to make of the women in *East of Eden* other than Abra? (I exclude here the female characters that are based on real-life members of Steinbeck's family.) *East of Eden* adds to the puzzling evidence of the strange disconnect between the women in Steinbeck's life and those he creates for his stories— the tension between women in his reality and his imaginative reconstruction of woman. His portrayals of the women in his mother's family, the Hamiltons, are drawn with a pen of pride, humor, and nostalgia. But, save for Abra, every woman who is Steinbeck-manufactured, the woman he could create "from the ground up," is pallid, hysterical, mean, and/or stupid. The first Mrs. Trask is a religious, suicidal hysteric; her successor is too dumb to know her own son, callous to his near murder of his stepbrother; Faye though a whorehouse madam, is easily duped by Kate; Kate's mother is sadistic and clueless about her daughter. The best mother in the novel is a man, Lee.

And how are women supposed to read *The Wayward Bus*? Bobbi Gonzales, who first read it in order to make a report for a Steinbeck seminar, was so appalled by the misogyny rife in the female characterizations that we ended up writing an article together about that novel as Steinbeck's misogynistic manifesto. Steinbeck begins the book with an inscription of lines from *Everyman*. If he also has "Everywoman" in mind, she presents a pitiful picture, running the gamut from hopelessly naïve waitresses to manipulative wives who suppress their husbands' sexual desires. And while the women are drawn with misogynistic venom, the men, including the protagonist, present and voice an appalling array of sexist thinking. However, there is pointed textual evidence that Steinbeck is satirizing aspects of male behavior and double standards. In one instance, when describing Pritchard, the narrator points out that while Pritchard considered the dancers at stag parties depraved, "it would never have occurred to him that he who watched and applauded and paid the girls was in any way associated with depravity" (40). Steinbeck's perceptions here are very much in keeping with feminist critiques that would be put forth a decade later.

Yet despite an occasional enlightened perspective, it is not only in the serious works that Steinbeck exhibits these sexist and misogynistic attitudes. *Cannery Row* is a wonderfully funny narrative—if you read it like a man. The humor is decidedly phallocentric, often at the expense of women. With few exceptions, the only good women are prostitutes. Wives are anathema. Again, though he uses memories of Ed Ricketts and life on Old Ocean Avenue as sources for the story, he leaves out the many women who worked in the canneries, the many active and professional women who were part of the group that partied and shared ideas at the lab.

There is a school of Steinbeck critics who respond to the castigations of Steinbeck's limited and repellent portrayals of women by explaining that Steinbeck's purpose in doing so is to critique woman-less or woman-oppressive culture. Chief among these are Abby Werlock, Jean Emery, and Charlotte Hadella. Werlock argues that the character I dismiss as baby-laden Lisa in *In Dubious Battle* is a Madonna figure, whose presence in the novel represents morality, caring, and conscience in opposition to the violent and often "cold-blooded" men. "If hope exists in this novel, it lies in the different world and different voice of the female embodied in Lisa," contends Werlock, using my own *Indestructible Woman* to buttress her arguments (63). Emery convincingly argues that *Of Mice and Men* is not a poignant, sentimental drama, but rather the achievement of a dream of male fraternity that represses and eliminates women and femininity. However, in her reading Steinbeck's tale is a critique of that sterility and lack of diversity, "a scathing commentary on misplaced values." She contends that "Steinbeck's sympathy clearly lies with the feminine" (41). Hadella, noting all the "guarded, fenced, and repressed" women in *The Pastures of Heaven* and *The Long Valley*, concludes: "Ultimately, cloistering women to prevent the human race from falling into sin proves to be a major cause for unhappiness in Steinbeck's disturbed 'valley of the world' " (69).

Of Mice and Men and its *one* unnamed woman has drawn a wondrously diverse set of readings about what it all means in terms of gender issues and feminist critique. Leland Person examines the novel "within a pluralized discourse of masculinity—as a novel about men's relationships to other men" (1), a homosexual reading in the sense that the term means intimate, but not necessarily same-sex, relationships. In his analysis, Curley's wife operates as a kind of outlaw virgin because by crossing "the carefully drawn lines between the ranch house and the bunkhouse, the owners and workers . . . she exaggerates the fault lines between homosocial and heterosexual desires" (2). Killing her imperils the "utopian homosexual dream" (4). Mark Spilka reads the same work with a different outcome. For him, there is something "painfully adolescent" about the dream of the female-less cooperative farm Lennie and George dream about. In his view Steinbeck "projects his own hostilities through George and Lennie" (64), and he sees a connection between Cathy Ames and Curley's wife. In the creation of Cathy, over a decade later, Spilka observes "a monstrous projection of his old hostility toward women as exploiters of the sex impulse" (70).

Complicating the matter of what to make of Curley's wife is the fact that she has evolved since her first manifestation in the novelette. Steinbeck enlarged her role for the play and tried to "explain" her to Claire Luce, who played the character on Broadway. Charlotte Hadella explores the "dialogic tension" of Steinbeck's portrait, citing Steinbeck's paradoxical explanation that you would love her if you knew her, but that you could never know her. Hadella theorizes that the differing analyses of the character may be attributed to the "levels of discourse in the story that compete for definition." In her estimation, the fiction "does not offer an authoritative or absolute statement on the woman's character" (73). My own study ("*Of Mice and Men*: Creating and Recreating Curley's Wife"), via three of her cinematic re-creations, concludes that how Curley's wife is portrayed on film often owes as much to the time of the film production as it does to Steinbeck's text. Betty Field's 1939 bejeweled, made-up, dark-stockinged vamp morphs over the decades into Sheryl Lynn Fenn's 1992 simple, sweet-faced, and bare-legged lost girl, the sexuality of each coded to the audience's semiotic expectations rather than Steinbeck's narrative descriptions. That she can change so much and yet remain an interpretive puzzle for succeeding generations is tribute to the universality of Steinbeck's creation.

My review of the various analyses of how Steinbeck depicts women is not meant to be exhaustive. Many critics whose work I admire are left out. Those I have mentioned are but some of the astute readers who have provoked my thinking and influenced my reading and teaching. The diversity and often-contradictory interpretations they present are also testament to the complexity and levels of interpretation Steinbeck's works inspire. For example, John Ditsky's reading (at the Third International Steinbeck Congress) of Steinbeck's work as itself being an "elusive and remarkable Woman" raises insightful issues about the gender coding of his creative process. What has been unendingly stimulating for me is that the question of how Steinbeck views women continues to inspire such disparate readings. Once all the readers settle on a single view, the issue ceases to be provocative, its mystery resolved. Not the case here.

Over the years I have received both verifications and refutations of my theories about Steinbeck's women. Particularly interesting have been responses from those who knew the man. After delivering my conclusions about the negative portrayal of women in *East of Eden* that resulted when Steinbeck had the opportunity to build a female character from the ground up in comparison to his portraitures of the women in his family, I was greeted by the outstretched hand of John Steinbeck IV, who introduced himself and let me know how much he liked my paper, how valid he found my conclusions. Virginia Scardigli and Jean Ariss were generally supportive of my ideas that Steinbeck had problems in relating to women. Margery Lloyd, on the other hand, found him quite gallant and responsive to women. She told me a charming story about how Steinbeck sympathized with her, holding her while she threw up and telling her that a pretty girl like her should not be sick. John Kenneth Galbraith, upon hearing my conclusions about misogyny in *The Wayward Bus*, insisted that Steinbeck loved women. Both the major biographies chronicle at once his dependence on and sometimes callous treatment of women.

After some twenty years of puzzling out the problem of women in Steinbeck, I decided to turn my attention to other approaches. For the 1990 Third International Congress, I explored the universality of the immigrant paradigm in *The Grapes of Wrath*. Though the Okies are migrants, rather than immigrants, Steinbeck presents their situation in terms of time-coded patterns of the treatment of foreigners. My students verified this conclusion in subsequent years, particularly when I taught in Venezuela and Spain. For Venezuelans, the Okies were analogous to the Colombians, who were swarming legally and illegally into their country, taking all the low-paying jobs. My students in Madrid saw the Okies as Moroccans and Algerians who used the poorly guarded Gilbraltar border as a pathway to Spain. A German student related the attitude of the Californians toward the Okies to the response many Germans have toward the Turks who have come in large numbers to avail themselves of economic opportunities not present in their country.[2]

Each new generation rereads Steinbeck through the lens of its own interests. The "Steinbeck and the Environment" conference—the brainchild of Susan Shillinglaw, Susan Beegel, and Wes Tiffany—inspired a second look at many of his works, a look that reveals Steinbeck's prescient environmentalism. *Sea of Cortez*, which has long since achieved mythic status with naturalists, yields further insights when subjected to a "green perspective." From the new approach of environmentalism to the time-tested exploration of how Steinbeck used the Arthurian myths as an underlying archetype, Steinbeck's works, both fiction and nonfiction, provide a never-ending treasure trove for study. Following the Arthurian theme from the early novels to its consummation in *America and Americans* was another revelation of the depths and levels of the man's endlessly questing mind.

In the 1956 film production of the Rodgers and Hammerstein musical *Anna and the King of Siam*, the king, memorably portrayed by Yul Brynner, sings a delightful song about his worries about what to do, whom to believe, how to lead his country.[3] Recently, as I replayed it on video, I thought the words quite apropos to the issue of Steinbeck and women. "Very often find confusion in conclusion," sings the king, a sentiment not unlike the one I feel when trying to unravel the many threads of John Steinbeck's tapestry of humanity. No sooner do I make my mind up about the woman issue when someone's astute reading convinces me to rethink my position. That is much of what has made the study of Steinbeck such a joy. In the song, after analyzing each issue and not being able to come to a conclusion, the king repeats the refrain: "Is a Puzzlement." That is the statement that ends his song. That is my conclusion after decades of studying Steinbeck and the woman question. Indeed, it is a puzzlement.

NOTES

1. Once, after the presentation of one of my feminist critiques of Steinbeck's limited and often negative depictions of women, Jack Benson chided me for being "hard" on Steinbeck. I jokingly reminded him that he was the one who provided me with all the ammunition, as much of my evidence came from his biography.

2. A number of my students at the Complutense in Madrid were with ERASMUS, a European Union student exchange program. Therefore, I was able to get the input from students in a number of European countries.

3. Steinbeck was familiar with the song. He refers to it in one of the "Letters from John Steinbeck" published in the *Salinas Californian* on February 18, 1967. He quotes the line, "Is a Puzzlement," in referring to the difficulty of explaining New York City politics to students in Bangkok.

Steinbeck's Concept of the Function of Fiction

Warren French

Although biographer Jackson Benson identifies John Steinbeck as one of the few novelists of his celebrated generation who received a significant part of his training in a college creative-writing program, Steinbeck never subsequently took part in any such program or, like Wallace Stegner, participated in summer institutes or workshops for young writers. Nor did he participate in book signings or literary fairs in the United States, and he refused invitations to speak at universities or to receive honorary degrees. Although early in his career, he did publish one article based on his conception of *Of Mice and Men* and encouraged others to experiment with such "play–novelettes" ("The Novel" 50–51), he avoided public discussions of the meanings or reception of his works. It has been difficult, therefore, to collect information about his concept of the function of fiction in the reader's experience, although on a few noteworthy occasions he did provide several pertinent clues.

A further complication to understanding what might be called Steinbeck's "literary development" is the drastic change in what kind of novels he thought might win him an audience very early in his career, as well as the misleading order of publication of his apprentice works, books that appeared before he had developed the vision that shaped his most significant publications. Before he enjoyed his first commercial and critical success with *Tortilla Flat* (1935), he had already completed six other novels (one of them a murder mystery), only three of which had been published; the others were apparently destroyed. The third of these to be published, *To a God Unknown* (1933), was actually written before the second (*The Pastures of Heaven* [1932]) and in a romantic style very similar to his first, *Cup of Gold* (1929). These two earliest works are both written in a stylized prose that might be described as the literary complement to the style and subject matter of Art Deco, which was internationally prevalent in the boom years of the 1920s. Such writings were popularized in the United States by the exotic romances of Brian Donn-Byrne and by James Branch Cabell's fantastic tales about a medieval kingdom of Poictesime. By reading Steinbeck's novels in the order of publication, one is particularly struck by the seemingly backward movement from *The Pastures of Heaven* to *To a God Unknown*, a problem arising from the difficulty of finding a publisher during the depths of the Depression.

That Steinbeck had made a deliberate, determined effort to break with the fantasy worlds of his romantic tales became evident in 1932 when he was living in his friend Ed Ricketts's California home next door to the distinguished anthropologist Joseph Campbell. Campbell was awakened one morning by a huge bonfire in his neighbor's backyard; Steinbeck was burning all his unpublished stories. With this flamboyant gesture, the writer cleared the way for a career of hitherto unimagined success. His great break came in 1934, when the New York publisher Pascal Covici was visiting Chicago and stopped in at Ben Abramson's Argosy Book Shop, which specialized in selling remainder copies of discontinued editions. Abramson was greatly impressed with Steinbeck's work and pressed upon Covici copies of his three novels. Covici sat up all night reading *The Pastures of Heaven* and immediately got in touch with Steinbeck's agent, Elizabeth Otis, desiring to reprint all three of his novels and offering a contract for the one he was just then completing, *Tortilla Flat*.

Steinbeck was thus embarked on a career that was to be based largely on the people and places of the region where he had grown up. Although, as indicated earlier, he rarely elaborated on his intentions in published works, a few comments at important moments do provide hints as to the underlying vision that shaped his success.

Writing to a friend, George Albee, in 1933 when he was engaged in one of his most successful and memorable works, the story cycle *The Red Pony* (1937), he explained that in one of the four stories about a boy growing up in the still pastoral California of his own childhood, he intended not to tell readers what was going on in the boy's mind but to "make the reader enter the boy's mind for himself" (Steinbeck and Wallsten 71). We get another clue five years later at one of the most trying moments in his career. When he is compelled to explain to Covici why he had destroyed the manuscript of the novel he'd just written, with the promise that he would replace it with another already underway (which, by the way, turned out to be *The Grapes of Wrath* [1939]), Steinbeck eloquently argues, "My whole work drive has been aimed at making people understand each other, and then I deliberately write this book [*Le Affair Lettuceberg*], the aim of which is to cause hatred through partial understanding" (Gannett xxi). The underlying motive revealed here for Steinbeck the writer involves inviting the reader to become a participant in the fictive process while simultaneously encouraging moral clarity and understanding. (It should also be noted that both these letters were not available to the public or critics until some years later.)

However, Steinbeck's clearest and most public statement about his concept of the function of fiction, not just his own but every writer's, was made most appropriately at the peak of his career, when he received the Nobel Prize for Literature in 1962. At this event he most fully explained his own conception of his profession to an audience he thought deserved it and might understand. Twice in his speech of scarcely more than five hundred words, he makes statements concerning the duty of all writers to society, beginning, "The ancient commission of the writer has not changed. He is charged with exposing our many grievous faults and failures, with dredging up to the light our dark and dangerous dreams, for the purpose of improvement" (*Speech* 8). Then after a discussion of Alfred Nobel, who commissioned these awards, Steinbeck explains that they are offered for "increased and continuing knowledge of man and of his world, which are the functions of literature" (10). It is noteworthy that he makes no specific references to his own work or to that of other Nobel Prize winners, although he does pay tribute to his "great predecessor," William Faulkner, who "more than most men, was aware of human strength as well as human weakness" (8). Steinbeck provides no further guidelines, although there remain a few more clues.

On an earlier occasion he had published some remarks he had made about the proper concerns for contemporary novelists, but these are not widely known here at home because they appeared in a French translation in Paris, where he was spending the summer of 1954 with his wife Elaine and his two sons. He agreed to join a number of prominent French writers at an outdoor book-signing festival of the kind he avoided in the United States. He found that he enjoyed the affair and wrote a report of it in one of the weekly columns that he had agreed to provide for the culturally oriented morning newspaper, *Le Figaro*, with the title "*Assez parle' de bon vieux temps*" (Enough said about the "good old days"). In reaction to the comments of Maria Crapeau, a French reporter, asking why American novelists were writing so much about the past when they should be concentrating on the present, Steinbeck, having just published *East of Eden* (1952), felt the remarks applied to him and was impressed enough to want to do something about the matter.

The problem of escaping the past wasn't easily solved, however, as he stressed later in 1954 in an interview for another European paper, the *Rome Daily American*. He told William Pepper that the old American dreams were exhausted because "there were no more frontiers or prairies or oceans to cross." Echoing Jody Tiflin's grandfather's frustration in "The Leader of the People," the climactic story of *The Red Pony*, Steinbeck continued, "We have come to a period where there is nowhere to go but up or down. Going down is great for oilmen and morticians. For a writer, for any man, the only practical thing is going up" (1). He finally found his own way up, not by traveling back home but in recollecting the times he spent in France during a period of continual political unrest. In a droll satire, *The Short Reign of Pippin IV* (1957), he depicted an attempt to solve France's instability of short-lived governments by recalling the last descendant of the Carolingian kings to restore the monarchy.

What is particularly significant about this entertaining burlesque in the context of Steinbeck's views on fiction and his strong support of Adlai Stevenson during his campaigns for the presidency is that Pippin is one of the "self-characters" that Steinbeck had explained in a letter to his editor. As the reign of the unexpected king proves quite short when he proposes a series of reforms, we see in Pippin the reflection of Steinbeck's own ideas about the writer revealing "our grievous faults and failures," revelations that often outrage both politicians and critics. Dissatisfied, however, in dealing with what he considered the problems of the contemporary world only in terms of France, Steinbeck began to feel that he had gotten out of touch with his own country and determined to reacquaint himself with his native land by the tour around the country that he reported in *Travels with Charley in Search of America* (1962), which followed up what he did not expect to be a final novel, *The Winter of Our Discontent* (1961), the action of which occurs during exactly the period between Easter and the Fourth of July when he was writing the book and is set in a small Long Island town like Sag Harbor, where he was then living. The novel ended ambiguously, leaving the prospects for the future in the hands of the readers, as Charles Dickens had in *Hard Times*. However, in its detailed examination of Ethan Hawley's fall from grace and loss of moral integrity, it had certainly exposed "many grievous faults and failures" and had dredged up into the light "dark and dangerous dreams, for purposes of improvement" as he specified to be "the ancient commission of the writer" in his Nobel speech.

He had not yet, however, actually specified any novels, by himself or others, that he would recommend as increasing our continuing knowledge of man and his world, which he maintained in the same speech was the principal function of literature. An enlightening discussion of this most important point was to await his last published book, one of his least understood and appreciated, *America and Americans* (1966), in which he supplies much autobiographical material and expresses his deepest feelings about his country and fellow citizens. In a sense, *America and Americans* provides the opportunity for a valedictory judgment upon them. In one of the climactic chapters, "Americans and the World," in the context of a conversation with an American friend who was an expert in Russian history, he asked his friend what Russian fiction he had read. The other explained that he had read Russian "history, economics, sociology, and law," but "never had time for any of its fiction." Steinbeck replied:

I have recently visited Russia for the third time, but I do know that if I had read only Russian history, I could not have had the access to Russian thinking I had from reading Dostoevski, Tolstoy, Chekhov, Pushkin, Turgenev, Sholokhov, and Ehrenburg. History only recounts, with some inaccuracy, what they did. The fiction tells, or tries to tell, why they did it and what they felt and were like when they did it. (135)

Steinbeck next provides a list of what he considers six landmark American novels: "[I]n considering the American past, how poor we would be in information without *Huckleberry Finn, An American Tragedy, Winesburg, Ohio, Main Street, The Great Gatsby*, and *As I Lay Dying*" (135). What is striking about this list is that all six novels by Mark Twain, Theodore Dreiser, Sherwood Anderson, Sinclair Lewis, F. Scott Fitzgerald, and William Faulkner are about determined young people who are trying to escape the limitations of their small town or backwoods origins to find a more rewarding life in what Huck Finn called "the territory," some successfully, some disastrously. It is actually Steinbeck's own story of the successful career that carried him from the family attic on a vanishing frontier to a guest bedroom at the White House. All faced the same problem as Jody Tiflin in *The Red Pony*, who seeks to sympathize with his grandfather's loss of the time when he had been "the leader of the people" on the vanished frontier. This choice of these six works reveals Steinbeck's conception of the novel not as mere entertainment or an escape from reality, but rather his desire, as stressed to the Russian scholar, for fiction to recount with accuracy the whole of human experience and to expand one's intellectual and moral horizons.

This emphasis on the function of fiction as a vehicle for self-improvement brings to mind how many of Steinbeck's own novels end without a conventional portrayal of the characters living "happily ever after": George kneeling over a prostrate Lennie, Ethan Hawley struggling against suicide and the incoming tide lest "another light . . . go out" (*Winter* 276), the Joads huddled together in a barn with Rose of Sharon nursing a starving man. As indicated earlier, many of Steinbeck's works, particularly those later in his career, conclude with the responsibility for determining what came afterward left up to the readers. As he stressed in his Nobel speech, Steinbeck felt that the function of fiction was to foster moral and spiritual growth by exposing "our many grievous faults . . . for the purpose of improvement." His including the reader as a participant in the fictive process, a very postmodern thing to do, is itself an example of this call for his audience to take moral responsibility, as well as an indication of his abiding faith in the perfectibility of man. John Steinbeck's fiction offers the reader not resolutions but challenges, like the old frontier. And the challenge remains for readers today.

"Of Ink and Heart's Blood": Episodes in Reading Steinbeck's *East of Eden*

Robert DeMott

The Affective Fallacy is a confusion between the poem and its *results* (what it *is* and what it *does*).
—William K. Wimsatt and Monroe C. Beardsley, *The Verbal Icon*

A work of art that enters us to feed the soul offers to initiate in us the process of the gifted self. . . . Reading the work, *we* feel gifted for awhile, and . . . with the artist's work at hand we suddenly find we can make sense of our own experience.
—Lewis Hyde, *The Gift*

In early 1985, halfway through my stint as the visiting director of San Jose State University's Steinbeck Research Center (now the Martha Heasley Cox Center for Steinbeck Studies), I came across an Associated Press news clipping dated April 24, 1969 that stopped me in my tracks: "Steinbeck Book Saves U.S. Newsman." During the Vietnam War, the life of Jack Russell, a National Broadcasting Company newsman, was saved when a grenade fragment embedded itself in his paperback copy of *Once There Was a War*, John Steinbeck's belated book of World War II newspaper reports. I was startled by the event's unpredictability and the irony of a man being rescued from annihilation by a book about annihilation. I imagined that embattled Steinbeck (who had died four months earlier in December 1968, amid unresolved tensions stemming from his controversial support of American troops in

Vietnam, his publicized friendship with President Lyndon Johnson, and his own private pessimism about the feasibility of that war) would have appreciated and understood the irony.

Metaphorically, what had happened to Jack Russell had happened to me too. A little more than four years before that day in Southeast Asia, Steinbeck's books—*East of Eden* in particular—saved my skin. His books didn't protect me from mortal harm, but they did alter me considerably by giving me a sense of purpose and motivation at a moment in my early twenties when, as a floundering, severely underachieving undergraduate in search of a senior thesis topic at a small New England Catholic college, I had no serious direction or prospects at all. With encouragement from two sympathetic young English professors—John Burke and Mike O'Shea—my life began slowly to take a beneficial turn after my exposure to Steinbeck's writing. Even so, the beleaguered thesis on Steinbeck's scientist heroes, which I submitted at the last possible minute in time to graduate with my class in June 1965, was abysmally bad and ill conceived, even pathetic in its unimaginativeness and in its near-total dependence on Joseph Fontenrose, Peter Lisca, and E. W. Tedlock and C. V. Wicker, whose three books—*John Steinbeck: An Introduction and Interpretation*, *The Wide World of John Steinbeck*, and *Steinbeck and His Critics*—were half of the total number of scholarly books then available on Steinbeck. But as ineffectual and derivative as the thesis proved to be (I later burned every copy), in gearing up for it by reading all the Steinbeck I could get my hands on (beginning with *Travels with Charley* and working randomly backward), I glimpsed for the first time the power of what Sven Birkerts has called "*deep reading*: the slow and meditative possession of a book" (146). As a result, I gained a second chance at an intellectual life (however woeful), which is one way of defining a writer's appeal and power, one way of saying grace to what Steinbeck himself, in "Some Random and Randy Thoughts on Books," called the "sacred" and authentically "magic" property of books (32, 34).

Through a combination of persistence, lucky breaks, and the good will of generous people, I finally left New England eight months after graduating from college, quit my dead-end job as a clerk in a liquor store, and turned my back on the temptation of going into business with my father (or with one of my other entrepreneurial relatives). One winter night, newly married, my wife and I fled our families and headed to Ohio, first to Cleveland and Kent for graduate school, then, in 1969, to Athens where I was hired to teach American literature at Ohio University to students, many of whom were not so different in their youthful anxieties, political unrest, and academic uncertainties than I had been a few years earlier. A circle seemed to have closed: from the moment the seriously neglected Steinbeck (whom the lit–crit establishment already considered officially "dead" several years before his actual demise) redeemed my ragtag intellectual life by providing access to a literary world I could encounter with a fervor and intensity I didn't know I had, his writing became especially significant to me.

More than that, precisely because his writing has always existed on the edges of discourse in a kind of unfashionable border area apart from the mainstream, it is doubly appealing to me. Sometimes the reading that matters most is visceral rather than cerebral, and comes as a surprise rather than being planned; such reading manages to move us in unaccountable ways toward a horizon we didn't imagine it was possible to see, much less reach. Indeed, far from being a reflection of reality—though of course it is that— the act of reading can become a reality all its own, which then becomes part of the ineluctable fabric of memory and experience, like "something that happened to me," as Steinbeck once said of his own reading (DeMott, *Typewriter* xx). This little testimony, then, is a homage to a life-saving experience and a celebration of the fortuitous entrance of an altering presence into my life, an unexpected offering I could not refuse, despite what name I gave it then. Among the books I have loved excessively during my life, *East of Eden* is another of those gifts, or to use Lewis Hyde's term, another of those touchstones of value and meaning around which some related personal events have clustered.

In fact, this chapter, even in its present streamlined form, is still really a confession, because as I conjure up my first reading of *East of Eden*, it had a slightly sinful quality, as though I had looked in a window and witnessed something unexpected or lurid pass between strangers, or as though I had stolen some precious object that I hardly knew what to do with once I had it in the palm of my hand. Not to put too ethereal or mystical a spin on these reminiscences, it is possible—even likely—that my guilt may have been compounded by the basest of material causes. The cover art of my paperback copy—a Bantam Fifty edition—was nothing short of thrilling. It featured an eye-popping, come-hither scene: a dark-haired, bare-shouldered, full-bodied woman in an alluring windswept peasant skirt promised untold pleasures and mysteries. In fact, the cover became a cause célèbre with some of my randy classmates. We tore into the book searching for the steamy parts in which this arresting rouge-lipped beauty played a key role, but, as a mere design trick of the paperback publishing industry, she was nowhere to be found in the novel proper. Her absence put a new twist on Bantam's claim that the text was "complete and unabridged."

After frenzied disappointment passed, reality set in: *East of Eden* is a huge, sprawling book that requires an enormous investment of time and psychological commitment to read. Charles Dickens's *Bleak House* was the only other "fat" novel I had ever read, and I knew what a daunting experience that had been, but I vowed I would slug through every line anyway. Personal, autobiographical, chatty, loose, and digressive, *East of Eden* was unlike anything I had read before and, so in its way, continued the assault on my piddling preconceptions. The book flew in several directions at once: the plot moved back and forth between the Trasks and the Hamiltons; the chapters alternated between dramatic narrative and editorial discourse. Except for my two personal favorites—Tom Hamilton and Cal Trask, whose morbidity appealed to the depressive side of my nature—I needed a scorecard to keep all the other "Cain and Abel" characters straight. I could not say that I understood the rationale of *East of Eden*'s alternating points of view or even very much liked or recognized its portrayal of my native Connecticut in the early part of the novel. I was astonished, however, when the door finally swung open on the X-rated parts featuring Cathy Trask and her victims because it gave sexual complicity a new name. And I was impressed at Steinbeck's unflinching honesty and candor in treating those scenes, which of course vastly diminished their salaciousness and made me feel I was being addressed as a serious adult, to be entrusted with forbidden knowledge, a situation my college's priestly censors rarely felt obliged to acknowledge, much less to offer.

I was equally impressed with the way Steinbeck used Genesis (4:1–16) as a touchstone for the action, characterization, and title of his novel. His wasn't the kind of formal biblical exegesis my religion professors espoused and about which I had been quizzed and tested into dumb submission, but something more inventive and certainly closer to my own loose requirements for a simple belief system grounded in freedom of choice. Furthermore, Steinbeck's statement in Chapter 19 of *East of Eden* that the "church and the whorehouse arrived in the Far West simultaneously" and that they were a "different facet of the same thing" (217) was at once one of the most exotic and most familiar things I'd ever read, because it was not at all unlike the kind of shocking but ultimately pragmatic and profound statements my mother's loquacious brother, Tony, was capable of making while driving me toward some trout fishing outing on a local river or, more outrageous yet, while seated around the dinner table at my grandmother's house. I was always predisposed to listen to a person who speaks directly, without cant or prevarication, so just as my uncle was capable of grabbing my attention with his assertiveness, I was equally engaged by *East of Eden*'s personal narrator who made the book, studded with personal commentary and offhand remarks, seem like a guided tour of a heaven and hell that looked more and more like the neighborhood I had grown up in. Just the brusque tone and gritty lingo I needed, I told myself, to balance my rarefied college education.

My field of vision was expanding in other ways, too, because it was literally my first realization that a novelist had the right to condense, rearrange, or heighten selective elements in his fiction. It began to dawn on me that, like glimpsing the bottom of a fast-moving river, there was a marvelous but shadowy process to be apprehended in the world of fiction, and even more so, that there was some shaping power at work in Steinbeck's novels, though I am positive I did not have the language yet to articulate that impression. I felt something more than mere journalistic realism was taking place, though, as in the scene in Chapter 17, when the narrator begins to change his mind about whether Cathy Trask is a human "monster." Or, on a more upbeat note, this moment in Chapter 23 when Steinbeck appears as a character in his own novel and recalls going fishing with his silent uncle, Tom Hamilton:

We started before the sun came up and drove in the rig straight toward Fremont's Peak, and as we neared the mountains the stars would pale out and the light would rise to blacken the mountains. I can remember riding and pressing my ear and cheek against Tom's coat. And I can remember that his arm would rest lightly over my shoulders and his hand pat my arm occasionally. Finally we would pull up under an oak tree and take the horse out of the shafts, water him at the stream side, and halter him to the back of the rig. . . . Tom had beautiful tackle and made his own flies. But he didn't seem to care whether we caught trout or not. (281)

If the aridity of the flinty Hamilton family farm near King City, California, shocked my water-soaked New England sensibility, here was a lovely reminiscence ("memory plus what I know to be true plus conjecture built on the combination," Steinbeck claims) that entered a note of balance, hopefulness, and "gallantry." This passage, which I reread several times, brought a small measure of consolation when I learned that Tom eventually killed himself. Perhaps by rereading it I could keep him alive somehow, which is probably the reason I tried not to think too long and hard about the fact that, like him, my uncle and I tied our own trout flies. "Was exotic California so different from puritan Connecticut after all?" I wondered.

More than that, in *East of Eden* Steinbeck seemed generous, even forgiving, in temperament. Here was a writer, I mused, in whose imagination the most striking opposites could reside undiminished, and one who embraced the society of outcasts, the renegade screw-ups of this world, of which I was a card-carrying member. Cal Trask and I seemed to be cousins under the skin: we were well-meaning, intent, even passionate with a kind of groping hunger, but we were also self-righteous, angry, quick to be wounded, brooding, and at least a couple of steps out of sync with the world around us. We lived in the land of Nod, always, it seemed, just outside of Eden. When I read the final deathbed scene, in which the dying Adam Trask at last blesses his wayward son Cal with the word "*Timshel*" (Thou Mayest), thereby empowering his free will, I was moved to tears, as I had been one earlier time when I read Walt Whitman's "When Lilacs Last in the Dooryard Bloom'd." Embarrassed by my own sentimentality, I went into the bedroom of my apartment and closed its door because I didn't want my roommate—a dean's list international relations major headed to law school—to see me weeping. Though I knew nothing at all about John Steinbeck's personality, his private habits, or his family, in the enclosure of my room I felt reassured by the fact that this book had the undeniable capacity to move my soul. "*Timshel* yourself," I thought.

Reading *East of Eden*, flaws and all, had a very liberating effect. That book helped me identify the quality of Steinbeck's work I admired—his sense of story, family history, and oral tradition, all elements very much out of fashion in that time and place because they eschewed ambiguity and aesthetic distance and so were suspected of being sentimental, that most grievous of critical sins. For me, though, who couldn't distinguish one type of ambiguity from the next or irony from a villanelle, and who hailed from a long line of sentimentalists capable of breaking into tears at the drop of a hat, Steinbeck's familiar tone was not only convincing but downright reassuring. It was just what I needed then because it seemed completely honest, trustworthy, believable. His world in *East of Eden* touched mine in numerous recognizable places. His literary voice was the first one I ever encountered that spoke to me and not at me. It was a conversational voice—there is no other way to explain it—a patient, instructive voice weaving those many oral facets together, directing his words toward me in such a way that I felt comforted, not abused, and reassured, not undercut, by the world's warring opposites: "Humans are caught—in their lives, in their thoughts, in their hungers and ambitions, in their avarice and cruelty, and in their kindness and generosity—in a net of good and evil. I think that this is the only story we have and that it occurs on all levels of feeling and intelligence," he proclaims in Chapter 34 of *East of Eden* (413). "*Amen!*" I scribbled in the margin of my book.

Deeper than that, though, *East of Eden* was the first book that gave me a handle on symbolic experiences, the first to make personal journeys, choices, and continuities seem like palpable endeavors. In a strangely unexpected way, I suppose, Steinbeck continued the work my uncle had already started; corny as it sounds, *East of Eden* gave me a sense that life was a journey through and around a series of alternative choices, and it also prepared me for a world in which the heroic beauty of Samuel Hamilton and the diabolical brutality of Cathy Ames could exist side by side. I wasn't Stephen Daedelus traveling the road out of Dublin to forge in the smithy of my soul the consciousness of my race; I just wanted to learn how to live among its daily contradictions and maybe catch a few big trout along the way. I didn't want to reject all aspects of orthodoxy, of patriarchy (my feelings toward my teachers, New Criticism, and the Catholic Church aside); like many Italian Americans, I simply wanted to choose the elements of continuity that were meaningful to me, even if they were nominally conflicting ones, and somehow manage to pass them on intact (though at the time I didn't know to whom).

Steinbeck's authorial tone, his assessments on the universality of good and evil, the dance of opposites in the world's body, the mythology of each person's inevitable fall from grace and potential resurrection, and perhaps most of all his emphasis—so different in this talky novel from his omniscient earlier ones—on the necessity of individual creativity, all seemed to me wonderful and honorable, earned and realistic, which is why I was willing to listen. His narrative voice didn't claim the past was such a transcendentally elevated time that we should reel in our lines because we could never live there again; his voice told how the past was different in degree, not in kind, from the present and how it was another part of a universal, unbroken emotional process we all participated in, as though we each stepped at different places into a river that flowed just outside our doors around, say, Norwalk, Connecticut, or Salinas, California. *East of Eden*, I decided, was a book that schooled the motions of the heart.

So while I left it out of my senior thesis, *East of Eden* affected me in a profound way, and for years afterward when I thought of Steinbeck as a writer, *East of Eden* was always the first book that came to mind, even before *Travels with Charley in Search of America*, *Tortilla Flat*, *Of Mice and Men*, *The Red Pony*, or *The Grapes of Wrath*. The mark of an intriguing novel, much like a fine trout stream, it seems to me now, is its capacity to surprise us on each subsequent reading by revealing greater depths, successive unfoldings, new flashes of color, motion, and brilliance without ever giving up its true meaning, if in fact a novel—or a river—can ever be said to have one true meaning. *East of Eden* continues to impress me as such a wonderful book because it is a landscape of incandescent words, a torrent of mutable meanings. I have read it countless times, both in its enormous original version and in its shorter, 691-page published form. I have taught it often—and successfully, I think—to college students in Ohio and California (who rank it among their preferred Steinbeck titles). I have repeatedly bent close over *Journal of a Novel*, Steinbeck's posthumously published record of its making, so I know something of the process by which *East of Eden* was created, and I know something of Viking Press and the publishing industry itself that gave the novel its material being. I also know that Steinbeck's mentoring tone, that sagacious voice and demeanor, was part of his original thematic and structural intent: the first draft of the novel (initially called "The Salinas Valley") is addressed directly to his two young sons and represents one possible way for a divorced father to give the gift of what he knows of the world to his children. And my research has delivered many of the lurid ins and outs of Steinbeck's private marital, domestic, and familial history that inform the book and surround it with a net of intentions, ironies, complicities, psychological ramifications, and disruptive interventions more complex than I think sometimes I wanted to know. (After I divorced in 1980, the novel, and that tangled era in Steinbeck's life expressed in it, took on yet another level of importance to me and became a mirror for my own upheaval, reflecting the convoluted relationship with my ex-wife and my desire to establish a lasting legacy with my daughter.) Always I have found something new in *East of Eden*'s pages to fuel my obsessions or to assail my sensibility.

A dozen years after college, when the dream of becoming an outdoor guide in Montana had been supplanted by a career as a literature teacher (which I suspect is another kind of fishing guide), I spent a good part of a December week holed up in a hermetically sealed, windowless room of the cathedral-like Humanities Research Center in Austin, Texas. It was eighty degrees and brilliantly sunny outside. I was far from Ohio's snowy wastes, so I had plenty of urge to play hookey and take in the sights around Austin, but good researcher that I had become in those years since college and graduate school, I instead hunched over the original manuscript and typescript of *East of Eden*. I owed my resolve to Ohio University, which had given me a grant to begin my exploration of Steinbeck's far-flung manuscripts, housed at archives in Texas, New York, and California, for a proposed book on Steinbeck's literary influences (eventually published in 1984 as *Steinbeck's Reading*); but more that that, I felt I owed staying put to Steinbeck, because I wanted to honor his herculean effort, his brave intention, his artistic experiment. And in a way I felt uncannily sure he was about to deliver something to me, there among those cascading leaves of paper.

Among the hundreds of cancelled typescript pages before me, I found some material that I selfishly wished Steinbeck hadn't cut from his novel, because it would have been part of my initial reading in 1964 and might have given me an even clearer sense of his purpose and achievement, his conscious reaction against the prevailing literary modes and practices of the era. The first snippet is a section that originally introduced Chapter 8 (which now begins, "I believe there are monsters born in the world to human parents"). Steinbeck penned this on March 28, 1951 (two full months into his nine-month writing stint); it was the opening paragraph of that day's writing about Cathy, the villainous "heroine." The gist of this section is that Steinbeck decried the modernist, New Critical tendency to favor what he called "the writerless book." He continued:

For all the arts are nothing but the long and hard and passionate search for true things. Art may have guess or conjecture but deliberate untruth has never and will never be permitted. Thus when the writer thought he had eliminated himself from his story he was falling into error. Himself chose the story, and he chose the details and picked out the words, and arranged the sequences. The writer was in every line.[1]

Steinbeck, of course, was in every line of his book, a fact that disturbed and unnerved his formalist critics, notably Peter Lisca. (I learned over the years that Steinbeck is a writer in whom the unresolvable issues of "academic correctness," including complications of politics, gender, technique, and canon formation, still make many people skittish and resentful; they always want Steinbeck to be something other than what he is.) But generally, to our far more catholic sensibilities this late in the game, his textual intrusiveness was a bold prophetic stance, a precursor of certain fabular, postmodernist fictional strategies. Had it been published twenty years later or published in tandem with *Journal of a Novel*, as Steinbeck intended, *East of Eden*, I fantasized, might have had a warmer reception.

Conjecture aside, just how deeply he was rooted in *East of Eden* is signified in this second excision, a draft of the prologue that Steinbeck wrote in unabashed homage to Miguel de Cervantes. It was another of those discoveries that stopped me in my tracks: "Reader—I have thought endlessly about my book which I now submit to you. It is compounded of ink and heart's blood—lighter than ink and darker than blood. Thousands of hours have gone into it to make it agreeable to your ear and sweet to your understanding." Here at last was that most elusive creature, the "whole man," which many of my college teachers and administrators had held out as our ethical model. But he turned out to be not a Platonic, Socratic, Aristotelean, Aquinian, or Eliotic philosopher, as those teachers had desired, but a deeply flawed, personally divided, unorthodox, modern novelist, humble about his own shortcomings just as he was a little proud when he hoped we would be mindful of his scriptive achievements: "Sometimes I have felt that I held fire in my hands to spread a page with shining, but I have never been able to shake off clumsiness and ignorance and aching inability." The ethical posture, the moral stance, it turned out, was not an absolute blueprint for behavior, the way some of my professors believed, but something they rarely talked about: a way of being in this world, an acceptance and cultivation of the demanding, strenuous, obsessive habit of mind that makes writing—or teaching—possible, rewarding, and necessary, even if imperfect, frustrated, and conflicted.

Before everything is said, I go back to that scene in the bedroom of my college apartment a lifetime ago, where I retreated in what I now see was pure dread from my roommate's cold critical stare. It was a failure of nerve born of ignorance and youthful timorousness. Much older now, I am not ashamed to confess that *East of Eden* still moves me as it moved me then, which is to say emotionally, mythically, sublimely. It is a passionate book that calls forth passionate responses. In my first encounter with such a work, at a time when many of my teachers and peers preferred William Wimsatt and Monroe Beardsley to Walt Whitman or the Beats, I could not help being fascinated by a writer who put so much of himself into his book.

His was, I realize now, an act of courage, or, better yet, an act of faith necessary whether you are filling a blank page, teaching the blind to read, or casting a trout fly into a ferocious headwind. Steinbeck, I discovered, existed ineluctably in the house of his fiction, in the architectural space of his own making, the deepest investiture of his self-imagining. No wonder *East of Eden* mattered so much to him, no wonder he repeatedly called it his "big" book. "A man's writing is himself," he remarked in "Critics— From a Writer's Viewpoint." It was one of the nuggets I gleaned from *Steinbeck and His Critics* (49) that had stuck in my head from my Assumption College days. I think I sensed that even in 1964. When I touched *East of Eden* for the first time, I seemed to have touched the man as well, though it was a long, long time and a circuitous journey before I could explain the why or how of erotic textual embrace. When heart's blood and dark ink begin to flow, when an author hands us his or her gift, who among us can tell the writer from the written or the reader from the read, who among us can refuse being moved or dare say no to the dream of being saved?

NOTES

This chapter is an altered, abbreviated version of an essay that originally appeared in *Connecticut Review* in 1992 with the title " 'Of Ink and Heart's Blood': Adventures in Reading *East of Eden*," then as an expanded chapter, " 'Of Ink and Heart's Blood': Adventures in Reading Steinbeck," in my *Steinbeck's Typewriter: Essays on His Art* (Troy, NY: Whitston, 1996), 265–85. In this redacted third go-around it seems less adventure than mere episode, hence the present subtitle. I dedicate this final version to fellow members of the Bar-20, who aided and abetted at the right times.

1. Steinbeck's statement appears in the 540-page autograph manuscript of *East of Eden* and in the 945-page typescript but was cancelled from the published novel. This excised section and the Cervantes-inspired prologue quoted below it are in a box of *East of Eden* "Dead Material" in the John Steinbeck Works collection at the Harry Ransom Humanities Research Center, University of Texas, Austin.

My Steinbeck Odyssey

Robert Morsberger

Although I have been active in Steinbeck studies for thirty-two years, I came to them comparatively late, when I was forty years old and Ted Hayashi and my wife converged on me to invite me and prod me, respectively, into submitting a paper to my first Steinbeck conference. Today, most readers encounter John Steinbeck in their teens, but my boyhood and adolescent reading had consisted mostly of nineteenth-century novels. I never encountered Steinbeck in high school or in my university work and had missed the Steinbeck movies between 1939 and 1949. At the John Hopkins University the yearlong American literature survey went no further than Henry James's *Portrait of a Lady* (1881). But in a course in modern American drama, I read the stage version of *Of Mice and Men* and thought it the most involving, moving work in the John Gassner anthology. George, Lennie, Candy, and Crooks were people Steinbeck made me care about deeply, and the tragic inevitability that destroyed their hopes was profoundly cathartic.

The next year I saw a rerun of John Ford's *The Grapes of Wrath* and was bowled over by the raw power of its narrative, language, people, and rage against injustice, as well as by Gregg Toland's photography and the indelible performances John Ford got from the cast. When I finally read the novel, it was during basic training at Fort Knox, where I obtained a battered paperback copy that I stowed in a pocket of my fatigues and read during endless hours of "hurry up and wait," much to the chagrin of the sergeant. "You men shouldn't waste time reading books or intellectual stuff like *The*

Reader's Digest," he growled. "Just read the field manuals, you get along OK; might get to Louisville sometime." But I persisted, unable to leave the exodus of the Dust Bowl migrants, to set aside Steinbeck's picture of the Joads' courage, "fambly" loyalty, and determination to overcome man's inhumanity to man.

After basic training, where I was unimaginably inept in the tank corps, I was transferred to a military intelligence school and then shipped to Germany as a counterintelligence agent. While playing "spy versus spy" as resident agent in Ansbach, I saw *Viva Zapata!* at the post movie house. At the time my knowledge of Mexican history between Hernando Cortés and Benito Juárez was nil. I had never even heard of Emiliano Zapata, but the film was utterly engrossing in its dramatization of Zapata's rebellion not only against the dictator Díaz but against successive waves of tyrants who tried to undo the revolution or twist it to their own ends. Like Steinbeck, I was intrigued with a revolutionary who did not want leadership or power but had them thrust on him when he was unable to do anything in the face of oppression and fought back. He was unique as a revolutionary hero who, when he had power, relinquished it rather than relished it, while those who lusted for it arranged his assassination. Since one of my eccentricities is an encyclopedic memory of movie credits, I remembered that the riveting screenplay of *Viva Zapata!* was by John Steinbeck.

During the next twenty years, I finally got to see a rerun of the 1939 film of *Of Mice and Men*; a curious TV version with George Segal as George and Nicol Williamson as Lennie; the wayward movie of *The Wayward Bus*; and Steinbeck himself as host for five stories in the movie *O. Henry's Full House*. During the course of teaching *The Grapes of Wrath* several times, I immersed myself in such Steinbeck criticism as there was by the 1960s and wondered why no one had written anything about *Viva Zapata!* "Why don't you?" said my wife. "I don't have a copy of the screenplay to work with," I answered lamely. In those days there were no videotapes.

This brings us to 1969, when my wife and Ted Hayashi between them got me involved in Steinbeck studies. We had just moved to California, and my wife was working on her MA in English at the Claremont Graduate School. One day she came home bearing a copy of an announcement asking for papers to be submitted for a conference on Steinbeck at Oregon State University. "Here's your chance to write that paper you've been talking about on *Viva Zapata!* Put up or shut up."

Being now in the movie capital of the world, I thought it was now or never and wrote to Twentieth Century Fox asking if its archives included a screenplay of *Viva Zapata!* What to my wondering eyes should appear in the mail just before Christmas but a copy of Steinbeck's shooting script.

Consequently, I spent my Christmas break analyzing the script and then writing intensely to submit a finished paper by the January deadline. Back came a prompt letter of acceptance from Dr. Tetsumaro Hayashi and Dr. Richard Astro, along with the gratifying news that Oregon State would pay my expenses. That left my university with no excuse for not letting me go.

At Corvallis I finally met Dr. Hayashi, who promptly informed me that his friends call him Ted. He was then youthful looking and clean shaven, but had already made a name for himself as founder of the John Steinbeck Society of America and editor of both the *Steinbeck Quarterly* and the *Steinbeck Monograph Series*. There, I also met not only Richard Astro, who with Ted was codirector of the 1970 Steinbeck conference, but also fellow participants Peter Lisca, John Ditsky, Robert DeMott, Webster Street, Joel Hedgpeth, Robert Benton, Charles Shively, and James Degnan, most of whom I would meet again periodically over nearly a third of a century. I found that becoming a member of the Steinbeck Society was like joining a fraternity of friends.

The conference was a great success, though those of us who rode in Dick Astro's car were not sure we would survive it, as he talked vigorously, with gestures, facing those of us in the backseat instead of looking at the road ahead while racing through the Oregon hills. But survive we did, and the next year the proceedings of the conference appeared in a hardcover book published by the Oregon State University Press—my first Steinbeck publication, and I believe the first for a number of us. Since then *Viva Zapata!* has been added to the Steinbeck canon.

When I submitted my paper for the Corvallis conference, I had no expectation of becoming a Steinbeck specialist. I had published several books on language and the first book on James Thurber, whose only connection to Steinbeck was a vicious attack on *The Moon Is Down*, prompted, I believe, more from Thurber's frustrations over a series of eye operations at the time than over the issues for which he lashed out at the novel. But thanks largely to Ted Hayashi, who was a major facilitator for Steinbeck scholarship, my list of Steinbeck publications kept growing steadily and I kept receiving invitations to participate in more conferences. The second, at San Jose State University, not yet the home of the Steinbeck Research Institute, was on Steinbeck films, and any I had not previously viewed I saw there, including such rarities as *The Forgotten Village* and *Flight*, whose directors, Herbert Kline and Barnaby Conrad, respectively, were present. The next thing I knew, Ted Hayashi had me write an article on all of Steinbeck's movies for one of his Scarecrow Press volumes. I came to the conclusion that more good-to-outstanding movies had been made from Steinbeck's works than from those of any other American author except Henry James (and most of the James films came later) and discovered that Steinbeck films earned a total of twenty-six Academy Award nominations, won four of them, and that Steinbeck himself was nominated three times for screenwriting.

By then I had long since read everything by Steinbeck and was coming up with ideas for papers without waiting for an invitation. I persuaded the Viking Press to publish the screenplay of *Viva Zapata!*, edited and with analytical articles by me, which has since been republished with Steinbeck's first version. My acquaintance with additional Steinbeck scholars expanded like ripples from a pebble tossed in a pond, as I found myself in company with Martha Heasley Cox, Jackson Benson, Mimi Gladstein, Roy Simmonds, Warren French, Louis Owens, Michael Meyer, John Timmerman, Robert Hughes, Susan Shillinglaw, and others at Steinbeck gatherings in Salinas, Alabama, Hawaii, Nantucket Island, Moscow, and at the American Literature Association and The Modern Language Association. Ted had made the John Steinbeck Society of America into the International Steinbeck Society, with many members from Japan, and the leading Japanese Steinbeckians turned up at various conferences, at which we were also privileged to meet Elaine Steinbeck and John Steinbeck IV.

Eventually, Ted Hayashi invited me to join the editorial board of the *Steinbeck Quarterly*, in which capacity I read, evaluated, and consulted with fellow board members about all sorts of submissions. After reading such an immense amount of Steinbeck criticism, both for the *Quarterly* and various Steinbeck anthologies, I can emphatically refute the dismissive disdain felt for Steinbeck by some literary snobs on the grounds that he is too popular, a simplistic writer suited mainly for high school students. It is not obligatory to like Steinbeck, but it was painfully bad sportsmanship to attack Steinbeck with an editorial in the *New York Times* the day after he received the Nobel Prize and to protest his inclusion in *The Library of America*. There is a vast and growing body of Steinbeck criticism by distinguished scholars who find his work full of complexities and examine it from a great variety of approaches: aesthetic, Jungian, mythic, archetypal, environmental, feminist, biological, historical, "tragical–comical–historical–pastoral," and the end is nowhere in sight.

Though my own writing about Steinbeck includes many literary articles analyzing his novels, stories, plays, and war correspondence, I have particularly focused on the adaptations of his works into other literary and artistic forms. One test of the vitality of an artist's work is its being translated into other media and passing into the heritage of his or her times. Thus, in addition to seventeen movies and numerous television dramas and documentaries, Steinbeck has inspired distinguished film scores, two of them by Aaron Copland; the song "Tom Joad" by Woody Guthrie; two operas; a ballet, *Curley's Wife*; several animated cartoons; two stage musicals; two stage versions of *The Grapes of Wrath*; stage versions of *East of Eden* and *Travels with Charley*; paintings by Thomas Hart Benton; and drawings by Jose Clemente Orozco. John Steinbeck has certainly found his way into "the souls of the people." As I dedicated my edition of *Viva Zapata!*, "Steinbeck Vive!"

Steinbeck, Ricketts, and Memories of Times Past

Richard Astro

My father died when I was young and most of my recollections of him have faded into the mothballs of memory. But two remembrances will always be with me. The first was his love for the New York Yankees. He had gone to college with and knew Lou Gehrig well before Gehrig left Columbia University to become one of the all-time greats in baseball history. The second was stories about his work with New York's Jewish poor and the articles he wrote for the *Daily Forward* during the Great Depression, which his mother (my grandmother) continued to read even after his death in 1953. It was from my grandmother that I first learned about the play he wrote on the poor and dispossessed during the 1930s. Entitled *Trombenick* (the Yiddish word for bum or hobo), my father's play had a mercifully short run on Broadway, despite what I was told were strong acting performances by Peter Lorre and Broderick Crawford. It had a somewhat longer stay in summer stock on Long Island, lasting most of a summer. I read *Trombenick* as a college freshman and even wrote an English composition essay about it. But even then, my affection for my father's memory notwithstanding, I knew the play was badly flawed, the language stilted, the dialogue forced, and the story line uninspired and uninspiring.

But it was my mother who told me that *Trombenick* was less important in and for itself than it was as a source for the plot and theme of *Of Mice and Men*, John Steinbeck's 1937 parable about the relationship between two itinerant farm workers in California's Salinas Valley, which catapulted

Steinbeck into the mainstream of twentieth-century American letters. I re-read *Of Mice and Men* during my first year of graduate school at the uni-versity of Washington and then went on to read almost all of Steinbeck's novels. And then, when my major professor left the university just as I was preparing to begin what would have probably been a dreary dissertation on Jonathan Swift and the Freethinkers, I found an Americanist, a senior cur-mudgeon in the department, by the name of Harry Burns who, according to local legend, had spent several years with Ernest Hemingway in Havana, Cuba, and was the prototype for the character of the economics professor in *To Have and Have Not*, who agreed to serve as my adviser on a thesis about Steinbeck. To be frank, my thesis was pretty mundane. The most noteworthy thing about it was that I finished the writing on the day Stein-beck died in December 1968. And during my research on the thesis, I searched in vain for any evidence that Steinbeck had heard of my father's play, let alone that he had seen it.

During the 1960s, it was not unusual for graduate students in English to take teaching positions after completing their doctoral coursework. It was still almost a decade before the job market would be glutted with freshly minted "PhDs" who were seduced into their graduate studies by unscru-pulous English department faculties to assume the onerous burden of teach-ing English composition. Faced with the option of teaching two sections of writing as a teaching assistant for an annual salary of $2,500 or four sections as an instructor at Oregon State University for three times that amount, I did the arithmetic and moved to Corvallis, communicating with my adviser for the next year or so by telephone and mail. And it was during the process of writing the dissertation that I encountered the prejudice that had devel-oped against Steinbeck when the political activist of my thesis committee (remember that this was the late 1960s) refused to accept my work because, he insisted, I had not dealt with Steinbeck's support of Lyndon Johnson and his foreign policies in Southeast Asia which, this professor argued, triv-ialized the writer and negated the value of his fiction. Eventually, Harry and the other members of the committee prevailed on their colleague to direct his ire on the novelist himself and not on this poor graduate student. I survived my dissertation defense early in 1969.

In my thesis, I had argued for Steinbeck's place in the mainstream of modern American writing because his novels celebrated a version of the American pastoral rather than the leftist ideology that dominated proletarian fiction during the 1930s. The battle in his first strike novel, *In Dubious Battle*, I suggested, was indeed dubious, and *The Grapes of Wrath* was more significant as an evocation of man's relationship with the land than as an attack on American capitalism. Moreover, I maintained that the themes and subject matter of *Of Mice and Men* and such lesser Steinbeck novels as *Tortilla Flat, To a God Unknown,* and *The Pastures of Heaven,* as well as such short stories as "The Chrysanthemums" and the four stories in *The Long Valley,* confirmed my case. Again, it was memories of my father who would tell me that the popularity of baseball owed more to a distinctively American impulse for repose in green places amid the rapid industrialization of its cities than to the heroics of Joe DiMaggio and Mickey Mantle in Yankee Stadium that informed my thinking as I grew up reading the novels of Fitzgerald, Hemingway, and Faulkner, as well as Steinbeck.

Little did I know when I passed my thesis defense in February of 1969 that I had merely scratched the surface of Steinbeck's fiction. At the end of the 1968–1969 academic year, I was rewarded with a promotion to assistant professor. And it was on the day when my promotion was approved that the fun really started. For into my office walked a strange little man who began by asking me about my work on Steinbeck and went on to regale me with stories of his friendship with the novelist during what he called his "salad days" as a graduate student in marine biology during the 1940s. I listened to all this with a mixture of amusement and incredulity until my visitor, who identified himself as Joel Walker Hedgpeth, director of Oregon State's Marine Science Center, asked if I would have any interest in perusing several boxes of unpublished letters that constituted a fifteen-year correspondence between Steinbeck and his closest friend, marine biologist Edward Flanders Ricketts. I mustered every bit of restraint I had to stay cool and casually responded that, yes, I would welcome that opportunity. He left, telling me that he would make arrangements for me to visit Ed Ricketts's son in San Rafael, California, who had the letters, and I just about fell out of my chair with anticipation and excitement.

It is impossible to conduct even a cursory examination of Steinbeck's life and letters without running across the name of Ed Ricketts. The two met in Monterey in 1930 and remained the closest of friends until Ricketts's untimely death in 1948. And, of course, they had collaborated on a curious volume about marine life in the Gulf of California that was published in late 1941 as *Sea of Cortez.* But I had always endorsed the accepted thinking that Steinbeck had written the log portion of this six-week adventure to the then little-known Baja California and that Ricketts had authored the larger portion of the book, an inventory of the many species of marine invertebrates he and the other members of the expedition had collected and cataloged during the trip. The Steinbeck–Ricketts expedition to the Gulf of California was generally regarded by most Steinbeck critics as a digression (he had just finished work on *The Grapes of Wrath* and was terribly fatigued and in need of relaxation). Clifton Fadiman's comments that *Sea of Cortez* was essentially trivia seemed to sum up popular thinking about this book, which, ironically, would become the definitive sourcebook for anyone interested in the marine life of the Gulf of California but was hardly worth more than passing notice by literary scholars.

My reading of the Steinbeck–Ricketts correspondence changed all that. For it became clear that the book was not only a true collaboration, but that the many conversations Steinbeck and Ricketts had about the book reflected thinking they had done together for a decade and that Steinbeck had incorporated into his most important fiction. And thus I began a three-year adventure that took me to the Sea of Cortez and on repeated trips to the Monterey Peninsula where I was fortunate enough to find and talk with Captain Tony Berry and the members of the crew of his purse seiner, *Western Flyer*, which carried Steinbeck and Ricketts to the Gulf of California. I also met and talked with other friends of both Steinbeck and Ricketts who, in varying degrees, were party to their conversations and understood the intellectual depth of their friendship during Steinbeck's most productive years as a writer.

Jackson Benson, who authored the definitive biography of Steinbeck, has shown that Steinbeck took good ideas for his fiction from wherever he found them. Some of those from whom he took materials, for example, Steinbeck's roommate at Stanford, Webster "Toby" Street (*To a God Unknown*), and Farm Security Administration camp administrator Tom Collins (*The Grapes of Wrath*), were willing contributors. Others, such as Monterey newspaper writer Beth Ingels (*The Pastures of Heaven*) and popular science writer Jack Calvin (Ricketts's collaborator on his other important study of West Coast marine life, *Between Pacific Tides*) complained about the novelist's propensity for what they regarded as literary theft. Still, as Steinbeck and Ricketts say in the introduction to the log portion of *Sea of Cortez*, "The design of a book is a pattern of reality controlled and shaped by the mind of the writer" (1). And it is the "pattern of reality" that constituted Steinbeck's view of the world that was in large measure shaped by the ideas and person of Ed Ricketts that accounts for Steinbeck's distinctive contribution to American letters.

The person of Ed Ricketts is a central character in much of Steinbeck's most important fiction. Doc in *Cannery Row* and *Sweet Thursday* is directly modeled on Ricketts. So is Doc Burton in *In Dubious Battle*, Friend Ed in *Burning Bright*, and finally, and most important, Jim Casy in *The Grapes of Wrath*. But it is Ricketts's ideas more than his person that really inform Steinbeck's fiction. Those ideas were not shaped on the California coast or in the Gulf of California. Rather, they have their genesis in Ricketts's studies in biology at the University of Chicago during the early 1920s when he took classes from the legendary Werner Clyde Allee, whose book, *Animal Aggregations*, published in 1931, became a bible of animal ecology. Allee, who did most of his fieldwork on that other coast, at the Marine Biological Laboratory at Woods Hole, Massachusetts, posited the thesis that organisms have an innate tendency to cooperate in matters of their own survival and reproduction. Ricketts's thinking incorporated Allee's thesis into his own investigations of the littoral of the California coast when he left Chicago (without a degree, contrary to what Steinbeck says in his tribute, "About Ed Ricketts," which prefaces modern editions of *The Log from the Sea of Cortez*) and was compatible with Steinbeck's less detailed thinking on the same subject that he gleaned in summer biology classes at the Hopkins Marine Station from a student of biologist William Emerson Ritter of the University of California at Berkeley, whose doctrine of the organismal conception of life dominated West Coast biological thinking at the time. In his work, Ritter stops short of the conclusion that cooperation among animals is innate and instinctive. Instead, he focuses on the tendency of animals to adapt to their environments and concludes that in this adaptation, wholes are much larger and more important than the sums of their collective parts.

The result of Ritter's thinking, when combined with Allee's thesis about social cooperation among animals, accounts for what is perhaps the most memorable passage in the log portion of *Sea of Cortez* when Steinbeck and Ricketts write that "Our own interest lay in relationships of animal to animal. If one observes in this relational sense, it seems apparent that species are only commas in a sentence, that each species is at once the point and the base of a pyramid, that all life is relational to the point where an Einsteinian relativity seems to emerge" (178). Furthermore, "not only the meaning but the feeling about species grows misty. One merges into another, groups melt into ecological groups until the time when what we know as life meets and enters what we think of as non-life: barnacle and rock, rock and earth, earth and tree, tree and rain and air. And the units nestle into the whole and are inseparable from it" (178). And finally, in what transports the reader to Ma's memorable speech to the Joad brood as the family seems to be fragmenting on the long trek from the Oklahoma Dust Bowl to the fertile cotton fields and orange groves of central California, Ricketts and Steinbeck assert that:

it is a strange thing that most of the feeling we call religious, most of the mystical outcrying which is one of the most prized and used and desired reactions of our species, is really the understanding and the attempt to say that man is related to the whole thing, related inextricably to all reality, known and unknowable . . . that all things are one thing and that one thing is all things . . . all bound together by the elastic string of time. (178–79)

My conversations with Tony Berry and with members of the crew of the *Western Flyer*, with filmmaker Herb Klein, a Steinbeck friend who accompanied the crew as far south as San Diego; with Carol Steinbeck, the novelist's first wife who, while she is never mentioned in the *Log*, made the entire trip to the Baja; with two of the three Mexicans who befriended Steinbeck and Ricketts in Mexico and took them on their famous *borrego* (bighorn sheep) hunt in Loreto; and with ichthyologist Rolf Bolin and librarian Alan Baldridge of the Hopkins Marine Station confirmed this sort of thinking by Steinbeck and Ricketts. They argued, as I have, that Steinbeck's gospel of social action—which depends above all on a willingness to forgo individual desire in favor of the higher goal of confronting common problems through unified group action—is what forms the thematic substructure of Steinbeck's best fiction and that the attraction Steinbeck's most memorable characters feel for the land and for the simple human virtues over the mean acquisition of monetary wealth are rooted in the thinking of Ritter and, via Ricketts, W. C. Allee.

John Steinbeck was no political ideologue. Rather, the themes of his best novels and short stories are rooted in the sort of scientific thinking about the relationships between living things and their environments that formed the genesis of the environmental movement nearly four decades before environmentalism became an American pastime. There were other sources of Steinbeck's thinking as well: insights from the thinking about comparative mythology from his friend Joseph Campbell; his own reading of the Arthurian legends; Richard Albee's "Argument of Phalax"; the philosophy of John Elof Boodin; and the strange mysticism of the German philosopher, Jacob Boehme. But it was his and Ricketts's unique blend of science and metaphysics gleaned from organismal and environmental biology that formed the thematic bedrock of his fiction and accounts for his distinction as a major twentieth-century writer.

My purpose in writing this piece has simply been to chronicle my own exploration into Steinbeck studies and to show how one moment of good fortune (Joel Hedgpeth's arrival in my office during that winter of 1969) opened doors that helped me better understand the range and scope of Steinbeck's thinking and, hopefully, and in some small way, helped later generations of readers of Steinbeck's fiction to better understand his life and work. Shortly after my book on the Steinbeck–Ricketts relationship, *Steinbeck and Ricketts: The Shaping of a Novelist* (1973), was published, my father-in-law, who never really understood why I or anyone would devote even part of a lifetime to reading and talking about novels (something for which I don't entirely fault him since I have my own moments of doubt on the subject) asked me how much money I would make on my book. When I told him that I'd be fortunate to make a couple of thousand dollars on royalties, he was taken aback and asked why I would spend so much time on such a project. My answer then and now is that the value of the sort of work I did was simply the experience of the joy of discovery and the shock of recognition. And, given my belief that art does indeed imitate life, to take from one discovery the key to another, so that in understanding Steinbeck's best fiction, I better understood myself.

As I write this, I am completing twenty-five years of service as an academic administrator: as a department chair, an arts and sciences dean, and, for thirteen of the past fifteen years, as the provost and academic vice president of two medium-size universities. If I've been able to bring any of the spirit of my literary investigations to my work in academic administration, it is that I should use the authority of my position to instill in faculty and in their students an understanding that higher education is really about learning and discovery rather than the simple acquisition of job skills. It is about engagement in which the learners (both faculty and students) see themselves more fully, understand themselves more deeply, and thus become equipped to live richer and more fulfilled lives. I've come a long way since my first reading of *Trombenick*. And all in all, it's been a pretty good ride.

Traveling with John: My Journey as a Steinbeck Scholar

Michael Meyer

As the current Steinbeck bibliographer, I am often asked what accounts for my passion for Steinbeck studies. After scouring libraries and journals for more than five years in order to compile a 558-page listing of Steinbeck scholarship from 1982 to 1996, I have come to think of John Steinbeck more as an intimate friend and philosophical adviser than a classic author I never met. Eventually, I became more than a Steinbeck scholar; I became a staunch advocate of Steinbeck's place among the very best of American authors and of his historic significance, not only as a recorder of his times but also as the moral conscience of the American reading public.

Such was not always the case. My first exposure to the Steinbeck canon came with *The Red Pony* in my freshman year of high school. It was followed by *The Pearl* a year later and *Of Mice and Men* the year after that. I vaguely remember my first readings of these texts, but I do especially recall Jody's passion for Gabilan in *The Red Pony* and his uncomfortable relationship with his father, a situation I identified with since my own father seemed distant and uncaring as well. My dad's expectations for my behavior were similarly high, and I seldom met his demands. I found Steinbeck's portrait of Jody's rebellious acting out to be accurate, depicting exactly how I felt. Mostly I identified with the anger Jody displaced on Doubletree Mutt and the destructiveness he practiced in the melon patch and on the helpless mice in the haystack. Such actions seemed to mirror my own sense of muted violence waiting to be vented against a demanding parental figure of my own.

If I noticed the beautiful prose, the crafted imagery, the melodic sentence structure, I do not think I was very impressed. I was an inexperienced reader, and I had not yet realized that my future vocation would be a teacher, scholar, and literary critic. It was enough if an author's words touched me deeply; I wasn't especially interested in how they accomplished it. During my sophomore year, *The Pearl* followed *The Red Pony*. I was exuberant because it was a very short novella that seemed easy to absorb. As a parable about the accumulation of wealth and the corrupting influence of materialism, it also fit well into my strict religious upbringing. If there were subtle nuances to the tale, I did not notice them, but I do remember thinking how interesting it was that such a simple parable could hold my attention, mesmerizing me and transporting me to a widely different world than my own. I think I sensed that I had been affected on a deeper level, but as a teenager I found it difficult to express just how the story of Kino and Juana became "my" story.

My junior year brought *Of Mice and Men*, a chilling tale of loneliness strangely mixed with a call for brotherhood and acceptance. I recall empathizing with the mental challenges faced by Lennie and sympathizing both with the demanding responsibilities faced by George and with the undeserved isolation endured by Curley's wife. I also remember the disconcerting ending; it reminded me of the tragic close of *The Pearl*, and I wondered what to make of an author who exposed his protagonists to the agonies of life without attaining a positive resolution. Somehow both Kino's undefined "discovery" at the death of Coyotito and George's commitment to Lennie even to the point of killing him resonated in my young mind as unusual but at the same time strangely moving. Yet, as my high school career drew to a close, Steinbeck was merely another author in a long list of required reading.

During my bachelor's degree program at Concordia University I had only a little more opportunity to read from the Steinbeck canon. No doubt the English Department there assumed that most students had been exposed to him in high school. However, in Modern American Novel (1900–1945), I did encounter *The Grapes of Wrath*, an imposing, daunting novel of 502 pages in small print. But from the moment I picked it up, I was entranced. As a budding English major, I found that I now had acquired at least some of the tools required for a higher appreciation of Steinbeck's literary accomplishments. The creative animal imagery now caught my eye, as did the cinematic quality of the word pictures and the poetic and musical craftsmanship of Steinbeck's prose.

By that point in my development, I was excited at my growing sense of appreciation for the written word; moreover, I had an adequate literary vocabulary that helped me define exactly what made a great work of fiction.

Based on my continued exposure to the author, I naturally assumed Steinbeck's stature was secure among literary critics. Having heard my professors speak of Steinbeck in glowing terms and realizing that they ranked him with Hemingway, Fitzgerald, and Faulkner as the leading writers of the early twentieth century, I was unaware of Steinbeck's declining reputation among scholars during the 50s and 60s. Until I began my master's degree in 1967, I had no clue that some of his more current works, including *Burning Bright*, *The Wayward Bus*, and *The Winter of Our Discontent*, were considered inferior products by a second-rate talent.

As I continued the MA coursework at Loyola University in Chicago, I began to understand that the traditional take on Steinbeck was that his work was middlebrow at best and filled with preachy sentimentalism unworthy of a great writer. Although he had received the Nobel Prize for Literature in 1962, his selection had been roundly questioned, even in his home country. I soon discovered Alfred Kazin's deprecatory reaction to Steinbeck's selection for the prize and was stunned that a fellow countryman would level such a harsh attack at an author who remained highly respected by the American reading public. Kazin's use of words such as "banal," "cuteness," and "propaganda" seemed completely inappropriate, as did his denunciation of the writer's "limited intellectual and creative resources." This last criticism hardly seemed to be grounded in reality, especially when so many of my fellow students found that Steinbeck's words spoke directly to them. Instead of denigrating his ability, they were impressed by Steinbeck's genius, especially his ability to weave so many elements into a text. After finishing my MA degree in 1969, I took a position in a Chicago-area high school, a decision that ultimately reaffirmed my belief in the power of Steinbeck's fiction. As a relatively new department chair in the 1970s, I had the opportunity to shape a developing curriculum. As a teacher I found that my classes responded in a similar warm manner to Steinbeck's prose and that discussions of his texts bristled with controversy and disagreement. The Steinbeck canon certainly elicited the very best from my students, and I began to include more and more of his novels in my required readings.

By 1980, a good ten years later, I began seriously considering work on a PhD, particularly when my high school offered a sabbatical at half pay after ten years of service. However, it wasn't until the second semester of my PhD studies that my path again crossed Agnes McNeill Donohue, a Loyola professor whom I admired and who had published *A Casebook on* The Grapes of Wrath with Thomas Y. Crowell in 1968. Remembering the great discussions in Nathaniel Hawthorne/Herman Melville course, I eagerly signed up for her seminar on Fitzgerald and Steinbeck. It was a decision that was to shape not only my dissertation but my life and career as well.

The seminar's enrollment was small, perhaps ten to twelve students, and each of us was required to lead a session on both Fitzgerald and Steinbeck. Though my work on Fitzgerald's *Tender Is the Night* later won recognition as best graduate paper of the year, it was my work on Steinbeck's *East of Eden* that influenced me most. Though it was Steinbeck's longest novel (603 pages) and though my presentation required reading the posthumously published *Journal of a Novel* (another 200+ pages), I found myself captivated by the many layers of meaning, the complex biblical allusions, and the experimental writing techniques the author employed. Although only a twenty-page seminar paper was required, I found it difficult to restrain my enthusiasm for the material. I told Dr. Donohue my paper was approaching sixty pages in length and that I had begun to view it as a potential chapter in a dissertation. With her encouragement, I refined the ideas that had fascinated me, and before long I had both a dissertation topic and director.

What had really caught my eye by that point were Steinbeck's philosophical musings in *The Log from the Sea of Cortez*, a nonfictional account of a collecting voyage he took with his friend Ed Ricketts off the coasts of Baja California. I was especially intrigued by his comments about human duality, about the intersections between good and evil, and about the paradoxes human beings face daily as they attempt to cope with life. The following quotes fascinated me most:

People get to believing and even to professing the apparent answers thus arrived at, suffering mental constrictions by emotionally closing their minds to any of the further and possibly opposite "answers" which might otherwise be unearthed by honest effort—answers which, if faced realistically, would give rise to a struggle and to a possible rebirth which might place the whole problem in a new and more significant light. (118)

[Y]et in our structure of society, the so-called . . . good qualities are invariable concomitants of failure, while the bad ones are the cornerstones of success. A man—a viewing-point man—while he will love the abstract good qualities and detest the abstract bad, will nevertheless envy and admire the person who through possessing the bad qualities has succeeded economically and socially, and will hold in contempt that person whose good qualities have caused failure. (80)

I soon discovered that these insights were only part of Steinbeck's extended struggle to understand the inexplicable. Yet to an individual who had grown up in a strict Lutheran background in which answers to life's questions were clearly defined, the words became liberating, broadening my perceptions and helping me to see my world more clearly. Whereas before biblical authority was asserted as unquestionable, I began to perceive the paradoxical nature of good and evil. Instead of black-and-white delineations of right and wrong, there were now gray areas regarding moral uprightness and turpitude.

The blindness of my previous single-mindedness began to come into focus and the main theme of my dissertation developed as I mulled over these passages and tried to determine the reasons for Steinbeck's popularity. He had attempted to explain—to break through—the religious claptrap promulgated by organized churches and to help his readers see the complexities involved in leading a "moral" life. Although a variety of factors may account for Steinbeck's appeal, there is no doubt that for me the key was his emphasis on moral ambiguity: America's failure to understand that along with independent "I" thinking, a trait which implies freedom but also suggests selfishness, the nation ought to cultivate "we" thinking and acknowledge that if mankind has an obligation to all fellow humans at times that obligation implies putting one's self after the needs of the group. Indeed, I came to recognize that one essential tenet Steinbeck espoused, which I too cherished, was a faith in humanity, a belief that despite the moral ambiguity and the trying ethical decisions that must be confronted daily human beings will continue to progress to a more positive balance between these two types of thinking and thus attain a life that maintains the necessary tension (yin/ yang) between opposites. As Steinbeck states in *The Grapes of Wrath*, although we often take a half step backward for every step we move forward, men and women can and should rise above the cruelty and evil that are part of human nature and find hope and consolation in discovering nonteleological "is" thinking, an acceptance of what happens and an unwillingness to question the "why" of occurrences.

Echoing Anne Frank's words in her famous diary, Steinbeck surely contends in all his fiction that "[i]n spite of everything . . . people are really good at heart!" This optimistic outlook is not soggy sentimentality; rather, it is a boundless acknowledgment of the human ability to overcome even its most destructive tendencies. This optimism buoys readers even as they explore the tragic deaths of Lennie in *Of Mice and Men* and Coyotito in *The Pearl*; it lifts them as they hear Adam Trask overcome his "sinful" paternal inheritance and pronounce the forgiving word "*Timshel*" to his shattered son Cal in *East of Eden*; and it gives them confidence that they too can overcome the temptations of "the devil, the world and our flesh" as Ethan Hawley does in *The Winter of Our Discontent*. The struggle, of course, is not an easy one. It may involve the loss of family as in *The Grapes of Wrath* and *The Pearl*, disillusionment and potential suicide as in *Winter* and *To a God Unknown*, painful self-discovery as in *The Red Pony* and *The Pastures of Heaven*, but asking "what" we will do with the hand we have been dealt rather than "why" we must confront difficult issues will ultimately serve us well.

Five summers later my study of moral ambiguity was finished and my commitment to Steinbeck was sealed. More important, I was also to find out that all my research served a practical purpose as well as an aesthetic one. As I attempted to deal with the untimely death of my wife from ovarian cancer at age forty-five and my own bout with colon cancer some six months after her funeral, the words from *The Log* gave me solace and peace. I asked "what" not "why" and, as Steinbeck noted, I found that I could answer the first question while the latter tormented me. While I cannot assert that Steinbeck's words were the most essential part of my recovery from intense grief and a grave illness, I know that his works were a significant element in the process.

In the years that followed the defense of my dissertation in 1986, though people have told me that I would never find a job in academe by presenting credentials in Steinbeck studies, though I have heard a prominent Steinbeck scholar advocate choosing a different author for a thesis rather than suffering rejection in job interviews, and though my own research has revealed Steinbeck's personal grief at the misunderstandings his work was subjected to, I continue to serve as an advocate for scholarly discussions and continued examinations of the canon. I have grown from a neophyte to a passionate defender, determined to do my share to promote an author whose genius and excellence have shaped a large part of my life. In the decade and a half after my PhD, I have served as assistant editor of the *Steinbeck Quarterly*; have attended conferences and presented papers at Nantucket, Tuscaloosa, and San Jose/Monterey; have published chapters in books as well as my own collection, *Cain Sign: The Betrayal of Brotherhood in the Work of John Steinbeck* (2000); and have undertaken the task of compiling a bibliography that had not appeared for fourteen years, as well as coediting, with Brian Railsback, Greenwood Press's *Steinbeck Encyclopaedia*, a reference work that has been in progress since 1995.

Throughout each of these tasks, I have considered the long hours of typing, poring over sources and library catalogs, correcting of rough drafts, and proofing of final drafts to be a labor of love. Perhaps at times, like a naïve child, I forgave obvious faults and overlooked deficiencies, and perhaps my impassioned defense of Steinbeck borders on obsession. Yet I remain convinced that when the Steinbeck bicentennial occurs in 2102, respect for his accomplishments will be heightened rather than diminished, and the genius of a small Salinas boy born at the turn of the twentieth century will be recognized and lauded by other champions who, like myself, have found their souls longing to attain the moral balance and ideal brotherhood that he espoused and struggled to express in his work.

Of Mice and Men and (Perhaps) Other Things

Roy Simmonds

This, as the saying goes and all writers of fiction stoutly deny, is "a true story." Whenever I tell it, people look at me in some disbelief, as if I am trying to fool them, and I have to assure them, "No, cross my heart—that is exactly what happened."

It occurred many years ago—in October 1941, to be precise—when I was barely sixteen years old. I had been introduced to the work of John Steinbeck during the summer of the previous year, before the Luftwaffe's air raids on London had become a daily occurrence, when with my grand-mother I went to see John Ford's film *The Grapes of Wrath*. When we emerged from the cinema on that brilliantly sunny late afternoon, my grand-mother's only comment was, "It was rather depressing, wasn't it?" She was far from being a perceptive film critic, for by her mid-seventies she had visited the cinema on only two previous occasions and, after the harrowing experience of *The Grapes of Wrath*, was never to go again. Although I may have mumbled a polite, if unconvincing, agreement with her dismissal of the film, I had been so shattered by what I had just seen on the screen that I could in no way have put my feelings into words. Indeed, at that moment I felt emotionally drained.

Later, back home, I could not get the story of the Joads out of my mind and I determined as soon as I could to get a copy of the book from the library. In the London borough in which I lived, we were fortunate enough to have three public libraries, but although I scoured the shelves of all three,

I was unsuccessful in my search. The book seemed to be in great demand and each librarian told me that the waiting list was very, very long. It is, of course, possible that they did not think that *The Grapes of Wrath* was a suitable book for a boy of my tender years to read. "We do have other books by Mr. Steinbeck," I was told. So I borrowed from this and that library every Steinbeck book that I could lay my hands on, reading my way through *To a God Unknown, Tortilla Flat,* and, gloriously, *Of Mice and Men,* my favorite. I thought the story of George and Lennie the most wonderful I had ever read. I cannot recall ever finding *Cup of Gold, The Pastures of Heaven, In Dubious Battle,* or *The Long Valley.* Perhaps they were always on loan when I searched the shelves, or perhaps it was that I had simply exhausted the holdings of Steinbeck works in all three libraries.

In September 1940, when I reached the age of fifteen, I started work for the first time in the accounts department of a moderately sized chain of furniture stores. The office was a twenty-minute walk from my home. The work was pleasant, though frequently interrupted by daytime air raids. There was, however, absolutely no prospect for advancement, and I soon determined that just as soon as I was sixteen, I would apply for a post in the Civil Service. After the required interview, I was allocated a position as a temporary clerk grade III in a tax office in central London at a weekly wage of £1.17.6. (approximately $7 at the 1941 rate of exchange). The tax office was in a small block, Central House, a stone's throw from Euston Station. There was a bus stop right outside for Routes 68 and 77, both of which ran from north London and across the river into the southern suburbs.

Although, as I was to discover, the office was within walking distance of many places of interest, including the British Museum, the Dickens House, and fabled Bloomsbury, I did very little exploring during my first few weeks in the big city. Even at lunchtime, I ventured only as far as the Express Dairy restaurant in Euston Road, where for about one and sixpence a day I fed royally on steak and kidney pie and mash and Charlotte Russe, or some other such incongruous menu.

After the easygoing but unrewarding atmosphere of the furniture store, my first days in the Revenue were complete purgatory. Almost pathologically shy, I spoke to no one unless I was first spoken to. My sole task, from nine o'clock in the morning to five o'clock at night, was to cast and recast columns of figures in immense, heavy ledgers, two or three times the size any Steinbeck ever wrote in. My desk was directly in front of the officer in charge of my particular station, a gentleman by the name of Mr. Phipps. It is no exaggeration to say that I was in fear and trembling of Mr. Phipps. He was a red-faced, balding, pipe-smoking tyrant with a slow guttural voice and piercing eyes, and he walked with a slight rolling gait. Whenever I happened to glance up from my work, those eyes of his always seemed to be riveted on me. I added figures and added figures all day and every day, Monday to Friday and Saturday morning too, until my head swam. If ever I crouched down behind the propped up ledger, in belief that I was safe for a while from those eyes, he would seem to suspect that I was up to no good, and I would hear his chair scrape backward as he stood up. The next moment he would be standing at my side and a little behind me, and he would wait there, without speaking, until, utterly unnerved, I would make a mistake. His hand, with a rigidly pointing finger, would shoot over my shoulder and jab at the ledger. "What did you do that for?" he would roar.

This may all seem like an inconsequential diversion from the subject of Steinbeck and his books, but it all has, in a way, a vague—and sometimes specific—significance. I remember that I used to arrive home each evening exhausted, and very often my dreams at night were dominated by the office, those ledgers, and Mr. Phipps. And so it was on this particular October night in 1941 I now come to, about three weeks or so after I had joined the office. The dream I had that night ran its usual course, except that when lunchtime came around I found myself not in the Express Dairy but standing at the bus stop outside St. Pancras Church. A Number 68 bus came along and I got on it. I had gathered from conversations overheard in the office that the southbound buses on both routes went to Holborn Station, but I had no way of knowing whether this was actually true or not. When the conductor came for the fare, I queried if the bus did go to Holborn, and when he told me "Yes," I purchased a ticket and asked him if he would alert me when we got there.

Immediately the ticket was in my hand and I was, as it were, committed. I began, in this dream of mine, to worry. How long would the journey take? Suppose it took more than half an hour to get there? I would be late back from lunch. What would Mr. Phipps say? Would I be dismissed in disgrace? Building after building passed by, the bus negotiated several sets of traffic lights, and then, on the far left-hand corner as we went across a wide cross-roads, I saw the blue facade of an underground station—Holborn. The conductor called out to me, but I was already on my feet. The bus stopped right outside the station entrance, and I alighted and began wandering back toward the crossroads, not really knowing what, if anything, I might be looking for.

Next door to the station entrance, and right on the corner, was an estab-lishment called Lyons Teashop. I turned right and discovered that on the other side was another entrance to the station. Beyond that was a Bewlay tobacconist shop, and beyond that was another shop with two entrances and a yellow-painted facade rather like an immense letter "E" lying on its open, three-legged side. Much to my delight, as I approached I discovered it to be a bookshop.

I wandered into the nearest of its two entrances. Shelves on either side flanked a narrow passage. I paused here and there to examine the books on display and then walked deeper into the shop. The passageway opened into a large room with shelves of books from floor to ceiling on each wall. There was a square, glass-topped counter in the middle of the room, and sitting behind a brass cash register was a bored-looking lady of ample proportions, idly turning the pages of a book. She did not look up as I entered. There were no other customers in the shop. The room was badly lit and I remember thinking that she would ruin her eyes if she persisted in reading here, but it was obvious that she was paying little attention to the book open before her. I wandered around the room, stopping occasionally to look at some book or other.

Finally, I ended up in the room's far right-hand corner, the gloomiest area of all, and there on a shelf at waist height I came across a little pile of old *Argosy* magazines. I knew of *Argosy* from having seen the magazine on sale at station newspaper kiosks. It was a monthly publication, costing one shilling, devoted to the reprinting of quality short stories. In my dream, I picked up the top magazine from the pile and looked at the front cover with its large galleon logo. The name "John Steinbeck" leapt out at me from all the other names listed there. I opened the magazine and examined the list of contents. "*Of Mice and Men*," I read. My favorite Steinbeck novel, no less! There was a penciled "6d." on the cover. My very own *Of Mice and Men* for sixpence! I could not believe my good fortune. I took the magazine over to the lady at the counter. She barely looked up as I handed her my sixpence and walked out of the shop. I woke up.

The dream was so vivid in all its detail that, the very next day, I made up my mind to retrace my dream steps. When lunchtime came, I went out to the bus stop, forgoing steak and kidney pie and Charlotte Russe, and waited for a Number 68 bus to come along. I did not ask the conductor to let me know when we got to Holborn because I was sure that I would know it when we got there. I just asked for Holborn and offered him the same fare that I had paid in my dream. So far, so good. And Holborn Station was there, as I knew it would be, on the far left-hand side of the crossroads. The bus stopped in Kingsway, right outside the entrance to the station, and I walked back toward the crossroads. There was the Lyons Teashop on the corner and the other entrance to the station beyond, and beyond that the little tobacconist shop, and beyond that—my heart was really thumping now—the bookshop with the two entrances and the yellow facade.

I walked into the nearest entrance. It was exactly as in my dream. I did not even pause to examine any of the books on the shelves, but, so sure was I of myself now, walked straight through into the badly lit room where the bored-looking lady sat behind the glass-topped counter and the brass cash register. I walked over to the far right-hand corner of the room, and there, as I knew it would be, was a pile of old *Argosy* magazines. I picked up the top one and saw the name "John Steinbeck" on the cover with a penciled "6d." I did not really have to look inside, but *Of Mice and Men* was there all right. I paid the lady my sixpence and left the shop with a triumphant, singing, unbelieving heart.

On the bus back to Euston I began reading: "A few miles south of Soledad, the Salinas River drops in close to the hillside bank and runs deep and green." There was no time for the Express Dairy that day. I bought a cheese roll from the little dairy in Duke Street at the rear of the office and sat in the churchyard in the October chill to eat it while I read my precious copy of *Argosy*, so miraculously obtained.

Later I discovered that the *Argosy* text was severely abridged. So despite the 1941 dream experience, I did not possess a complete text of *Of Mice and Men* until the Reprint Society of London issued it in a double volume with *Cannery Row* in 1947. It may seem strange that after this miracle I had to wait another six years before I was at last able to possess my own volume of what was one of the most influential books of my impecunious youth. Such is life.

But I still have the tear sheets from that magazine. They are on the desk in front of me as I write this. My vandalism appalls me now, for the magazine itself, with that scribbled "6d." on the cover, has long been cast out with other household refuse. I am not a clairvoyant or whatever, and I have never ever had that same sort of experience again. But this *is* a true story. Cross my heart.

John Steinbeck and Japan

Kiyoshi Nakayama

I

John Steinbeck, the 1962 Nobel Prize laureate, is one of the greatest writers in U.S. history. Small wonder that he has been popular in Japan as well as in other parts of the world. Japanese people have read Steinbeck with pleasure since his works, together with those of Ernest Hemingway and William Faulkner, started being introduced to Japan right after World War II. In the Japan of those days, everything American was new and highly valued; we were drastically Americanizing ourselves, absorbing whatever the occupation army either offered or forced on us. We had not had democracy—no freedom of speech, thought, to say nothing of freedom of the press—before or during the war. We were at last liberated from every fetter when we were defeated. While very few books were available, we read hungrily whatever was published here and abroad, and those books brought into the country by GIs. Those who read *The Grapes of Wrath*, for instance, were deeply impressed to learn that there were days when thousands of people were stricken with hunger and poverty even in the affluent society of America.

In the 1950s, Hemingway was more popular in Japan than any other world-famous writer. A collection of his complete works in Japanese translation was first published in 1956, and a new translation was published in 1974. The Japanese version of Faulkner's collected works began to appear in 1970, though it took more than twenty years to complete the collection. As for Steinbeck's works, all his novels and short stories were translated and published separately by 1981. Then in 1985, Yasuo Hashiguchi accomplished a monumental work: *The Complete Works of John Steinbeck*. This twenty-volume reprint collection of the first trade editions of all of Steinbeck's books included such small works and pamphlets as *Saint Katy the Virgin* (1936), *Their Blood Is Strong* (1938), *How Edith McGillcuddy Met RLS* (1943), *Vanderbilt Clinic* (1947), and *Positano* (1954). In the same manner, the twenty-volume Japanese translation of *The Complete Works of John Steinbeck* started in 1996 and was completed in March 2001. Surprisingly or naturally enough, on this past International Translation Day (September 30, 2001), the publisher was awarded the 37th Japan Translation Publication Culture Prize. The presentation address notes in part that, in addition to such world-famous novels as *The Grapes of Wrath* and *East of Eden*, the collection includes seven books that are translated for the first time into Japanese, among them *Steinbeck: A Life in Letters*, *Working Days: The Journals of The Grapes of Wrath*, and *Journal of a Novel: The East of Eden Letters*.

II

Back in 1957, John Steinbeck, John Dos Passos, and John Hersey—they were called "three Johns"—arrived at Haneda Airport in Tokyo at 9:40 P.M. on Saturday, August 31, to participate in the 29th International P.E.N. Congress in Tokyo. Elaine Steinbeck was also invited as a guest, but she did not come with her husband. The famed Pulitzer Prize winner received an extraordinarily warm welcome, as he disclosed in his letter to Elaine, included in *Steinbeck: A Life in Letters*: "I have been interviewed unendingly all day long" (Steinbeck and Wallsten 566). Steinbeck was one of the most popular writers among those invited to the congress. He must have enjoyed his popularity. Even on Sunday morning (the congress started on Monday, September 2), reporters from the major newspapers crowded into his room at the Imperial Hotel. In an article entitled "Steinbeck Talk Shop," he says, to please the Japanese, that this is his first time in Japan and that "he plans to return soon with his wife for a month's visit" (Hitchman 1). But he did not. A typhoon was attacking southern Japan, and the weather was terrible in Tokyo, as he relates, "It stays hot and muggy. . . . I should go out and walk around and I dread it. It's like swimming in warm blood, humidity 300 percent. I'm sorry to have to tell you this and crush your hopes, but we will *not* live in Japan" (Steinbeck and Wallsten 570).

As Steinbeck says in another note to Elaine, he found out only the night before that he was supposed to make the closing address of the opening session of the congress. He "was not told about this," and made up his mind that "it will be the shortest speech on record" (Steinbeck and Wallsten 566). So it was. The *P.E.N. Report: 29th International Congress, Tokyo, 1957* reads:

I am pleased and honored and a little startled to stand here. Until this morning I did not know I was to speak today, and this fact has imposed a virtue, which, while accidental, is very real. My remarks shall be very brief. I have [a] close relationship with this Congress. It is the first Congress in Asia; it is my first Congress anywhere.

When I was leaving New York, apprehensive of the unknown, a very good friend said, "You'll be all right, just listen." But on thinking about it, it seems to me that listening is not enough: one should also hear. There are many reasons for listening, some good and some devious. The only purpose of hearing is understanding. I thank the P.E.N. Club of Japan for its hospitality and I go now to listen and, I hope, to hear. (Japanese P.E.N. Centre 27)

This is, as the writer says, "the whole damn thing," and "has been compared to Japanese poetry" (Steinbeck and Wallsten 568).

Steinbeck was chased by reporters, was repeatedly interviewed, and soon grew tired of it. In an interview by Masami Nishikawa, professor of English at Tokyo University, which was broadcast nationwide on the NHK's (Japanese Broadcasting Corporation) fifteen-minute radio program *Morning Interview* at 7:45 A.M. on September 4, *The Mainichi* reports that Steinbeck said, "I hope this doesn't destroy me at home since I have constantly refused. I never appear on the radio, I never appeared on television at home" ("John Steinbeck" 2). When asked what he was going to see in Japan, the country unsurpassed for scenic beauty, he observed, "I am going to see more Japanese people than little trees. My tendency is that I am more interested in people than in things. Landscapes never attract me so much as [the] people who move on them" (Nishikawa 5).

Steinbeck was to deliver a paper in one of the literary sessions on September 4, but luckily found a good excuse not to speak—he came down with the Asiatic flu. He was also expected to speak at a session on September 6, but he asked Dos Passos "to bring his regrets that he hadn't been able to come to more sessions" (Japanese P.E.N. Centre 235). Dos Passos did so, and read Steinbeck's analects in the session when he was called on, following an introduction in which he said, "While [Steinbeck] was in what he called his delirium, he wrote some analects which he thought might be amusing to read":

"I didn't know I had political ambition, but I must have, I am ill."

"Courtesy grows out of a potential kick in the pants. Hydrogen bombs—if enough nations have them, may well be jet-propelled doves of peace."

"Hospitality is the most charming torture the human being has ever devised."

"Since Thoreau's time, desperation has grown noisier."

"The difference between a congress and a dogfight is that a dogfight has rules."

"There are two ways to privacy: smallpox and poverty."

"Confusion is the child of speech. Silence has never produced misinformation."

"All people have one thing in common: they are good, and those other sons of bitches are bad."

"A bird can fly, but cannot thread a needle."

"Government is the final proof that individual men have failed."

"To have led a good life, one must be dead."

"The evil man is never [as] evil to himself as a good man."

"Force is the persuasion of failure."

"An armed people will kill many, a disarmed people is already dead."

"Much as we try to make it so, ideas have neither nationality nor race." (Japanese P.E.N. Centre 235–36)

Come to think of it, the P.E.N. Club of Japan had made a mistake. They expected Steinbeck would speak, hopefully as eloquently as Mac in *In Dubious Battle*, instead of trying to hear. They invited those whom they thought were "progressive" writers. What he contributed to the congress, however, was nothing but the brief closing address and the "analects"—he was sick in bed throughout.

Steinbeck left Tokyo on September 10 and did not return to Japan for ten years, when he stopped by with Elaine on their way home from Vietnam. It was early April when Mr. and Mrs. Steinbeck, together with his son John IV, then in the American armed forces and spending his five days of R&R, went to Kyoto in the prime of the cherry blossom season. Elaine recollected, when I saw her at her Sag Harbor cottage on August 17, 1984, that they stayed at the Miyako Hotel and spent all night sitting on a bench in the garden peacefully surrounded by the beautiful blossoms: "probably one of the very most beautiful things I have ever seen, things to stare at for storing, to remember later" (Steinbeck, "Dear Alicia" 4). But Steinbeck could not move about freely during those days because he had slipped a spinal disk in Hong Kong. A few days later, they returned to the Hotel Okura in Tokyo and then flew back home, bidding farewell to Japan for good.

III

The first International Steinbeck Congress, which Yasuo Hashiguchi and Tetsumaro Hayashi organized, held in Fukuoka, Japan, in 1976, was a great success and triggered the birth of the John Steinbeck Society of Japan in 1977. Now we have more than 170 members—most of them college professors. We hold an annual conference at which we enjoy a banquet to strengthen the bonds of friendship. Our activities were reported partly in the *Steinbeck Quarterly* until 1993 and have since been reported regularly in our *Newsletter* and *Steinbeck Studies*.

Today, most of the Japanese people enjoy a relatively comfortable standard of living though we have been economically in a mild depression. For more than ten years after World War II, however, almost all of the Japanese people were indigent, and everyone was eager to be a "proletarian," a Socialist, or a Communist. This was simply because we had scant food and lived in want at that time. And this is partly why we read and are deeply moved by Steinbeck's writings, just as readers in Russia, France, and other parts of Europe read and are moved by them.

This, however, is not the only reason why Steinbeck has been popular in Japan. More important, his works have been widely read because his writings touch our hearts with their invariably affirmative attitude toward life—his humanism, admiration of courage, and warm love. In addition, he deals with universal themes, depicts beautiful California landscapes, and portrays the ordinary people with sympathy and compassion. His sense of humor is second to none in popular esteem. What he writes about—friendship, courage, and altruism, among other things—seems to be based on his positive acceptance of the goodness of man. He did describe the fall of man as well: Steinbeck's California as a land "East of Eden," where people driven out of paradise live. In fact his California is everywhere that anyone lives. In the same manner, Steinbeck's "group-man" or "phalanx" theory, which is revealed and demonstrated as a theme in *In Dubious Battle* and *The Grapes of Wrath*, is not merely based on his scientific approach to life but his fundamental worldview of mankind and the universe. It underscores the fact that men and women want to live together decently with the people around them. A human cannot live alone; he/she needs friends, love, and a feeling of togetherness. George needs Lennie, Doc needs Hazel and Suzy, and Cal needs Lee and Abra. We, as readers, need Steinbeck—his warm humaneness and his love for ordinary people.

Once a Japanese gentleman visited the Salinas Public Library and was asked why he was interested in Steinbeck. He was silent for a long time, and then, consulting his pocket dictionary, he simply said, "Oneness." As this rather funny incident reveals, our philosophy of oneness is very close to that of Steinbeck and Edward F. Ricketts—their holistic worldview. When Steinbeck was writing *To a God Unknown*, he noted in a journal that he gave to his close friend, Carlton A. Sheffield:

The story is a parable, Duke. The story of a race, growth, and death. Each figure is a population, and the stones, the trees, the muscled mountains are the world—but not the world apart from man—the world *and* man—the one inseparable unit, man plus his environment. Why they should ever have been misunderstood as being separate I do not know. Man is said to come out of his environment. He doesn't know when. (Sheffield 195)

It is this universal idea of Steinbeck's, seemingly derived from his love of Nature, that attracts Japanese readers today and connects California and Japan so closely together. If California were not so beautiful as he describes in his stories, and if it were nothing but a desolate desert without poppies, lupines, mallow weeds, wild oats, and fuchsias, then he could not have written such attractive stories. Then we would not have liked Steinbeck so much. We do not have golden poppies, and yet we love such wildflowers because they are little and look weak, but in reality are strong. They represent inviolable, eternal beauty, the lilies of the field, and "even Solomon in all his glory was not arrayed like one of these" (St. Matthew 6:29). We like a person who grows flowers, even "four cucumber plants" in the pots just inside the windows, as Steinbeck did in his New York apartment (Steinbeck and Wallsten 852). We raise chrysanthemums with flowers almost as big as Elisa Allen does. It is this aesthetic feeling of ours—to love and live with the beautiful things in Nature—that Yasunari Kawabata felt obliged to express in his 1968 Nobel Prize acceptance speech, "Japan, the Beautiful, and Myself." When we visit Steinbeck Country in California, we see with our own eyes that the landscapes he described are indeed beautiful, even in the age of postindustrialization. We imagine that they must have been more beautiful when the writer actually described them. People are kind and friendly, and look pleasant and happy. We feel pleasant and happy as well. After all, California and Japan are good neighbors. We live so close together—there lies just an ocean between us.

Steinbeck in Scandinavia

Donald Coers

Elaine Steinbeck recalls that for her the most dramatic moment of the Nobel ceremonies for December 1962 occurred on the very last evening of that festive week. A young secretary in the Swedish Foreign Ministry named Stig Ramel had been assigned to attend to the Steinbecks' needs and to keep them abreast of protocol. At the final event, the Royal Ball, Mrs. Steinbeck recalls that Mr. Ramel advised them, "The guests form a semi-circle and the royal family go by and then they go stand in the middle of the floor and someone is chosen to accompany them in to dinner" (E. Steinbeck 256). But the Steinbecks were not to worry about that, since no literature laureate had ever been chosen. Mrs. Steinbeck describes what did happen that night:

Well, we were standing in a line, everybody's dressed in gown and white tie and so forth, when a man in a wig carrying a long staff and dressed in medieval clothes came and stood in front of John and me and he stamped the floor with his staff and he said, "Madam, would you advance to the middle of the floor and take the arm of the king and lead the party in? Sir, would you please take the arm of the queen and lead in?" . . . I looked at John and he was bursting with pleasure, and pride. John was selected for that because he was such a popular choice [for the Prize]. (256)

That affection for Steinbeck in Sweden in fact had already been demonstrated when the secretary of the Swedish Academy broke protocol during the presentation ceremony and addressed him as "*Dear* Mr. Steinbeck" (Benson 920). Of course, by 1962 Steinbeck's popularity had for years been worldwide, his works translated into thirty-six languages, from Arabic to Urdu. But among John Steinbeck's many international audiences, Scandinavians have always had a special regard.

It was in Scandinavia that the first foreign language editions of Steinbeck's work appeared. In 1938, *Tortilla Flat* was published in Danish, Norwegian, and Swedish. The next year, all three countries published translations of *Of Mice and Men*, and during the following year, all three brought out *The Grapes of Wrath*. Steinbeck appealed immediately to Scandinavians, and that appeal has endured. Since 1938, Steinbeck's Scandinavian publishers—Gyldendal of Copenhagen, Gyldendal of Oslo, and Bonniers (Sweden)—have published hundreds of issues of individual titles, multivolume collected works, and book club editions. Gordon Hølmebakk, editor in chief of Gyldendal of Oslo, says that he is still "astonished" by the numbers for Norway (letter to the author).

The major reason for the early acceptance of Steinbeck's works in Scandinavia is probably political. During the Depression, Sweden, Norway, and Denmark all adopted gradualist approaches to socialism. Steinbeck's early works struck sympathy with Scandinavians, who perceived in *Tortilla Flat*, *Of Mice and Men*, and *The Grapes of Wrath* kindred social and political sensitivities. Otto Lindhardt, formerly chief editor of Steinbeck's Danish publisher Gyldendal of Copenhagen, says that Danes have always appreciated Steinbeck's "social democratic ideas" (personal interview). Gordon Hølmebakk notes that the early Steinbeck works "coincided with the rise and consolidation of the idea of 'social democracy' and the Welfare state in Norway" (letter to the author). Stig Ramel, the Steinbecks' aide during the Nobel festivities, attributes a similar reason for the enthusiastic reception of Steinbeck's works in Sweden: "Swedish writers at the end of the Depression were very interested in social problems, and their mood was very anticapitalistic" (telephone interview).

Steinbeck was already popular in Scandinavia, then, when historical forces during World War II assured that he would become even more so. Beginning roughly a year and one-half before the Japanese attack on Pearl Harbor, Steinbeck worked for various American intelligence and information agencies. Using information gleaned from refugees from Norway and Denmark, both overrun by the Nazis on April 9, 1940, he wrote a work of fiction about the psychological effects of enemy occupation. His setting was an unnamed country, in Steinbeck's words, "cold and stern like Norway, cunning and implacable like Denmark, reasonable like France" (Benson 491). That work, *The Moon Is Down*, was published in the United States in March 1942. It was welcomed by resistance organizations in several occupied European countries. Illegally translated, printed on underground presses, and widely distributed, it served successfully as propaganda in France and Holland, but it was especially effective in Norway and Denmark. Readers there were certain that Steinbeck had intended Norway as its setting, and they were grateful that an author with an international reputation would call the world's attention to their plight. Also, they were touched that Steinbeck understood exactly how they felt about military defeat and occupation. Although technically neutral, the Swedes printed the Norwegian translation of *The Moon Is Down* and helped smuggle it into Norway. On at least one occasion Steinbeck communicated even more directly with Norwegians through their patriotic underground. One of his inspirational messages appeared in the May 1943 issue of the resistance paper *Bulletinen*. In occupied Denmark the popularity of *The Moon Is Down* was such that there were thousands of copies of two different translations, although it is impossible to say how many editions or copies were ultimately turned out because they were illegal publications cranked out by hand on mimeograph machines (Staffeldt, personal interview). A Danish bibliography lists sixteen separate editions of the two translations (Buschardt, Fabritius, and Tønnesen 79). When the war ended, Steinbeck's works were in great demand in Norway and Denmark.

Because of Steinbeck's prewar literary popularity, as well as his wartime contributions to the Danish and Norwegian resistance, he enjoyed a hero's welcome when he made his second trip to Scandinavia in 1946, arriving in Copenhagen at the end of October. He had made his first trip in 1937 when he and his first wife, Carol, visited Denmark and Sweden en route to Finland and Russia. During the earlier trip he was free to move about unrecognized. This time he was traveling as a celebrity, with *Time* magazine reporting his triumphal receptions and a newspaper in Copenhagen announcing, "John Steinbeck, all of Denmark is at your feet" (Benson 586). In the middle of November, the king of Norway gave Steinbeck the Haakon VII Cross, a grateful nation's acknowledgement of the role *The Moon Is Down* had played in bolstering the morale of the Norwegian people during Nazi occupation.

In June 1957 with his new books and reprints of older ones still selling in large numbers throughout Scandinavia, Steinbeck returned to Denmark and then went on to Sweden, where he stayed with his closest friend in Scandinavia, Bo Beskow, the Swedish artist and writer he had visited during previous trips. Steinbeck's friendship with Beskow was his most significant personal association with Scandinavia. It lasted from 1937 until Steinbeck's death in 1968. The two men had much in common. They were both over six feet tall and roughly the same age—Steinbeck born in 1902, Beskow in 1906. They shared a love of the sea and a fondness for gardening. Both were dedicated artists who liked to experiment (Beskow was a writer and a creator of stained-glass church windows as well as a painter). In the fiction of both there is a characteristic earthiness and lack of pretension and an interest in Old Testament themes. And they shared an impatience with formality and ceremony, a fascination with gadgetry, and a droll sense of humor (a memorable scene in my 1981 interview with Beskow was his rendition of Steinbeck imitating a seagull gliding in for a landing). Finally, the two men experienced traumatic divorces at about the same time, sharing these and other highly personal details with each other in long letters and during visits. It was during Steinbeck's trips to Scandinavia, spaced at ten-year intervals, that Beskow painted three portraits of his friend.

The two men had met quite by chance in New York in the spring of 1937. Beskow was attending to business with an American publisher when he saw in the hallway an "unkempt young man about my age with a shadow in his blue eyes." The publisher introduced them and gave Beskow a copy of Steinbeck's recently published *Of Mice and Men*. The publisher also mentioned that Steinbeck would be traveling through Stockholm that summer on his way to Russia. Beskow invited Steinbeck to come and see him, and left his address. Steinbeck mumbled a perfunctory response, and the two men parted. That evening Beskow picked up *Of Mice and Men* to fall asleep by, but could not sleep until he had finished the book (Beskow, *Krokodilens middag* 56).

Steinbeck did visit Beskow in Stockholm that June, and Beskow remembers a fine time, although Steinbeck and his first wife, Carol, were so casual that it was difficult getting into the better eating places. Beskow took a particular liking to Carol, describing her as "sincere, free-talking, and a fun girl without pretense." She could also be outrageous. Beskow recalls a night he and his wife spent with the Steinbecks at an amusement park. Carol disappeared, and the others eventually found her in the room of distorted mirrors, unperturbed, urinating on the floor while three guards looked on horrified (Beskow, personal interview). But it was a carefree, memorable visit, Beskow remembers. "The summer was warm and beautiful as it usually is that time of year, and we sat in the daylit nights and ate herring, which they loved, while John sang Irish songs." Before the Steinbecks left, Beskow painted his first portrait of him "while he was contemplating *The Grapes of Wrath*" (Beskow, *Krokodilens middag* 57). That portrait "resembled Lennie from *Of Mice and Men*, shy with a luminous, blue look in a light blue shirt against a warm orange background" (67).

When Steinbeck returned to Scandinavia in 1946 on his triumphal postwar trip, he telephoned Beskow from Copenhagen: "Bo, for God's sake, come down here!" Beskow took the night train and found Steinbeck overwhelmed by the local press.

[H]e had barricaded himself in the Hotel d'Angleterre. I found him there living in an ousted German count's suite. . . . John was barefoot, dressed in pajamas and very depressed even while surrounded by silk wallpaper, uniformed waiters and [his second wife] Gwyn. He was unkempt, wild-eyed and miserable. Gwyn was lying in the rose-colored bedroom which smelled of perfume and Virginia cigarettes. She was dressed in lace and tulle. John held up a whisky to me, put on some eau-de-cologne and hair tonic and said, "I didn't know how nice it was to have luxury. I am enjoying it." He didn't look like he was enjoying it. (93–94)

Together Steinbeck and Beskow toured the refugee camps in Copenhagen, which made up nearly one-third of the city's population at that time. Ordinarily they would not have been allowed such a visit, but because of *The Moon Is Down*, Steinbeck was regarded as a member of the Danish resistance. Beskow, the neutral, war-sheltered Swede, tagged along, uncomfortably conscious of Danish disapproval (94). From Copenhagen they went on to Stockholm, and then they flew to Oslo for the awarding of the Haakon VII Cross. Forced to land some distance from the city, they arrived at their hotel late. The press corps, furious because it had been waiting five hours, took out its frustration on Steinbeck. It was a low point in his long association with Scandinavia. Beskow remembered it as a terrible press conference that might have been even worse. Fortunately, Steinbeck mumbled so badly that no one understood what he was saying (96). After the two men returned to Stockholm, Beskow painted his second portrait of Steinbeck, this time on commission, because Beskow had refused to give up the first one.

The next year Steinbeck and photographer Robert Capa stopped over in Sweden on their trip to Russia. After that came Steinbeck's divorce from Gwyn and the death of his close friend Ed Ricketts, followed by a long silence. Then Beskow recalls, Steinbeck phoned him from Madrid one night before Easter, 1952:

"Bo, come down here." His voice was interrupted by a woman's voice, unmistakably southern: "Hello darling, do come." It was Elaine, John's . . . third wife. I flew to Spain and met them in Seville. . . . Elaine and John met me at the airport with a bottle of champagne. . . . I felt like I already knew Elaine through John's and her letters, and had decided that [he] seemed to have landed in safe waters. We drank whisky and bonded again, and he told me about his new book—"the best I have ever written" [*East of Eden*]—and his new wife—"the best wife I have ever had." (120–24)

After the meeting in Spain, Beskow sensed a cooling in his relationship with Steinbeck. A few months later when the Steinbecks were in Rome, the Italian writer Ezio Taddei attacked Steinbeck in the Communist newspaper

L'Unita for failing to denounce what he referred to as American war crimes in Korea. Steinbeck's reply, in which he defended his country and called Taddei a liar, struck Beskow as patriotic cant. Beskow believed his friend had been intimidated by the McCarthy hearings and that, in any event, he had become more "American" (128–29). Beskow believed that Steinbeck "felt a need to defend America at a time when all the other intellectuals criticized it. This is my explanation for his later writings . . . when he went very pro-American . . . about America's role in Vietnam" (Beskow, personal interview).

Despite the growing political distance between them, Steinbeck and Beskow continued to write and to see each other. When Steinbeck and Elaine had gone to Sweden around Midsummer Eve in 1957, Beskow, then living in Rytterskulle with his new wife Greta, had painted Steinbeck for the third and final time, this painting done in heavy gray (Beskow, *Krokodilens middag* 67).

That August Beskow and Greta came to New York, where they spent the rest of the summer and the fall while Beskow painted the modernistic fresco mural on the wall of the Meditation Room in the United Nations building. He had been recruited for that task by his close friend and fellow Swede, then UN General Secretary Dag Hammarskjöld. During their stay in New York, the Beskows visited the Steinbecks in Manhattan and at their summerhome in Sag Harbor. They also introduced the Steinbecks to Hammarskjöld, who occasionally came along.

Five years later, while preparing for his trip to Stockholm to receive the Nobel Prize for Literature, Steinbeck wrote to Beskow at least three times, reminiscing about earlier visits, sending his schedule, asking for help in avoiding extra speeches, wondering whether Beskow would have time to do a fourth portrait, and requesting that he arrange a trip to the grave of Hammarskjöld, who had been killed in a plane crash in Africa the previous year. Hammarskjöld had been a member of the Swedish Academy at the time of his death, and in that capacity had been instrumental in securing the Nobel Prize in Literature for the 1960 laureate, St. John Perse. Hammarskjöld died before the decision to award the 1962 prize to Steinbeck, but the academy almost always considers previous nominations as a positive factor in decisions. The records of the academy are closed for fifty years, so we will not know for another decade whether his connection with Hammarskjöld was a significant factor in Steinbeck's selection.

When John and Elaine Steinbeck arrived at the airport in Stockholm on December 8, 1962, the greeting party included their assigned aide, Stig Ramel, and Bo Beskow, who, according to Ramel, made his job difficult during the entire visit by being intrusively proprietary with Steinbeck. By this time, the relationship between Steinbeck and Beskow had so transformed that, according to Beskow, the time they spent together during the Nobel festivities "was the last blaze of a smoldering friendship." But Beskow's final act of friendship, a public defense of Steinbeck, was yet to come. The selection of Steinbeck for the Nobel Prize had ignited a controversy in Sweden.

The debate opened in Swedish newspapers on October 26, the day after the announcement of the selection of Steinbeck, and it continued until around the middle of November. Generally, those attacking the Swedish Academy's judgment in the matter argued that Steinbeck was too conservative a choice; the prize should have gone to a deserving writer in Asia, Africa, or South America. Steinbeck, it was alleged, lacked the passion of a great writer; moreover, anticipating Arthur Mizener's criticism that would appear in the *New York Times* on December 9, Steinbeck's time had passed, and "a moral vision of the thirties," to borrow Mizener's phrase, did not deserve a Nobel Prize in the sixties. Swedish supporters of the selection of Steinbeck responded that his work during the thirties should have secured the prize for him then and that the academy was serving justice by correcting its earlier oversight. Other supporters praised Steinbeck's warmth and spontaneity and unusual appeal to literary as well as general audiences. Of the various Swedish attacks, one was so intemperate that Beskow called it "an execution." It came from Swedish writer Artur Lundkvist, a Marxist who had received the Lenin Peace Prize in 1958. Lundkvist's criticism, reported in *Expressen*, one of Stockholm's morning papers, included the allegation that the selection of Steinbeck was "the Swedish Academy's biggest mistake." That attack infuriated Beskow: "Did [Lundkvist] mean that Pearl Buck was greater than the author of *The Grapes of Wrath*?" (Beskow, *Krokodilens middag* 129). Beskow defended Steinbeck in Stockholm's radio–TV magazine in his final gesture of friendship.

The rift between Steinbeck and Beskow seems at least partly attributable to the latter's perception that Steinbeck changed over the years from an idealistic Socialist into a glib American patriot. That perception is shared by those American critics who never forgave him for what they considered political apostasy: his supposed abandoning of Socialist or even Communist doctrine after he had achieved fame and financial security.

But neither Beskow's views nor those of the censorious Swedish literary critics nor even his later support of the U.S. role in Vietnam, so unpopular throughout Scandinavia, has significantly affected John Steinbeck's standing with his most loyal audience there—the general reader. The proof of that in Scandinavia is the same as that in the United States and throughout much of the world—the remarkable continuing sales of his works. And it is bolstered in Scandinavia by the judgment of those in a good position to know. They include people such as Stig Ramel, who attests to Steinbeck's appeal to "ordinary people": "[Steinbeck] had a personal touch; his readers felt close to him. He did not write in the highly literary, sophisticated style. The Scandinavian tradition appreciates literature which focuses on the fate and the lives of common people" (telephone interview). They include the Norwegian publisher Gordon Hølmebakk, who calls Steinbeck "[t]he most widely read [literary] American author [in Norway] since the war," attributing his widespread popularity to "something in Steinbeck's whole ethos, his compassion with the underprivileged, his unsnobbish solidarity with [his] fellow man, his humanity and humour" (letter to the author).

If the controversy that surrounded his being awarded the Nobel Prize had any effect on Steinbeck, he didn't show it during the glitter of the Nobel ceremonies in Stockholm. Stig Ramel says that typically each year one of the laureates stands out from the rest, and that "John was the great hero of that year's festivities. He behaved like a complete gentleman . . . absolutely one hundred percent wonderful and charming with everyone, carrying on interesting conversations all around him. Of the ten or twelve laureates that year, John stood out. [He] was the shining light" (telephone interview).

Stig Ramel went on to become director-general of the Nobel Foundation, a position he held until 1992. Steinbeck played a crucial role in his election to that position. The Nobel Foundation had assigned Steinbeck to Ramel because of reports that Steinbeck was a wild man who drank a lot. Ramel had been told before the Steinbecks' arrival, "You have a difficult job." But, as Ramel says, "Elaine and I became good friends from the time of our first meeting at the plane. She and I saw to it that Steinbeck drank no hard liquor, only vermouth. . . . The Nobel Foundation was so pleased with my handling of Steinbeck that years later they made me director-general. I have often been sorry I could not write John Steinbeck a letter and thank him. . . . By that time he had died" (telephone interview).

John Steinbeck did thank Stig Ramel for his help during the festivities. After the Steinbecks left Stockholm, Ramel was so exhausted he slept for twenty-four hours. He was awakened early the next morning by a hotel porter delivering a big wooden box. "When I opened it," Ramel says, "it had twelve bottles of whisky and a note from John: 'Dear Stig, Here's all the whisky you prevented me from drinking' " (telephone interview). It was a characteristic beau geste, and a fitting farewell to Scandinavia.

John Steinbeck and His Immortal Literary Legacy

Tetsumaro Hayashi

Because my own estimation of John Steinbeck's magnificent art and craft differed so vastly from the general critical climate of the "Eastern" establishment in the 1950s/60s, a few of my colleagues and I decided to take action to promote Steinbeck studies. With the support and encouragement of Preston Beyer, Peter Lisca, Warren French, and Sakae Morioka (Japan), we started the Steinbeck Society of America (1968–1988), which derived from the Steinbeck Bibliographical Society (1966–1968) and later developed into the International Steinbeck Society (1988–1998). Later, at the start of my twenty-five-year tenure at Ball State University, we initiated the *Steinbeck Quarterly* (1969–1994) with the dedicated support of several university sponsors and such young scholars as James Salem, Reloy Garcia, Robert DeMott, John Ditsky, Yasuo Hashiguchi, and Kenji Inone. When I first started my Steinbeck studies in 1954 as an MA candidate under the guidance of the late Harry Warfel, Distinguished Professor of American Literature at the University of Florida–Gainesville, there was only one book written about Steinbeck (by Harry T. Moore), published in 1939. In my opinion, our collaborative endeavor, very audacious in the 1960s, has ultimately made a significant difference in Steinbeck studies and international activities over the years.

Like my Shakespeare seminars, which I have taught more frequently than any other course in my forty-five-year professional teaching career, I have been able to enjoy teaching Steinbeck seminars virtually every semester consecutively. While I always needed a break, a semester or two, before I wanted to again teach such seminars on Arthur Miller, Ernest Hemingway, Yukio Mishima, and Eugene O'Neill, teaching Steinbeck has always provided an unusual sense of new reading and exhilarating rewards in search–discovery. I have thoroughly enjoyed discussing, debating, and analyzing the art and craft of Steinbeck—his gifted story-teller's magic, his memorable characters and controversial themes, his powerful symbols and dominant metaphors, his poetry and music in dramatic prose fiction. His literature has spoken to me and many of my treasured students and friends with a very personal voice, revealing slowly to us his depth and richness, diversity and humor, audacious techniques and compelling ecological foresight. His prophetic vision and unmistakably clear political, moral, and social messages are truly remarkable.

Of Steinbeck's unique messages, I wish to cite the following:

Man (mankind) is imperfect but perfectible.

Man/woman is free but responsible.

Man/woman has a moral choice as he/she encounters evil, destruction, and atrocity in the "Waste Land"—the postlapsarian cosmos.

His value scheme remains essentially Judeo–Christian in his obsessive thematic concerns with good and evil, right and wrong, choice and fate, democracy and tyranny, love and hate, teleology and non-teleology, and a transcendental breakthrough to a more holistic view of life.

One of the major reasons why we started the Steinbeck Society in 1966 and the *Steinbeck Quarterly* in 1968 (eleven months before Steinbeck's death) and why I carried on managing both the society as director (later president) and the journal as editor-in-chief despite decades of budget cuts was that in the 1950s/1960s we were working in almost total isolation, with very few creditable critical and biographical guides; we were an absolute minority in our Steinbeck-related endeavors. We thus created a forum for our gifted young scholars and creative researcher–explorers in Steinbeck's "Wide World." It was indeed a journey in the "road less traveled," but our committed collaborative efforts—scholarly, editorial, budgetary, and in supporting members in forty-four countries including the United States, Japan, England, and Canada—were well worth the effort.

My richest reward has long been encountering the brilliant, creative people who love Steinbeck passionately. I should like to dedicate this statement—in honor of John Steinbeck—to those who have with unselfish devotion offered their extraordinary talents and resourcefulness to promoting Steinbeck studies among younger students, teachers, translators, editors, book dealers, and scholars here and abroad. My sincere thanks to the incredible goodwill and unmatched generosity of Dr. and Mrs. John J. Pruis and Dr. and Mrs. Richard W. Burkhardt, two former Ball State University presidents/first ladies; to Mr. Thomas E. Spangler, for his unflinching support; and to some of the shining stars in the galaxy of Steinbeck scholars: Ditsky, DeMott, Fontenrose, Owens, Simmonds, Benson, Gladstein, Heavilin, Morsberger, Shillinglaw, and others, especially in California, Indiana, Illinois, Idaho, Oregon, and Japan. It has been a demanding life of public service on my part, but a very rewarding, creative one at that.

John Steinbeck: Yesterday, Today, and Tomorrow

John Ditsky

I have chosen a title which, one way or another, seems to promise the impossible (except to tax patiences, which is never impossible). But I am aware of being a member of some sort of middle generation of Steinbeck readers. The pioneer work of Peter Lisca and Warren French and others was already in print well before I ever thought of devoting my time to writing about John Steinbeck. Like many of the members of my generation, I was introduced to Steinbeck by a teacher's class assignment. In my case, it was *The Grapes of Wrath*, and as a child born at the end of the Depression, it was not difficult to relate to Steinbeck's angry depiction of the plight of the displaced Okies. I began to read other works by Steinbeck, and like many of those of us who were born a few years either side of *Grapes*, I largely read him *backward*, without the sense of an entire career and its changes that one gets from the criticism of such commentators as French and Lisca. Yet at the same time, I was aware of Steinbeck as a living member of that generation of giants who, all born around the turn of the century, were mostly still among us and able to be taken for granted as presences in our lives. So while the experience of reading *Grapes* for the first time was still fresh, I quite naturally acquired and read *The Winter of Our Discontent* and *Travels with Charley* when they first appeared. The point I wish to make is that for a reader of that day coming to the writings of John Steinbeck as a whole rather than as a linear development, it was entirely possible to feel in Steinbeck's passionate indictment of the complacencies of the Eisenhower era in *Winter* very much the same sort of admirable heat one had found earlier in *Grapes*, in which it embodied the fervent militancy of Julia Ward Howe's lyrics to "The Battle Hymn of the Republic," the source of Steinbeck's most famous title.

Jackson Benson's rich biography of John Steinbeck, ironically, may also have marked the end of the era of concern with the linear account of Steinbeck's career. Now that the story of that career has been substantially told in an accurately proportioned way, perhaps—as Warren French suggested years ago—we can turn our attention to the whole rather than to this or that part. There are, of course, some gaps in the account we would still like to see filled in, such as what drove Steinbeck into literature as a career or what the later "public" Steinbeck was really like. Thanks to Pascal and Pascal Covici, Jr. and to Thomas Fensch, we have a pretty good idea of what Steinbeck thought he was doing when he was actually doing it, and Bob DeMott's edition of the journals that accompanied the writing of *The Grapes of Wrath* fills in our understanding of the high point of Steinbeck's output as never before. If Ted Hayashi's hard work on the political John Steinbeck is finally allowed to see daylight, the "linear" view of Steinbeck will be largely in place, and with it, what I would have to term "John Steinbeck—Yesterday" will be, in one sense, a matter of history, and in yet another sense, will have changed, as history itself changes.

Perhaps because he was such a writer of the American road, we have been tempted to read Steinbeck like something we can unroll from a spool as opposed to trying to see him whole. Steinbeck moving through time will always fascinate us, and we are grateful for whatever recent treasures of this sort we are given—such as Bruce Arris's volume showing us the Steinbeck of the pre-celebrity years. But we can also, I think, expect to see less and less of the sort of attention that so many studies of Steinbeck, relentlessly and chronologically making their way through the entire canon of his works, have been providing us with. Note that Peter Lisca rewrote his first major book, and note how substantially he did so; note also that Warren French did the same. In great part, these revisions show an admirable capacity for growth on the part of their creators, as well mark a shift away from an earlier sort of criticism that seemed obsessed with pinpointing the date on which the John Steinbeck one had grown up with ceased to be recognizable. You can see the signs of this approach without any trouble, whether it takes one or another of a great many forms: John got famous; John got remarried; John changed his ideas; John made new friends; John got preachy; John went to Hollywood; John lost Ed Ricketts; John got remarried; John left California; John had the gall to win the Nobel Prize; John got reactionary; John *changed*, all of them say. Bad, bad John.

It's at this point that I begin to feel the real weight of the burden of the topic. It is, after all, safer to hide in a narrow crack of concern. It's dangerous to be out in the open making graybeard prophecies about where we're going and how what we think we know is not going to stay the same. What can I say to defend my claim that Steinbeck's "changes" are going to seem a lot less interesting than they have, and that revisionist criticism is going to take the form of overviews and core samples? If there is any credibility behind what I am about to say, perhaps it comes from the experience of teaching Steinbeck courses over thirty years and noting what changes have taken place in that time in the attitudes of my students. What I have noticed most is this: Today's students seem almost wholly without a sense of history or any notion of historical perspective. The experience I mentioned earlier, of having read *The Grapes of Wrath* and *The Winter of Our Discontent* as practically simultaneous publications, is routine to them; the Depression and the Eisenhower years are equally distant and therefore the same. In one sense that's a shame; yet in another, there's something to be said for it, and good or bad it will surely contribute to our growing understanding of "John Steinbeck—Tomorrow." They have no interest in the chronology of John Steinbeck's life, but they are not without understanding, insight, or real contributions to make. When one recent student commented that he liked John Steinbeck because of his "understanding of human nature," he was also bringing a Bible reader's sensibility to a single entity that included *Winter* as well as *The Pastures of Heaven*. He wasn't interested in drop-off points; he saw a continuity, a wholeness, a oneness, what Steinbeck would've called "a shining." When a young woman in the same class expressed her general dislike of Steinbeck, with some exceptions—describing the writer rather cleverly, I thought, as someone who had had "greatness thrust upon him"— she did so by means of an overview ("He's always this, he's always that") that a critic of twenty or thirty years ago might not have dared.

The late Joseph Fontenrose might have so dared. Maurice Dunbar wrote of this man's passing, and movingly, in the *Steinbeck Quarterly*. Fontenrose once made, in his Barnes and Noble volume on Steinbeck, the sort of critical generalization about the writer that I think typifies the "John Steinbeck—Tomorrow" approach of my young students. He summed up Steinbeck's philosophy as "inadequate" for a novelist. I have never quite understood this observation, and I should have done something about my failure to understand when Fontenrose and I were together for the Second International Steinbeck Congress in 1984. Too late now. Did he mean, I wonder, that Steinbeck didn't have enough philosophy to write fiction? Hardly likely, however much you write off a lot of what got said in Ed Ricketts's lab as homespun reinventing of the wheel. Fontenrose, who threw in the biblical with the whole universal apparatus of myth Steinbeck used, might not have appreciated my male student's appreciation of the writer, or at least not have taken his reasons to be valid ones. On the other hand, he may have meant that John Steinbeck didn't have a fine enough novelistic philosophy; and there my woman student, who thought the philosophy was not bad but simply omnipresent, might have disagreed with Fontenrose. Apples and oranges?

In the volume of essays I compiled for G. K. Hall & Co., Louis Owens, Cliff Lewis, and Carrol Britch contributed essays that show how "John Steinbeck—Today" can sketch out "Tomorrow" simply by taking a clean, new, revisionist view; all of a sudden, critical pieties about John Steinbeck's "sentimental" view of the Joads turn out to be just that—critical sentimentalism of a negative sort. That kind of work represents a focusing on a single novel, as indeed the series format for my book on *The Grapes of Wrath* demanded. But consider larger subjects that, for all their obvious immediacy, have been either ignored or left lying around, as if in hospital corridors, almost unattended to. For all of Joseph Fontenrose's attention to biblical usage in Steinbeck, for instance, and for all the fuss about this or that example in the *College English*es of some years back, it is astounding that no one has done a thorough overview of this subject in all of Steinbeck to date. John Timmerman published an annotated summary of such work in *Steinbeck Quarterly*, but where is the entire book that this subject so clearly demands be written (with the possible exception of Michael Meyer's *Cain Sign* [2000], which focuses on the Genesis theme of brotherly betrayal)? This is but a single example of a major area of interest in Steinbeck's work that has been largely taken for granted as self-evident, but that seems to me to demand a closer and more imaginative kind of reading.

Part of the problem has been, of course, that what with his letters, his journals, and his narrator's voices, it has seemed all too easy to let John Steinbeck explain himself—to take at face value all the plausible essayings that accompany his fiction as a kind of running moral for each work. We know we shouldn't do so; we have a term in criticism, "intentional fallacy," to cover this particular sin and its attendant evils, but that wonderfully sane Steinbeckian voice is so rational and so convincing that we do it anyway. Maybe it is time to reverse the process and let all of Steinbeck—the stories and the supposed mirror images provided by the letters and the journals and the narrational voices—be read as a very different kind of fiction. Only then, perhaps, will readers of Steinbeck begin to free themselves from the tendency to judge Steinbeck on the basis of whether or not one agrees with him.

Put another way, one problem with Steinbeck is that so many of us have been attracted to his fiction originally because of the apparent lifelikeness of his creations. But when his creations come to seem like mere constructs, symbols, mouthpieces, we look for ways to cry "Failure." When presumed wimps become kings of France and when grown men talk to the canned goods, some of us get our backs up. Then we conveniently forget about authorial intention and want to believe that John Steinbeck really didn't know what he was doing, even when he said it was precisely what he wanted to do. We forget, perhaps, what a sense of play there was in the man and therefore also in his works. We forget as well that there are many ways to tell the truth, including by lying. We so insist on seeing him as a realist that we resist acknowledging the romantic who, after all, broke into book print by telling a pirate yarn. We find ways to forgive him the whopper about the young girl giving her milk to a starving man, but we can only shake our heads when we find him dumping a used-up stud overboard or marrying a scientist off to a whore. It is, I think, this sense of play that bothers us, because it argues lack of "Serious Intent." Some of us have forgotten about that thing called irony.

Incidentally, you will have noticed a certain seeming contradiction in what I am saying, for while I am speaking of new directions in Steinbeck criticism, I also seem to be noting that Steinbeck will survive without them. The paradox comes from inside me because I am both a critic of Steinbeck and his lay reader who would enjoy him even if I didn't have to devote a part of my career to writing about him. Some of you doubtless feel the same. If pressed on the issue of whether we need the critics, then, my answer will be characteristically forthright: yes and no. Robert DeMott has led the pack of critics calling for more careful attention to Steinbeck as artist and stylist. I agree. What Steinbeck does looks so easy we hardly think to talk about just how he does it. If we insist on comparing Steinbeck with documentary photographers, we miss the implications of the fact that all his life he was an amateur inventor. I also suggest that style might mean a great deal more than we think it does in Steinbeck's work, and that there is a great deal to be gained in following DeMott's lead in calling for greater awareness of Steinbeck's inventive artistry. A student of mine designed an imaginary production of *Burning Bright* that argued that the play would work if produced in the spirit of Brechtian Epic Theatre. I'm not sure that such a production, if carried out, would turn this vehicle into a commercial success, but I am convinced that she was right in taking her approach, and that her constructive attitude toward Steinbeck's artistry is the way we ought to deal with the later writing. In that sense, critics can be helpful.

However, here are a couple of ways in which our sense of "John Steinbeck—Yesterday" may have inhibited our critical sense of him "Today" and made his "Tomorrow" slower in the coming—or, I might say, ways in which we demand that John Steinbeck play by realist rules. For one, consider how in recent years the changing nature of the profession of teaching has resulted in changing attitudes toward certain writers, some of them major. I refer to the rightfully growing voice of women critics around the world, and the subsequent attention now being paid to aspects of literature formally smiled at according to the all-purpose maxim "Boys will be boys." Steinbeck tends to let women stand for things, no doubt about it, and what shall we make of this? A former student of mine, Sandra Beatty, and Bob Morsberger began the study of the ways in which John Steinbeck seems to categorize his women characters and presumably thus diminish them as rounded human beings. There are wives and there are whores, and often it is the whores who seem to be on the pedestal. Mimi Gladstein furthered this cause with her study of Steinbeck's "indestructible" female type, and her efforts have brought attention to a phenomenon we will doubtless be hearing a good deal more of: the fact that though John Steinbeck's life was filled with a remarkable number of remarkable women, his works are not, and presumably art thus fails to reflect life accurately. A study by two more former students, Beth Everest and Judy Wedeles, argued for the centrality of women in *East of Eden*, but it is probably not going to do much to change the minds of those who expect their female characters to be fully fleshed out—not simply "monsters."

But these studies, useful and necessary as they are, may also be limited by their realistic biases. Mimi Gladstein began the process of reading Steinbeck from the standpoint of feminist criticism, a different matter entirely since it involves bringing into play critical principles that are not formulated in terms of a single writer's work, nor its fidelity to life—or lack of it. This relatively recent development is one of the waves of the future, not merely for John Steinbeck, and it will provide us with a great many insights beyond the simple measurement of the effectiveness of an artist's female portraiture. And in truth, I expect this sort of study from without—the kind that depends on the application of critical or philosophical theory rather than the measurement of Steinbeck's accuracy in depicting an observable reality—to provide the wave of the critical future in Steinbeck studies. Once we have piled up enough data about the "linear" Steinbeck, in other words, we can begin the effort to see him whole—whatever that may prove to mean for his future reputation. I suspect very strongly, however, that what the community of professional teachers and critics choose to do about Steinbeck will have remarkably little impact on those who read him. To play with an idea put forth by Jack Benson—however playful he himself meant to be—the fortunes of a writer like Ezra Pound may depend entirely on the academics, but what have these latter, in turn, ever been able to do to diminish the standing of John Steinbeck among his following?

There are also areas in which forests need to be recognized as being greater than the sums of single trees, and that returns me to a topic I mentioned earlier of Steinbeck's biblical allusions. John Timmerman admits that Steinbeck was hardly a believer, yet Joseph Fontenrose may have been obscuring the special nature of Steinbeck's use of the Bible in lumping its myths and patterns in with all the other universal stories Steinbeck employed, like some Joseph Campbell of fiction, because they were universal. The nonbeliever's fascination with the believer's sacred book is a most interesting paradox, especially when it accompanies what Ted Hayashi has identified as markedly Judeo–Christian morality—as seen from, perhaps, God's perspective. Or, to put it more accurately, from the perspective of humans who have taken on the role of gods. I don't for a moment mean to suggest that Steinbeck was a closet believer, of course, but I do think he was religious in the most genuine sense of the term—he was deeply serious about an aspect of human nature some see fit to ignore. If that is so, it is less surprising that one cannot separate his use of the Bible from his deeply felt moral sense, for he used religious references critically. By this I mean that he saw the failing of God-centered institutional religion as a denial of the human, and so he employed the stories and the usages of such religion to show up these shortcomings for what they are, as well as suggest what better thing might take their place. In such a sense, then, the notorious ending to *The Grapes of Wrath* becomes not merely an interesting parallel to Christian notions of the Eucharist that a person could write a critical note about, but rather a functional—and also revolutionary—upsetting of the relatively meaningless (he might say) event that takes place in churches and that makes for no real differences in society. What Steinbeck does with religion, then, amounts almost to parody, a subject that in itself is far greater than its religious component alone, though it has hardly been discussed. Most important, however, is the way Steinbeck employs religious references to beat religion at its own game.

Steinbeck's biblical allusions, then, can be seen as a kind of rewriting of the bible rather than as a literary crutch or a claim on higher reader attention. An example of this can be found, appropriately enough, in the Nobel Prize address that ends with these two paragraphs which begin by referring to Alfred Nobel himself:

Less than fifty years after his death, the door of nature was unlocked and we were offered the dreadful burden of choice. We have usurped many of the powers we once ascribed to God. Fearful and unprepared, we have assumed lordship over the life and death of the whole world, of all living things. The danger and the glory and the choice rest finally in man. The test of his perfectibility is at hand.

Having taken God-like power, we must seek in ourselves for the responsibility and the wisdom we once prayed some deity might have. Man himself has become our greatest hazard and our only hope. So that today, Saint John the Apostle may well be paraphrased: In the end is the *word*, and the word is *man*, and the word is *with* man. (10)

Notice this typically Steinbeckian scientific equation between atomic research—looking inside the atom—and the moral responsibilities that curiosity entails. The deed is done, he seems to say; now we must accept the burden and fact and get on with the existence of the race. Literature itself is the extension and the expression of the process, and the stylistic approach proposed is paraphrase. The nuclear arms race becomes, not surprisingly, Armageddon; but it is also an Armageddon that can and must be evaded because "Thou mayest" triumph over sin.

We are reminded, perhaps, that many years earlier John Steinbeck had been called "Saint John" for speaking out in church and chiding the minister for making a fatuous remark, a remark the writer thought antihuman. We remember, perhaps, that at the beginning of the Nobel Prize address Steinbeck made his quasi-Lutheran stand on the importance of literature in these terms: "Literature was not promulgated by a pale and emasculated critical priesthood singing their litanies in empty churches—nor is it a game for the cloistered elect, the tin-horn mendicants of low-calorie despair" (7). What is important to note here is his equation of the peddling of despair with a con game and the con game with organized religion and religion with bloodless, sexless elitism—and criticism. In Steinbeck's parody of religion, religion itself becomes the caricatured denial of humanity while literature is its redeemer—if only the temple can be cleansed of those artificial voices, those *castrati*, the critics. Small wonder, then, that Steinbeck categorized priests and critics alike as representatives of a dead faith, as enemies of the word, as those who would keep the people prisoners in a dull and soulless Eden.

We have a long way to go toward finally understanding the thinking of John Steinbeck, as well as extricating it at last from the critical thicket where it is difficult to tell it from that of Ed Ricketts. I believe that we are at the day in which there will be no more, or at least little more, talk of "non-teleological" or "is" thinking in Steinbeck, and little more as well about the "phalanx" theory, but a lot more of reading him straight and direct—from his books and with imagination. Perhaps now, on his centennial anniversary, Steinbeck's "Today" has finally arrived. If that is so, we will shortly see whether John Steinbeck will ever be judged as objectively as other major American authors—Twain, Hemingway, Faulkner, Wharton—are judged: by intellect and not by hearsay, by reading instead of rumor. My bet is that we will find that he has been out there ahead of us all the time, a "leader of the people," all too aware that he acted, and spoke, as the voice of that people, and that only through his imagination could he transcend the limitations of that people's existence, their realities; that what the "group-man" was capable of finally producing was an evolutionary leap that could escape the brute confines of the group's existence and become man, woman, person—fallible and yet "perfectible." That will be his "Tomorrow," and if we are lucky, it will also be ours.

In the end, though, Steinbeck's meaning is in the hands of his readership. I don't think that anything the scholars can do will stop that readership from growing or from discovering their own new applications of his works to their lives. Like my students, they don't need our help to see him whole. But this begins to sound like false modesty, and it is modesty—humility, rather—that I want to turn to, finally. For a long time now, I have wondered what it must have been like to have been John Steinbeck, Nobel Prize winner, and to have been reviled in print for daring to receive the prize at all. What thoughts went through his mind as he prepared his speech of acceptance? We know from the finished speech that he began by expressing his own doubts about whether he was the most deserving of the award, and then went on to state his pleasure in receiving the award as a representative of a kind of group-man, the writers. Almost comically, but also characteristically, he portrayed himself in animal terms, his function being "not to squeak like a grateful and apologetic mouse, but to roar like a lion out of pride in my profession and in the great and good men who have practiced it through the ages" (7). It's at this point that he makes that comparison to religion, not surprisingly, and shortly thereafter is paraphrasing a great predecessor, William Faulkner, who surely shared some of the same attitudes on the subjects being discussed, but whose very mention was, to my thinking, a gesture of humility.

By the same token, in speaking of Steinbeck criticism by Richard Astro, Robert DeMott, and Roy Simmonds—criticism that promised to change the way the future will read Steinbeck—Warren French insisted at the Second International Steinbeck Congress that "future critics have to seek new directions," and he called for "readings that may make us see in works that seem to be becoming historically dated, fresh meanings for a changing world." French was a scholar speaking to scholars on that occasion, whereas I hope to speak as a reader of Steinbeck to others of that fellowship. What may seem to be contradictions in this essay are actually, I think, like the paradox in Steinbeck's thinking. The mass produces nothing—except its own leaders, who arise out of the mass through an evolutionary process born of need. In such a manner, society produces its moral individuals and also its artists. And in the same way, the mass of Steinbeck's readers will continue to produce genuine critics of his work. And "Tomorrow" they will tell us what we need to hear.

Selected Bibliography

Astro, Richard. *John Steinbeck and Edward F. Ricketts: The Shaping of a Novelist.* Minneapolis: U of Minnesota P, 1973.

Baumgartner, Jennifer. " 'The Custodians of the Public Interest': Unraveling John Steinbeck's Literary Reputation." Master's thesis. Western Carolina U., 1999.

Benson, Jackson J. *The True Adventures of John Steinbeck, Writer.* New York: Viking, 1984.

Beskow, Bo. *Krokodilens middag [Dinner for a Crocodile].* Stockholm: Bonniers, 1969.

———. Personal interview with Donald Coers. 23 May 1981.

Birkerts, Sven. *The Gutenberg Elegies: The Fate of Reading in an Electronic Age.* New York: Fawcett Columbine, 1995.

Booth, Wayne C. *The Company We Keep: An Ethics of Fiction.* Berkeley and Los Angeles: U of California P, 1988.

Buell, Lawrence. "In Pursuit of Ethics." *PMLA* 114 (Jan. 1999): 7–19.

Buschardt, Leo, Albert Fabritius, and Helge Tønnesen. *Besættlesestidens illegale blade og bøger [Illegal Pamphlets and Books of the Period of Occupation].* Copenhagen: Det Kongelige Bibliotek, 1954.

DeMott, Robert. *Steinbeck's Reading: A Catalogue of Books Owned and Borrowed.* New York: Garland, 1984.

———. *Steinbeck's Typewriter: Essays on His Art.* Troy, NY: Whitston, 1997.

Ditsky, John. "John Steinbeck: Yesterday, Today, and Tomorrow." *Steinbeck Quarterly* 23.1–2 (1990): 5–16.

———. "Your Own Mind Coming Out in the Garden: Steinbeck's Elusive Woman."

John Steinbeck: The Years of Greatness, 1936–1939. Ed. Tetsumaro Hayashi. Tuscaloosa: U of Alabama P, 1993. 3–19.

Eliot, T. S. "The Hollow Men." *The Norton Anthology of English Literature: The Major Authors.* 7th ed. New York: Norton, 2001. 2630.

Emerson, Ralph Waldo. *Nature: Anthology of American Literature.* Ed. George McMichael et al. 7th ed. Vol. 1. Englewood Cliffs, NJ: Prentice, 2000. 813–40.

Emery, Jean. "Manhood Beset: Misogyny in Steinbeck's *Of Mice and Men.*" *San Jose Studies* 18.1 (1992): 33–42.

Everest, Beth, and Judy Wedeles. "The Neglected Rib: Women in *East of Eden.*" *Steinbeck Quarterly* 21.1–2 (1988): 13–23.

Fiedler, Leslie. "Looking Back after 50 Years." *San Jose Studies* 16.1 (1990): 54–64.

Fireside Theatre. *Everything You Know Is Wrong.* Columbia, 1975.

Fontenrose, Joseph. "*The Grapes of Wrath.*" *John Steinbeck: An Introduction and Interpretation.* American Authors and Critics Series. New York: Barnes and Noble, 1963. 67–83.

Galbraith, John Kenneth. "John Steinbeck: Footnote for a Memoir." *The Atlantic* 224.5 (1969): 65–67.

Gannett, Lewis. "Steinbeck's Way of Writing." *The Portable Steinbeck.* enl. ed. New York: Viking, 1946. xxi–xxiii.

George, Stephen K. " 'The Disintegration of a Man': Moral Integrity in *The Winter of Our Discontent.*" *Steinbeck Yearbook.* Ed. Barbara A. Heavilin. Vol. 1. Lewiston, NY: Mellen, 2000. 93–111.

Gladstein, Mimi R. "*Cannery Row*: A Male World and the Female Reader." *Steinbeck Quarterly* 25.3–4 (1992): 87–97.

———. "Deletions from the *Battle*; Gaps in the *Grapes.*" *San Jose Studies* 18.1 (1992): 43–51.

———. *The Indestructible Woman in Faulkner, Hemingway, and Steinbeck.* Ann Arbor: UMI Research Press, 1986.

———. "Missing Women: The Inexplicable Disparity between Women in Steinbeck's Life and Those in His Fiction." *The Steinbeck Question: New Essays in Criticism.* Ed. Donald Noble. Troy, NY: Whitston, 1993. 84–98.

———. "*Of Mice and Men*: Creating and Recreating Curley's Wife." *Beyond Boundaries.* Ed. Susan Shillinglaw and Kevin Hearle. Tuscaloosa: U of Alabama P, 2002. 205–220.

———. "The Strong Female Principle of Good—Or Evil: Women in *East of Eden.*" *Steinbeck Quarterly* 24.1–2 (1991): 30–40.

Gladstein, Mimi, and Bobbi Gonzales. "*The Wayward Bus*: Steinbeck's Misogynistic Manifesto." *Steinbeck: Revisionist Views of His Art, Politics, and Intellect.* Ed. Cliff Lewis and Carroll Britch. Lewiston, NY: Mellen, 1989. 157–73.

Hadella, Charlotte Cook. "The Dialogic Tension in Steinbeck's Portrait of Curley's Wife." *John Steinbeck: The Years of Greatness, 1936–1939.* Ed. Tetsumaro Hayashi. Tuscaloosa: U of Alabama P, 1993. 64–74.

Hayashi, Tetsumaro, ed. *John Steinbeck: The Years of Greatness, 1936–1939.* Tuscaloosa: U of Alabama P, 1993.

Herbert, George. *The Temple. The Selected Poetry of George Herbert.* Ed. Joseph H. Summers. New York: New American Library, 1967. 39–265.

Hitchman, Sue. "Steinbeck Talks Shop." *Asahi Evening News* 3 Sept. 1957: 1+.

Hølmebakk, Gordon. Letter to Donald Coers. 13 Dec. 1994.

Hyde, Lewis. *The Gift: Imagination and the Erotic Life of Property.* New York: Random, 1983.

Japanese P.E.N. Centre. *P.E.N. Report: 29th International Congress, Tokyo 1957.* Tokyo: Kasai, 1957.

The Jerusalem Bible. New York: Doubleday, 1966.

"John Steinbeck Interviewed for First Time over Radio." *The Mainichi* 5 Sept. 1957: 2.

Kazin, Alfred. *On Native Grounds.* New York: Harcourt, 1942.

Lindhardt, Otto. Personal interview with Donald Coers. 20 May 1981.

Lopez, Barry. *Crossing Open Ground.* New York: Random, 1989.

Meredith, Burgess. *So Far, So Good: A Memoir.* Boston: Little, Brown and Co., 1994.

Moore, Judith, Abe Opincar, and Bob Shanbrom. "Where The Grapes of Wrath Are Stored: John Steinbeck Was My Father." *San Diego Leader Weekly* 30 Mar. 1989: 26–29.

Nishikawa, Masami. "Half an Hour with Steinbeck." *Eigo Seinen* [*The Rising Generation*] 1 Jan. 1963: 4–5.

Noble, Donald, ed. *The Steinbeck Question: New Essays in Criticism.* Troy, NY: Whitston, 1993.

Parini, Jay. *John Steinbeck: A Biography.* New York: Holt, 1995.

Pepper, William. "Steinbeck on the Novel." *Carmel Cymbal* 10 Mar. 1955: 1.

Person, Leland S., Jr. "*Of Mice and Men*: Steinbeck's Speculations in Manhood." *The Steinbeck Newsletter* 8.1–2 (1995): 1–4.

Pritchard, H. A. "Does Moral Philosophy Rest on a Mistake?" *Moral Obligation* by H. A. Pritchard. Oxford: Oxford UP, 1950.

Railsback, Brian. *Parallel Expeditions: Charles Darwin and the Art of John Steinbeck.* Moscow: U of Idaho P, 1995.

Ramel, Stig. Telephone interview with Donald Coers. 9 Dec. 1994.

Rosenblatt, Roger. "The End of the Age of Irony." *Time* 24 Sept. 2001: 79.

Scardigli, Virginia. Telephone interview with Stephen George. 28 July 2001.

Schulberg, Budd. *Writers in America.* New York: Stein, 1983.

Seelye, John. Personal interview with Susan Shillinglaw. May 2000.

Sheffield, Carlton A. *Steinbeck: The Good Companion.* Ed. Yasuo Hashiguchi. 20 vols. Kyoto: Rinsen, 1985.

Spilka, Mark. "Of George and Lennie and Curley's Wife: Sweet Violence in Steinbeck's Eden." *The Short Novels of John Steinbeck.* Ed. Jackson J. Benson. Durham: Duke UP, 1990. 59–70.

Staffeldt, Mogens. Personal interview with Donald Coers. 20 May 1981.

Steinbeck, Elaine. " 'John Believed in *Man*': An Interview with Mrs. John Steinbeck." *After* The Grapes of Wrath: *Essays on John Steinbeck.* Ed. Donald V.
Coers, Paul D. Ruffin, and Robert J. DeMott. Athens: Ohio UP, 1995. 241–
71.

———. Personal interview with Brian Railsback. New York City. 2 Mar. 1993.

Steinbeck, Elaine, and Robert Wallsten, eds. *Steinbeck: A Life in Letters.* New York:
Viking Penguin, 1975.

Steinbeck, Gwyn. Taped interview conducted by Terry Halladay.

Steinbeck, John. *America and Americans.* New York: Viking, 1966.

———. *Cannery Row.* 1945. New York: Penguin, 1994.

———. *The Complete Works of John Steinbeck.* Ed. Yasuo Hashiguchi. 20 vols. Kyoto:
Rinsen, 1985.

———. "Critics—From a Writer's Viewpoint." *Steinbeck and His Critics: A Record
of Twenty-Five Years.* Ed. E. W. Tedlock, Jr. and C. V. Wicker. Albuquerque:
U of New Mexico P, 1957. Reprinted by E. W. Tedlock, Jr. in 1969. 48–51.

———. "Dear Alicia: Letter from John Steinbeck." *Salinas Californian* 20 May
1967: 4.

———. *East of Eden.* 1952. New York: Penguin, 1992.

———. "Flight." *The Long Valley.* 1938. New York: Penguin, 1986. 41–66.

———. *The Grapes of Wrath.* 1939. New York: Penguin, 1986.

———. *In Dubious Battle.* 1936. New York: Penguin, 1992.

———. *Journal of a Novel: The* East of Eden *Letters.* New York: Viking, 1969.

———. ". . . . like captured fireflies." *CTA Journal* (Nov. 1955): 7.

———. *The Log from the Sea of Cortez.* 1951. New York: Penguin, 1995.

———. *The Moon Is Down.* New York: Viking, 1942.

———. "The Novel Might Benefit by the Discipline and Terseness of the Drama."
Stage 16 (1938): 50–51.

———. *The Pastures of Heaven.* 1932. New York: Penguin, 1995.

———. *Sea of Cortez.* New York: Viking, 1941.

———. *The Short Reign of Pippin IV.* 1957. New York: Penguin, 1977.

———. "Some Random and Randy Thoughts on Books." *The Author Looks at Format.* Ed. Ray Frieman. New York: American Institute of Graphic Arts, 1951.
27–34.

———. *Speech Accepting the Nobel Prize for Literature.* New York: Viking, 1962.

———. *Sweet Thursday.* New York: Viking, 1954.

———. *Travels with Charley in Search of America.* 1962. New York: Penguin, 1980.

———. *The Wayward Bus.* New York: Viking, 1947.

———. *The Winter of Our Discontent.* 1961. New York: Penguin, 1989.

Steinbeck, Stanford. Telephone interview with Stephen George. 28 July 2001.

Steinbeck, Thom. Personal interview on behalf of Peter Jones Productions, Inc. 22
July 1998.

Stout, Jeffrey. *Ethics after Babel: The Languages of Morals and Their Discontents.*
Boston: Beacon, 1988.

Street, Webster. "John Steinbeck: A Reminiscence." *Steinbeck: The Man and His Work*. Ed. Richard Astro and Tetsumaro Hayashi. Corvallis: Oregon State UP, 1971. 35–41.

Tedlock, E. W., Jr., and C. V. Wicker, eds. *Steinbeck and His Critics: A Record of Twenty-Five Years*. Albuquerque: U of New Mexico P, 1957. Reprinted by E. W. Tedlock, Jr. in 1969.

Timmerman, John H. *John Steinbeck's Fiction: The Aesthetics of the Road Taken*. Norman: U of Oklahoma P, 1986.

Walhout, Clarence. "The End of Literature: Reflections on Literature and Ethics." *Christianity and Literature* 47 (1998): 459–76.

Werlock, Abby H. P. "Looking at Lisa: The Function of the Feminine in Steinbeck's *In Dubious Battle*." *John Steinbeck: The Years of Greatness, 1936–1939*. Ed. Tetsumaro Hayashi. Tuscaloosa: U of Alabama P, 1993. 46–63.

Wimsatt, William K., and Monroe C. Beardsley. *The Verbal Icon*. Lexington: U of Kentucky P, 1954.

Wolfe, Tom. *Hooking Up*. New York: Farrar, 2000.

Index

About the Editor and Contributors

Richard Astro is currently the provost of Drexel University. He codirected with Tetsumaro Hayashi the 1970 Steinbeck Conference at Oregon State University, the proceedings of which were later published as *Steinbeck: The Man and His Work*, a thiry-year forerunner of the present *A Centennial Tribute*. Dr. Astro is best known in Steinbeck circles for his groundbreaking *John Steinbeck and Edward F. Ricketts: The Shaping of a Novelist*.

Donald Coers is Vice President for Academic Affairs at Angelo State University in San Angelo, Texas. He is the author of *John Steinbeck as Propagandist:* The Moon Is Down *Goes to War* (1991) and coeditor with Paul D. Ruffin and Robert J. DeMott of *After* The Grapes of Wrath: *Essays on John Steinbeck* (1995).

Robert DeMott, Edwin and Ruth Kennedy Distinguished Professor at Ohio University, has published the trilogy *Steinbeck's Reading* (1984), *Working Days: The Journals of* The Grapes of Wrath (1989) (a *New York Times* Notable Book), and *Steinbeck's Typewriter* (1996), winner of the Nancy Dasher Book Award. He is editor of the Library of America's uniform three-volume Steinbeck project, is an accomplished poet, and plans a career as a fly-fishing guide upon retirement.

John Ditsky, professor of American literature, modern drama, and creative writing at the University of Windsor, Ontario, has published four critical volumes on Steinbeck (*Essays on* East of Eden; *John Steinbeck: Life, Works,* *and Criticism*; *Critical Essays on Steinbeck's* The Grapes of Wrath; and *John Steinbeck and the Critics*), as well as more than one hundred critical articles, notes, and chapters on a variety of subjects. He has also had more than fourteen hundred of his poems accepted by major and "little" magazines of a dozen countries and is poetry editor of *The University of Windsor Review*.

Warren French is the founding president of the International John Steinbeck Society. He has published several books on Steinbeck in the Twayne Authors Series, as well as *A Companion to* The Grapes of Wrath (1963), *A Filmguide to* The Grapes of Wrath (1973), and books on J. D. Salinger and the Beats. Since retiring from Indiana University in 1986, he has been honorary professor of American studies at the University of Wales, Swansea. Only recently he learned that he is a direct descendant of colonial New England poet, Anne Bradstreet, "The Tenth Muse."

John Kenneth Galbraith was born in Ontario and received degrees from the University of Toronto, the University of California at Berkeley, and Cambridge University. His major works include *The Affluent Society*, *The New Industrial State*, and *Economics and the Public Purpose*. A former ambassador to India during the Kennedy years, he is currently a professor emeritus of economics at Harvard, where he has taught since 1949.

Stephen K. George (PhD, Ball State University, 1995) is a professor of English at Brigham Young University–Idaho. His publications include articles, reviews, and introductions in *Steinbeck Studies*, the *Steinbeck Yearbook*, the *Steinbeck Encyclopaedia*, and *John Steinbeck's* The Grapes of Wrath: *A Reference Guide*, as well as in anthologies from Greenwood and Alabama UP. He is also the director of Brigham Young University–Idaho's literary journal, *Outlet*, and currently resides with his family in the quiet town of Rexburg, Idaho.

Mimi Gladstein has been teaching and writing about Steinbeck for some three decades. She is one of the pioneers in bringing a feminist critical perspective to bear on Steinbeck's work. Professor Gladstein has been honored with both the John J. and Angeline Pruis Award as Outstanding Steinbeck Teacher for 1978–1987 and the Burkhardt Award for Outstanding Steinbeck Scholar in 1996.

Terry Gorton is finishing his dissertation, "The Uses of Entrapment—Readers Caught in the Webs of Literature," for Stony Brook University in New York. He lives with his wife Lisa and their two girls in Rexburg, Idaho, where he teaches English literature and composition at Brigham Young University–Idaho.

Tetsumaro Hayashi, graduate professor of English and vice president and director of graduate studies in English at Yasuda Women's University in Hiroshima, is a former president of the International John Steinbeck Society (1981–1993). Dr. Hayashi has published 34 books and 23 monographs on British and American literature, as well as more than 130 scholarly articles. He has also served as the editor-in-chief of the *Steinbeck Quarterly* (1968–1993) and the *Steinbeck Monograph Series* (1970–1991) while at Ball State University in Muncie, Indiana.

Barbara Heavilin is an associate professor of English at Taylor University in Upland, Indiana. Her previous Steinbeck publications include *The Critical Response to John Steinbeck's* The Grapes of Wrath and the *Steinbeck Yearbook*. In addition, she has also published articles and reviews on Margaret Fell Fox, William Wordsworth, and James Thurber.

Peter Lisca spent most of his academic career as a distinguished professor and scholar of American literature at the University of Florida. In many ways the founding father of Steinbeck criticism, he published six books on the author, including the groundbreaking *The Wide World of John Steinbeck* (1958), which was the first major examination of the writer's literary career. Dr. Lisca died in Gainesville on April 17, 2001, just a month before this tribute had its beginning.

Burgess Meredith, perhaps most famous for his roles as the manager Mick in the *Rocky* movies and the Penguin in the *Batman* series, has long been an acclaimed actor on stage and screen, as well as a close personal friend of John Steinbeck. In 1939 he played the starring role of George in Lewis Milestone's film classic *Of Mice and Men*.

Michael Meyer is adjunct professor of English at DePaul and Northeastern Illinois Universities in Chicago. He is the current Steinbeck bibliographer and his essays on Steinbeck have appeared in numerous books and journals. His most recent Steinbeck scholarship is *Cain Sign: The Betrayal of Brotherhood in the Work of John Steinbeck* (2000). He is presently working as an editor on *Literature and Music* for Rodopi Press's series, *Perspectives in Modern Literature*, and is coeditor of the new *Steinbeck Encyclopaedia* (Greenwood, forthcoming).

Arthur Miller, the celebrated American dramatist, was born in New York City in 1915. After graduating from the University of Michigan in 1938, he moved back to Brooklyn to continue his writing career. His first major success was *All My Sons* (1947), which won the New York Drama Critics' Circle Award. However, he is most famous for his third play on Broadway,

Death of a Salesman (1949), for which he received the Pulitzer Prize. In June 1957 Steinbeck wrote an essay for *Esquire* that eloquently defended the playwright against the charges of the House Un-American Activities Committee. Mr. Miller currently resides in Connecticut.

Robert Morsberger (PhD, Iowa State University, 1956), professor emeritus at the California State Polytechnic University–Pomona, has published chapters in or introductions to 119 books, 70 articles, 15 short stories, and 10 books, including the first book on James Thurber and the biography *Lew Wallace: Militant Romantic* (1980), in collaboration with Dr. Katherine M. Morsberger. A film historian, he is coeditor of two volumes on *American Screenwriters* in the *Dictionary of Literary Biography.* His publications include twenty-eight articles on Steinbeck, in addition to editing two versions of *Viva Zapata!* for Viking/Penguin, and he has served on the editorial board of the *Steinbeck Quarterly.*

Kiyoshi Nakayama is professor of English at Kansai University, executive director of the Steinbeck Society of Japan (1987–1994), director of the John Steinbeck Society of Japan (1977–   ), and head of the executive office of the American Literature Society of Japan (1997–2002). Dr. Nakayama has edited and compiled several Steinbeck volumes, as well as authored the trilogy *Steinbeck's Writings: The California Years* (1989), *Steinbeck's Writings II: The Post-California Years* (1999), and *Steinbeck's Writings III: The New York Years* (forthcoming).

Brian Railsback teaches American literature and creative writing at Western Carolina University, where he has served as the department head of English and the founding dean of The Honors College. He has published numerous articles and book chapters on John Steinbeck, as well as the book *Parallel Expeditions: Charles Darwin and the Art of John Steinbeck* (1995); he has also lectured on Steinbeck in Japan, Mexico, and throughout the United States. Presently he is coeditor, with Michael Meyer, of the *Steinbeck Encyclopaedia.*

Virginia Scardigli was a close friend of John Steinbeck during his days with Ed Ricketts on "Cannery Row." She was born in Kansas City, Missouri, on February 12, 1912, and graduated from the University of California at Berkeley in 1933. Afterward she worked for various area papers, such as the *Carmel Cymbal*, and taught high school in Palo Alto, where she currently resides.

Budd Schulberg, son of legendary movie producer B. P. Schulberg, began working at Paramount Studios at the age of seventeen and published his first novel, *What Makes Sammy Run?*, in 1941. He wrote, with F. Scott Fitzgerald, the screenplay *Winter Carnival* (1939), as well as the screenplay for the classic *On the Waterfront* (1954). Schulberg is perhaps most famous for his courageous founding in the mid-1960s of the Watts Writers' Workshop (now known as the Frederick Douglass Center). Always a champion and friend of Steinbeck, Mr. Schulberg currently resides in Westhampton Beach, New York.

Susan Shillinglaw is a graduate of Cornell College and the University of North Carolina–Chapel Hill. For the past fifteen-plus years she has been the director of the Center for Steinbeck Studies at San Jose State University, where she is also a professor in the English department. She teaches a Steinbeck class every spring semester and summer and edits the award-winning *Steinbeck Studies*, published by San Jose State University. She has published several articles/introductions on Steinbeck and edited several Steinbeck texts.

Roy Simmonds was born in London and has been an independent scholar since the early 1970s. He has published essays on William March, John Steinbeck, Edward J. O'Brien, and Ernest Hemingway in a number of US literary journals. His published full-length works include *The Two Worlds of William March* (1984), *John Steinbeck: The War Years, 1939–1945* (1996), and *A Biographical and Critical Introduction of John Steinbeck* (2000). The preeminent Steinbeck scholar of Britain, Roy passed away in November 2001 shortly after submitting his essay to this volume.

Elaine Steinbeck grew up in Fort Worth, Texas, studied drama production at the University of Texas, and eventually managed several Broadway productions, including the smash hit *Oklahoma!* She met Steinbeck over Memorial Day weekend in 1949 and the couple were married on December 28, 1950. Over the next twenty years they were inseparable, with Elaine helping make possible the writing of his later fiction as well as the flowering of Steinbeck scholarship to come. Mrs. Steinbeck lives in New York City.

Gwyn Steinbeck, John's second wife, sang professionally with bands, on the radio, and as a vocalist for CBS. She and John married in New Orleans on March 29, 1943, just a few days after his divorce from Carol. Although their marriage was in constant upheaval, they did have two sons, Thom and John IV. Gwyn died on December 30, 1975, in Boulder, Colorado, at the age of 58.

John Steinbeck IV, the younger son of John Steinbeck, wrote the acclaimed book, *In Touch* (1969), which is a memoir of his experience in

Vietnam. He was also awarded an Emmy for *The World of Charley Company* (1968), a CBS documentary, while his autobiography, *The Other Side of Eden: Life with John Steinbeck*, just appeared in 2001. Affectionately nicknamed "Catbird" by his father, he died in February 1991 from surgery complications.

Stanford Steinbeck is a first cousin of John. He graduated from Stanford University in 1930 and worked for Shell Oil Company most of his life. He now resides with his niece and her husband in Atherton, California.

Thom Steinbeck, elder son of John Steinbeck, lives in California and is a writer and published author. He has written screen adaptations of *The Pearl* and *The Moon Is Down*, as well as a book of short stories, *Down to a Soundless Sea*. Currently he is the executive producer and screenplay writer of the HBO production, *Travels with Charley*, which should be released in 2002, the centennial anniversary of his father's birth.

Webster Street was an attorney-at-law in Monterey, California, and friend of Steinbeck from their college days at Stanford until John's death.

John Timmerman, professor of English at Calvin College in Grand Rapids, Michigan, has published two books and many essays on John Steinbeck. Additionally, during the past decade he has published *T. S. Eliot: The Poetics of Recovery*, *Jane Kenyon: A Literary Life*, and *Robert Frost: The Ethics of Ambiguity*.

Tom Wolfe was born and raised in Richmond, Virginia. He earned a PhD in American Studies from Yale University in 1957 and then worked for ten years, mostly as a reporter, for such papers as *The Washington Post* and *Herald Tribune*. In 1965 he published *The Kandy-Kolored Tangerine-Flake Streamline Baby* and established himself as a leader in the literary movement of New Journalism. His most famous works include *The Right Stuff* (which won the American Book Award for nonfiction), *The Bonfire of the Vanities* (which has been "recognized as the essential novel of America in the 1980s"), and the New York Times bestseller *A Man in Full*.

Yevgeny Yevtushenko, the celebrated Russian poet, was a close friend of Steinbeck despite their occasional political differences. A member of the European Academy of Arts and Sciences and an honorary member of the American Academy of Arts and Letters, Yevtushenko currently resides in Oklahoma, where he is a Distinguished Professor at the University of Tulsa.

Recent Titles in
Contributions to the Study of American Literature